ON TRUTH

A Neo-Pragmatist Treatise in Logic, Metaphysics and Epistemology

Richard Bosley

UNIVERSITY
PRESS OF
AMERICA

Copyright © 1982 by **Richard Bosley**

University Press of America, Inc.

P.O. Box 19101, Washington, D.C. 20036

Library of Congress Cataloging in Publication Data

Bosley, Richard.
  On truth.

  Includes index.
  1. Logic. 2. Metaphysics. 3. Knowledge, Theory of.
I. Title.
BC61.B67 1982   191   81-43800
ISBN 0-8191-2568-7
ISBN 0-8191-2569-5 (pbk.)

DEDICATED TO

MY MOTHER AND

THE MEMORY OF MY FATHER

iii

ACKNOWLEDGEMENTS

Dialogue writing must always have seemed attractive to those of us who keep records of philosophical conversations. For the dialogue which I place before the reader I am indebted to many people for ideas and arguments which have emerged in conversations about philosophical matters. Regarding the general account of using a language (Parts I and II) I owe a great deal to Mary Richardson and G.A. Spangler. An argument for distinguishing thought from perception (I.3) was devised by Rockney Jacobsen (to whom I owe many improvements in the theory of truth). Improvements in the account of assertion (III) I owe to discussions with David Murray and Michael Durrant. Elements in the account of negation (IV) are due to Ken Alpern and Stephen Leighton. Improvements in the theory of universals (VI) I owe to Arliss Davis and improvements in the argument about perceiving universals (V.5) to Susan Haley. An argument concerning linguistic idealism is due to Marshall Hopkins (VIII.13).

I hope the form of a dialogue suggests to the reader what must in any case be obvious: progress in philosophy rests upon good conversation. The obligation of the recorder of such conversations is too broad to make public in a satisfactory way. I hope, therefore, that the form itself will show my indebtedness to many colleagues and students, particularly to my colleagues Herman Tennessen and Peter Schouls--to the first because he moved me to write the first draft of the dialogue for a seminar of his and to the second because of his criticism of an early draft. The dialogue was revised and set in November of 1978 in order to commemorate the first anniversary of my father's death. Further revisions have been made since then. I have decided to retain the numbering of parts and sections established by the summer of 1980 and to mark added sections by adding a fraction to the original number.

Finally, I acknowledge the fine assistance given me by Miss Liane Brink, who has prepared the manuscript for printing by an offset reproduction process.

ANALYTICAL TABLE OF CONTENTS

instance, does Time depend upon Motion?

CHARACTERS

In order of appearance:

a Recorder, Julian Ingram, an assistant to the
Chancellor
a Porter
William Alexander, a philosopher
the Chancellor of a new academy
Katherine Woods, a student
Keith Anderson, a student

The dialogue is set in Alberta during one day in
November of 1978.

(1)
RECORDER: (I arrived here early enough to put things
in order and to arrange to have a porter bring us coffee this morning, tea this afternoon and spirits this
evening. The Premier of the province has decided to
found an academy. Since principal tasks of an academy
are, first, to institute procedures and to train and
educate people in their mastery, maintenance and use
and, second, to discover, to know and to teach the
truth, it is necessary to have guidance in accounting
for such possibilities. He has appointed a scientist--
a man whom I do not know--as chancellor of his academy.
The Chancellor, in turn, has appointed me as chairman
of his department of philosophy. The Chancellor asked
me to recommend a philosopher to lead our discussions
today. I naturally thought of an acquaintance of mine
whom I met several years ago during a session of a summer institute in philosophy. The Premier has charged
us with answering the question what account is to be
adopted by the Chancellor. In light of that account, I
gather, the Chancellor is meant to help influence the
activities of the academy. I have also invited two
students along.)
PORTER: Your guests have arrived, Mr. Ingram.
RECORDER: Fine. Do show them in. (He left and shortly returned, introducing William Alexander, the Chancellor, Katherine Woods and Keith Anderson.)
RECORDER: Good morning, Mr. Alexander.
ALEXANDER: Good morning.
RECORDER: You know that the Premier has selected this
man as Chancellor of an academy which the Premier
wishes to establish.
ALEXANDER: I do know. I understand that the Chancellor is to be tutored in ways of philosophers.
CHANCELLOR: In order to arrive at an account of truth.
I would otherwise have no suitable foundation for an
academy. This is Katherine Woods, Mr. Alexander, and
her friend, Keith Anderson.
ALEXANDER: We met some years ago at a session of a
summer institute.
CHANCELLOR: The Premier wishes to have a representa-
tive from another part of our academy present.
ALEXANDER: I am happy to hear you say so. Philosophy
is a central square of a city; let all those have access to it who require it. All sections of your academy require it. Some philosophy everyone must do on
his own; for the rest he needs access to the central
discipline. It would be worse for members of your aca-

demy to do philosophy without knowing that they do so
or without knowing their way to the square of their
city where its business is concentrated.
KEITH: I suspect there are parts of your city overrun
with social science--parts philosophy might usefully
try to reclaim.
KATHERINE: Are we fit for a reclamation project?
ALEXANDER: Not today.
CHANCELLOR: Before you begin, you would perhaps be
willing to say what you take philosophy to be.
ALEXANDER: I will give only the genus of the activity
of philosophizing; it will not be necessary, for the
benefit of today's discussions, to differentiate its
species from other species of the genus. Philosophizing is a two-fold activity: the first division has two
parts, namely giving accounts and explanations and also
laying down procedures, principles and rules by means
of which a critical inquiry can be conducted. With
respect to the first part of the first division I can
say that you will today be given a general account of
our speaking and thinking a language. The account will
be given by advancing what we call the Thesis of Continuance. And with respect to the second part I would
have a philosopher lay down guidelines by following
which certain other things can be considered, weighed
and perhaps criticized and put right. Suppose that a
man has risen to give testimony before a judge. A
philosopher can help us guide a critical inquiry regarding the testimony: he will keep before us the possibility of putting certain questions, for example
whether the testimony is consistent and true and
whether it can be followed.
CHANCELLOR: And the second division?
ALEXANDER: In the second division I include the activity of conducting a critical inquiry; it is conducted
by means of accounts, theories and explanations some of
which will be given today. With an eye on our limited
purposes I can say that we first require an account of
acts of a leader and then an account of applying and
following his work. So our basic accounts are of instigation and following.
CHANCELLOR: In addition to having your statement of
what you take philosophy to be I request another. For
I wish to know what we can take for granted as we set
upon our journey. Miss Woods and Mr. Anderson, I
understand, have first degrees in philosophy, although
they now pursue advanced studies in other disciplines.
But I have no training in philosophy. So I would like
to know what I need not treat as if suspended.
ALEXANDER: We come to philosophy capable of some

thought and conversation.

CHANCELLOR: Of course.

ALEXANDER: We will not let philosophy alienate us from so elementary a concession.

CHANCELLOR: I hope we will not.

ALEXANDER: It is part of the concession that we can manage basic achievements of knowledge and disclosure.

CHANCELLOR: You speak in a way which is unfamiliar to me when you speak of more or less simple achievements of knowledge and disclosure. Is there a perfectly simple achievement of knowledge mention of which is appropriate to our concession of what we have at hand as we begin our conversation?

ALEXANDER: Yes, knowledge of the letters of our language; next we know words and, in some instances, a certain part of a word.

RECORDER: What is it to know a word?

ALEXANDER: What is it to ask, "What is it to know a word?"

RECORDER: It is our custom to say that when one knows something, one knows something that can be stated by means of a that-clause. For example, to know your name is to know that your name is Alexander. Of course there is another sense of the word "know": a sense revealed by the following example. I say, "I know the table; it belongs to Katherine." Such knowledge, I believe, Bertrand Russell would call "knowledge by acquaintance." Others would say that such knowledge is recognition without discursive thought. I presume you wish to set aside such a use of the word "know"; for you surely mean to presuppose the same sense and meaning of the word when you pass from granting that someone knows the letters of a language and words of a language to granting that someone knows what his name is.

ALEXANDER: I do mean to presuppose the same sense and meaning of the word.

RECORDER: Then what is the sense of the word "know" or of the word "knowledge" which we are all to know when we hear you claim that we come to philosophy capable of more or less simple achievements of knowledge and disclosure?

ALEXANDER: We stand at too early a station along our route for me to give a complete answer to your question. To reach knowledge is to manage an achievement; managing an achievement depends upon the use of certain resources. Let us presuppose that we can employ a language sufficiently well sometimes to know what the words are which we utter. In light of the presupposition it becomes evident that certain achievements of knowledge are prior to that of telling the truth. So I

mean to have us presuppose a notion of knowledge and to
define and to account for truth partly in terms of a
presupposition of knowledge. It is granted we come to
consciousness by managing basic achievements of knowledge; we aspire to account for truth. In speaking
with one another we manage more or less basic achievements of knowledge and disclosure. Think of making a
speech as effecting a hierarchy of acts and achievements. There are elementary acts simpler than those
whose achievement is telling the truth.
RECORDER: You reverse our standard account, Mr.
Alexander. We are accustomed to saying that truth is
prior to knowledge. Similarly, logic is prior to epistemology. We say that logic establishes certain elementary truths and that epistemology establishes elementary instances of knowledge.
ALEXANDER: No, epistemology must be prior. For certain elementary achievements of knowledge and disclosure are prior to the more complex achievement of telling or knowing the truth. It is accordingly reasonable
to hold that an account of simple achievements is prior
to one of more complex achievements.
CHANCELLOR: Of course Mr. Alexander is right. We cannot suspend the allowance that we know the words which
we hear spoken. Our philosophical discussions presuppose as much.
ALEXANDER: When we have done what we can do today to
master an account of certain acts and achievements, we
will define truth and falsity.
CHANCELLOR: You made a remark with which none would
wish to disagree: we come to philosophy capable of some
thought and conversation. You obviously mean to have
us reflect upon the language we speak. Upon what would
you have us focus our attention?
ALEXANDER: There are four great families of words
whose use is common to all critical disciplines. Words
of the families are instruments whose use is essential
to our work. The supreme family of the four is that of
defect, sufficiency and excess. Of the three remaining
the first is the family of sameness and otherness; the
second is that of combination and separation, and the
third is that of dependence and independence. I would
have you reflect upon the use you make of the words
"too" and "enough", the words "the same" and "other",
the words "together with" and "apart from" and the
words "depending upon" and "independent of". This afternoon we will take up particular considerations of
the four families. I propose to define truth in terms
of our leading family.
CHANCELLOR: I understand.

4

RECORDER: Can you give us a motto as to what it is to disclose the truth?
ALEXANDER: Yes. To disclose the truth it is necessary first to apply and follow procedures laid down in creating, maintaining and developing a community; it is necessary to do so with sufficiency. To tell the truth and have knowledge it is necessary to have improved one's position sufficiently; standards of sufficiency are set by those who initially laid down a procedure.
CHANCELLOR: We will keep your motto in mind as we set upon our journey. Do begin.
ALEXANDER: Although we are a young land wishing to help support an old civilization, we are not prepared to take metaphysical theories on faith; our excess may therefore be that of seeking a reason and an account of all things. That search, however, is not constantly attended by doubt, and I have no wish to follow our great predecessor in setting our entire intellectual framework upon the back of doubt and so dismissing it from our presence, hoping that with secure foundations laid in his absence, it can be returned in one piece and then laid down again.
KATHERINE: I rejoice to learn that you have no intention of dragging our framework away from us.
CHANCELLOR: Please lay out your own method so that we can follow you when you give your account of truth. (2)
ALEXANDER: I shall first lay down our method, then make some distinctions and finally bring the method to bear upon our subject.
CHANCELLOR: Fine.
ALEXANDER: Since our age has lost touch with a notion of teleology, it is necessary for me to emphasize four of our basic notions. The first is that of the principal task which is undertaken or of the dominant objective which is to be reached. We say, for example, that a man puts this here or that there in order to build a house. The principal objective is building a house. Many other things are done in subordination to completing the principal task. In the notion of subordination, then, you have our second basic idea. Notice too that doing something in subordination to completing the main task contrasts with doing something which is incidental to completing the main task. Further, many actions are coordinated in order to reach the principal goal. For example, one man lifts a board into place while another holds another board in place.
RECORDER: Mr. Alexander, you would again make fashionable a view to which Aristotle's name is annexed. He too would have us distinguish means and end; he would

have us inquire what the end is in the reaching of
which actions and materials are made subservient. I do
not have in my record philosophical remarks about coordination.
ALEXANDER: You may set them down now. Children coordinate use of their hands in mastering complex actions.
RECORDER: I understand. I'm sure we'll have no difficulty with your employment of the notion.
ALEXANDER: Our fourth basic notion is that of continuance. In building a house a worker goes from doing
this to doing that. Several coordinate actions are
taken up one after another. Let us say that he continues from one to another.
RECORDER: We are familiar with the first two notions
as philosophical notions. I accept the place to which
you assign coordination. You also make the notion of
continuance a philosophical notion. Does it contrast
with a traditional idea?
ALEXANDER: Yes, with that of unity and of combination.
You know that one of the most important traditional
notions is that of unifying and of combining. They
have been employed in constructing philosophical systems for whose origins we are indebted to ancient philosophers.
CHANCELLOR: By emphasizing principal tasks do you wish
to suggest that for purposes of philosophy we should
first be clear what the principal task is which is set
upon under given circumstances?
ALEXANDER: Yes. To ask that question is to follow a
basic part of our method. We then proceed to a consideration of more and more deeply subordinated and coordinated acts. We therefore reject that method according to which one begins an analysis by considering
most simple parts and then proceeds to larger wholes.
KATHERINE: How are we to tell what the principal objective is? Shall we confine ourselves to this morning's conversation, to that of today or to the interests of a life? Some men take things in years, some in
weeks and some in days. Have you not seen farmers who
buy by the ton, Mr. Alexander, and housewives, by the
ounce?
ALEXANDER: The grasp of some is more capacious than
that of others. Some will seize upon the action performed as that of laying a brick; others, as building
a house, and still others, as promoting the glory of
God.
CHANCELLOR: One moment ago you said I put a question
which forms part of your method. What is your method?
ALEXANDER: I can state our general method in three
steps. First, inquire as to the dominant objective

6

of a given act, action or activity. Second, inquire
whether, and if so, how our notions of beginning, continuing, developing and completing apply and also our
notions of subordination and coordination. With respect to the second family of notions we wish to know
what acts are sufficient in order to bring the principal objective to completion. Third, inquire as to
appropriate modes of criticism. Such a method I shall
apply and follow in our conversation.
CHANCELLOR: The first two steps imply a distinction
between end and means. Certain means are effected as
if sufficient for reaching the dominant end.
ALEXANDER: And in following the third step of our
method we put three supreme critical questions: whether
there is defect of means for the end, whether there is
sufficiency and whether there is excess of means for
the end.
CHANCELLOR: I will keep your statement of your method
in mind as we proceed.
RECORDER: We recognize a predecessor of the second
step of your method in a part of Descartes's method.
He too would have us analyze a whole into its most simple parts.
ALEXANDER: Indeed. He would have us conclude such an
analysis with an eye on synthesis and composition. I
have an alternate plan in mind: do not look to synthesis and composition but to the application of two families of notions, that of subordination and coordination
and that of continuance and development. In the execution of the plan you will have an alternative to
Leibniz's notion of an analysis of a predicate out of
its subject.
CHANCELLOR: We will keep your plan before us as we
proceed.
RECORDER: You spoke of next making distinctions.
KEITH: Before you do so, I would like to put a question about your general method. I have the impression,
both now and from your earlier thought, that philosophy
makes a three-fold demand upon any effort at complete
understanding. First, the demand for an account of the
objective of certain means; second, the demand for an
account of means, and third, the demand for an account
of sufficiency when means are said to be sufficient for
an objective. Now I suppose that Julian is even more
keen than I am to have the impression affirmed. For he
is an historian of philosophy and is everywhere in
search of continuity. Surely you do wish to help support our tradition's commitment to a distinction between means and end.
ALEXANDER: I do and also recommend to you a three-fold

distinction: means, sufficiency and reaching an end.
KEITH: Would you say that when anyone claims that certain means are sufficient for a certain objective, he
implies that means are one thing and the objective,
another?
ALEXANDER: Yes.
KEITH: Then surely it follows that the objective is no
part of the means.
ALEXANDER: I think so much does follow.
KEITH: In his <u>Physics</u> (II.8) Aristotle remarks that
certain plants grow leaves. Now it sometimes happens
that in growing leaves a plant effects means adequate
for protecting its fruit. According to your view it
follows that protecting fruit is no part of growing
leaves.
ALEXANDER: There is such a consequence of my view;
have you any reason to reject it?
KEITH: No, none. I wish to make sure I can widely apply and follow your view and remain at home with the
consequences of applying and following it. One sometimes plays a game well enough to win. Playing a game
is to effect means; winning is to reach an end. So it
follows that playing a game is one thing; adequacy of
playing, another, and winning, still another. It further follows that winning is no part of playing.
ALEXANDER: There is such a consequence. Again I ask
you: Have you any reason to reject it?
KEITH: I can't think of any. It does occur to me that
it makes some difference whether we say, "He won IN
playing" or whether we say, "He won BY playing." I am
satisfied that my impression about your method is right.
Perhaps we should go on.
RECORDER: You spoke of next making distinctions.
(3)
ALEXANDER: We mark broad distinctions among three
worlds in which people act and achieve things. We also
mark three levels of mind. The first world we call
natural; the second, social, and the third, communicative. When I speak of three worlds, you will remember
that I speak of certain acts, actions and activities
and also of certain achievements: in the natural world
one moves one's arms, lifts things and walks; in the
social world one sets boundaries, lays down a procedure
and follows a rule, and in the communicative world one
speaks, writes and draws. When I speak of three levels
of mind, you will remember that I speak of certain
powers, acts and achievements: with respect to the
first level I mention the power to see, to hear, to
feel, to attend, to concentrate and to remember; with
respect to the second I mention certain acts and

achievements of perception: looking at and seeing something, listening for and hearing something, picturing something, remembering something and recognizing something, and with respect to the third I mention certain acts and achievements of language, for example formulating an opinion and coming to know something. I combine reference to the third level and the world of communication in speaking of acts and achievements of inner and outer speech or of language.

CHANCELLOR: Such distinctions are familiar to me. It is customary for writers to distinguish a natural from a human world; it is also customary to distinguish perception from thought.

RECORDER: But I am not yet clear how to make a record of them. I understand that you wish us to distinguish acts and achievements of perception, which you account for with respect to the second level of mind, from acts and achievements of language, which you account for with respect to the third level of mind. You would accordingly have us distinguish seeing something from knowing something.

ALEXANDER: Indeed. There is a method which we can employ to make a distinction clear between achievements of thought and achievements of perception. To employ the method ask what restraints are placed upon reporting an instance of knowing or an instance of seeing. Restraints are invited in answer to the question whether one can go on correctly reporting by means of correct premisses.

RECORDER: I'm not sure I follow you.

ALEXANDER: Consider an example. I correctly report to you that the Chancellor is sitting in a room in Edmonton. Now it happens to be true that the room he is sitting in is the Green Room. By means of the observation I can be said to continue to report correctly when I say that the Chancellor is sitting in the Green Room; the report is allowed to be correct whether or not it is allowed that the Chancellor knows that this room is the Green Room.

RECORDER: Of course.

ALEXANDER: When one reports on an instance of your knowledge, however, we must introduce restraints against so continuing if you do mean to give a correct report. For suppose the Chancellor tells me that Mr. Smith arrives tomorrow. But suppose that he does not know that Smith is the author of a Treatise on Education. I do not correctly report to you on the Chancellor's knowledge if I say to you, "The Chancellor knows who is coming tomorrow: the author of a Treatise on Education." For I would imply that the Chancellor does

9

know what he does not in fact know.

RECORDER: I very well see your reason for inviting constraints against using certain premisses for going on to give a correct report.

ALEXANDER: Then you will also see how we can account for a distinction between belief and knowledge at the third level and perception at the second level of mind.

RECORDER: I think I do see. Reporting of acts and achievements of perception is not thus controlled. If it is correct to claim that a certain cat can see a mouse and if it is true that that mouse is my pet, it is correct to claim that the cat can see my pet. Whether the cat knows that the mouse is my pet, is not to the point.

ALEXANDER: Good. By means of our account of a distinction between thought and perception you have means to prove a further point which is implicit in earlier remarks of mine. The point is that to form an image or to picture something is not to reach an achievement of knowledge at the third level of mind. For if it is correct to say of you that you can now picture the face of a friend, it would also be correct to say that you picture the face of the Premier, provided your friend is the Premier. It is not necessary for you to know whether he is the Premier.

CHANCELLOR: We can all allow you your account of a distinction between the second and the third levels of mind or between perception and thought.

ALEXANDER: Then I can bring our method to bear in giving an account of the possibility of perceptual and epistemological improvement.

CHANCELLOR: I think that we are ready to have you review our perceptual and epistemic positions.

(4)

ALEXANDER: Let us attend to acts of the natural world whose mastery and completion are sufficient for putting oneself in a natural position necessary for guidance, judgment and disclosure. Some acts are conveniently mentioned by alluding to the senses. With respect to the eyes I can improve my position by looking, by focusing my eyes or by turning my head; with respect to the ears I can improve my perceptual position by listening or by turning my head; with respect to a number of parts of the body one can improve one's position by touching, by holding or by pushing; with respect to the tongue one can put oneself in a good position by using the tongue in this or in that way, and with respect to one's head I improve my position by attending, by concentrating and by considering. To do such things as to look and to attend is to initiate, to continue or to complete an act of the natural world; let us not

seek today to give an account of its foundations. We
further allow with respect to the first level that we
have the power of sight, of hearing, of feeling and of
mind.
CHANCELLOR: We follow you in taking so much for
granted.
ALEXANDER: The second level is that of coming to see
something, to hear something, to feel something, to remember something, to recognize something or to picture
something. It is possible for us and animals to reach
the second level without having knowledge, clarity or
insight as to what it is, for example, that one can
see, remember, recognize or picture; indeed, it is possible to reach the second level without the employment
of any symbolic instrument.
CHANCELLOR: We agreed with you a moment ago that there
is a distinction between perception and thought. We
are surely obliged to agree with you now that reaching
achievements of perception does not depend upon reaching achievements of thought.
ALEXANDER: Then let us classify acts and achievements
of perception as acts and achievements of the second
level of mind. We also wish to account for the social
world. I shall postpone giving such an account. The
third level, you remember, is that of coming by clarity, insight or knowledge as to Where, When, How or
What. And the third world, finally, is that of communication.
CHANCELLOR: I think we understand your two triads of
distinctions: first, second and third levels of mind,
and first, second and third worlds of action.
ALEXANDER: Then I can state two theses with respect to
our perceptual and epistemic positions. Our first
epistemological thesis is that to reach the third level
of mind we must master acts and actions of the world of
communication. The world of communicative acts is
therefore prior to the third level of the acts and the
achievements of thought. Our second epistemological
thesis is that the social world is prior to that of
communication.
CHANCELLOR: The second thesis is not controversial; it
is not necessary for us to discuss it. It is evident
that social organization is prior to linguistic organization. Your first thesis, however, is controversial.
RECORDER: Indeed. It would overturn a contrary thesis
on which I have been educated: I mean the thesis that
thought is prior to communication.
ALEXANDER: There can be several reasons for holding
the contrary thesis: which of such reasons are appropriate to our conversation?

RECORDER: There is a principal reason; it is that thought begins in sensation. Plato has a character of his Sophist say that there is a kind of opining done through sensation; seeming is a mixture of sensation and opinion. There are also philosophers of the British school who hold that to have pictures and images is to be in thought. If such a thesis is correct, it cannot be correct to hold, as you do, Mr. Alexander, that mastery of an instrument of communication is prior to thinking.

ALEXANDER: Let us by all means examine my thesis.

CHANCELLOR: Before we examine it, we should make sure we understand it. How much can be achieved by reaching various degrees of goodness, acuity and sensitivity? Can one thereby come to know things? Can one do so without use of a symbol?

ALEXANDER: No. The first level is not that of acquiring knowledge.

CHANCELLOR: And you say that to reach the second level is still not to have come far enough. I agree with you in saying that I can see something without knowing what it is that I can see.

ALEXANDER: I insist upon a further point: it is possible for an animal to see something and to recognize something without either knowing that it does see or recognize something or knowing what it is that is seen or recognized.

CHANCELLOR: Then how do we reach the third level?

ALEXANDER: Awareness or knowledge as to what things are is reached by means of the construction and the mastery of a framework of language. I will shortly say how such construction is possible; we will then consider a few elementary examples.

CHANCELLOR: Then what is the relation between exercising a certain control, reaching a certain degree of acuity and coming to see and to hear things, on the one hand, and, on the other, building up a framework of inner and outer speech adequate for reaching and sustaining the third level?

ALEXANDER: There is a relation of support; there is not one of truth. We can improve ourselves sufficiently to lay foundations for a framework; the foundations do rest somewhere; they are supported. But remember that to speak of support is not to speak of truth.

CHANCELLOR: So you would have us account for an improvement in our positions which is sufficient to support the building up of a framework of inner and outer speech.

ALEXANDER: Yes. Doing so requires mastery in all three worlds and at both the first two levels of mind.

KEITH: I fear that I am still unclear how the third level does and does not fit with the second level.
ALEXANDER: Little wonder. Ours is a long tradition in which philosophers write as though of a magic tree: to shake it is, let me say, to see it. When it is shaken, that-clauses fall out, leaving budding facts behind.
CHANCELLOR: Surely we are now in a good position to distinguish perceiving from thinking.
ALEXANDER: It is one thing to acknowledge that there is a distinction; it is another to work out a satisfying way of stating it--that way forming a permanent path of our systematic philosophy. You doubtless realize that the distinction has had a difficult career: sometimes philosophers write about thinking as if they should be writing about perceiving alone; at other times philosophers write about perceiving as if they should be writing about thinking alone.
KEITH: I recognize the first case. When Plato has a character continue an inquiry into stating and thinking, the character seeks help from seeing and hearing. As they have objects, so too does thought. What do you have in mind in the second case?
ALEXANDER: Some philosophers write about seeing as if there were a question of seeing correctly. We grant that one can be wrong in thinking something; some have written as if one can be wrong in seeing something. Some such assumption is made, I presume, when a philosopher writes of veridical perception and of seeing something as it is.
KATHERINE: I have never understood such a use of the word "as". I have thought that someone who writes in that way assumes the possibility of making a comparison. We do say, "Keith is not telling it as it happened."
ALEXANDER: And what is the force of saying so?
KATHERINE: Now, when you ask, I'm not sure.
ALEXANDER: Do you mean that the way in which he is telling a story is not the way in which something happened?
KATHERINE: No. I mean that his report is not accurate.
ALEXANDER: Do you think that a philosopher means something comparable when he denies that one sees something as it is? For if seeing a rose were like relating an incident, then as I can be accused of giving an inaccurate report of an incident so I can be accused of having or of seeing an inaccurate sight of the rose.
KATHERINE: (laughing) You polish an idea until its absurdity becomes manifest.
ALEXANDER: Doing so is an old habit of mine--a residue

from the story-telling phase of ordinary language philosophy.
KATHERINE: I'm not as repelled by absurdity as you
are. Think of the world as so created that however we
strain our eyes we catch only inaccurate glimpses of
things.
ALEXANDER: We do speak of seeing well and badly.
Would you say that in using such words we make it possible to draw a comparison?
KATHERINE: I can't imagine what it would mean to say,
"I see a rose as well as it is." There's nothing a
rose and my seeing a rose have in common. It's therefore pointless to try to compare them.
KEITH: My question did not concern a purported relation between a rose and seeing a rose; I meant to ask
about the relation between the third level of acts and
achievements of thought and the second level of acts
and achievements of perception.
ALEXANDER: I had not forgotten. I meant to purge our
use of the word "see" from implications appropriate to
acts of thought. You must know that many of my contem-
poraries write as if seeing were an act of thought. In
order for you to follow me in making my complaint I
must make sense of a notion of appropriately describing
sense impressions or of minimally but objectively reporting what is perceived. Let us suppose that I have
formulated an opinion as to the likelihood of the Premier joining us tomorrow. Having formulated an opinion, indeed, I complete an act of the third level of
mind.
KEITH: I understand.
ALEXANDER: In the course of speaking I may be concerned not to say more than is necessary; I may be concerned to express myself faithfully; I may be concerned to
say precisely--perhaps we would even say exactly--what
I think.
KEITH: I understand. You have recourse to what you
think in order to judge or to criticize either what you
say or the saying of it.
ALEXANDER: Yes.
KEITH: And so by speaking of having recourse either to
the act of opining or to what is thought you lead us to
understand the notion of minimal verbal reports, of
making them minimal or of making them cautious.
ALEXANDER: Then do you think that I have laid foundations which are adequate for conducting and completing
our inquiry?
KEITH: I think so.
ALEXANDER: Whatever the relation is which we have been
trying to state between saying what I think and think-

14

ing what I think, I observe that there is no such relation between saying and seeing. There is therefore no
comparable support for correcting or modifying what is
said. I observe further that there is no way in which
an act of thought or speech and seeing are so related
that upon the basis of seeing something it is possible
to govern and to regulate the execution of the act.
There is no recourse to seeing well, to seeing something or to what is seen in order to make sure that one
is not, for example, saying too little or too much,
speaking, as it were, incautiously or carelessly.
KEITH: I understand. The second observation is stronger than the first one.
ALEXANDER: Consider them a little further. There is
no suitable analogy between saying that it is not likely that the Premier will join us tomorrow and thinking
that such is not likely and between saying, "That is
the Premier" and seeing the Premier. As saying, "That
is the Premier" stands to thinking that that is the
Premier, saying, "That is the Premier" does not stand
to seeing the Premier.
KEITH: What is the difference upon which you wish to
have most emphasis laid?
ALEXANDER: In the first instance I have recourse to
thinking that it is not likely that he will arrive tomorrow in order to judge whether I say too much were I
to say, "It is very unlikely that he will arrive tomorrow." But in the second instance it means nothing to
say that I have recourse to seeing the Premier in order
to judge whether I say too much were I to say, "I see
the Premier." Similarly, I talk nonsense when I say,
"I have recourse to seeing him in order to judge whether I say too little were I to say, 'I barely caught a
glimpse of him.'"
KEITH: And the second observation which you made is
that to see or to hear something is not to be in pos-
session of means adequate for criticizing either saying
something or what is said. I am inclined to think that
something more should be said on behalf of the stronger
observation that to see or to hear is not to secure any
part of a platform from which to criticize what one
says one sees or to judge the adequacy of saying whatever it is that one says one sees. You have laid it
down, after all, that independent of language it is
possible to achieve adequate goodness of sight and of
hearing for the performance of certain actions of the
natural world.
ALEXANDER: In making such a concession I deploy our
notions of achievements, success and failure; I do not
deploy notions of truth and falsity and of correctness

and error. I accordingly argue that to provide a platform adequate for criticism and adjustment it would be
necessary for seeing and hearing to be acts of thought.
For criticism as to the adequacy, accuracy or appropri-
ateness of an act of thought can be given only from a
part of our platform provided by another achievement of
thought or by another act of thought whose execution is
independently secure.
CHANCELLOR: I think that we have sufficiently considered the second observation. Let us stand by the observation that the continued execution of one act of
thought is challenged only by some achievement of
thought or by the execution of another act but not by
seeing and hearing.
(As the Chancellor finished his summary, the Porter
entered our room, pushing a tray before him. He poured
and served coffee. I felt relieved to have him interrupt our discussion. I was not satisfied and, indeed,
felt perplexed. I felt as many students must feel:
taking notes beyond my power of absorption. The Porter, a pleasant boy still in highschool, I should suppose, looked around at us, embarrassed at having moved
us to silence.)
PORTER: Have you founded your academy?
KATHERINE: Good Lord, no! We don't even know what
truth is. Will you come to our academy, if we do get
one founded today?
PORTER: I don't know. My parents want me to become
either a scientist, a lawyer or a businessman.
KATHERINE: (turning to the others) You see how we are
in the West: in pursuit either of prestige, power or
money. (turning to the Porter) Why don't you give up
all three and major in philosophy?
PORTER: What is philosophy? I'm in my final year at
school. Philosophy is not laid on.
KATHERINE: Good thing too. I don't think a definition
of philosophy is useful. Here is a philosopher, in
pursuit of wisdom and understanding. Follow his lead.
PORTER: What have you been discussing the past hour?
KATHERINE: Tedious distinctions.
KEITH: (looking annoyed) Philosophy consists in part
in the drawing of fine distinctions.
KATHERINE: You people differentiate a lot; you don't
give equal time to identifying. (turning to the Porter) You should see these people in action: they dress
for war against confusion in the house of sameness and
otherness and emerge waving tools fit for differentia-
tion. (smiling at the Porter with an expression of
tenderness) There is a high price set on the head of
confusion.

16

KEITH: Does our distinction between a natural and a human world deserve your derision?
KATHERINE: No.
KEITH: Or that between perception and thought?
KATHERINE: No. I'll further grant you that society precedes communication. But your next move leaves me in doubt: I mean that communication precedes thought.
ALEXANDER: It is still too early to resolve your doubt.
KEITH: Do try to stay awake a little longer.
PORTER: I'll return with more coffee in one hour, if that helps.
KATHERINE: I'm sure it will (she replied, smiling).
(The Porter left.)
(5)
RECORDER: You may not expect of me the same speed of comprehension which you expect of yourselves. I am both listening and taking notes.
KATHERINE: And talking. You are not as quiet as your record would suggest.
RECORDER: I have in my notebook a record of your attempt to draw and defend a distinction between acts and achievements of the second and acts and achievements of the third level of mind. We have the distinction in the words "perception" and "thought". Now it seems to me that your position estranges me from my education. Mr. Alexander would have us appreciate how unclear epistemological writing has been; on the other hand he acknowledges that there is a serious tradition which would have sight productive of that-clauses. Now I would like to return to the fountainhead of our tradition.
KATHERINE: Gentlemen, he means Plato.
RECORDER: There is a brilliant argument in the Phaedo which is inconsistent with Mr. Alexander's plan for an easy distinction between perception and thought. Suppose we are looking at two sticks; I remark, "They are equal in length." Now surely when I say, "they" and then say, "equal," I don't mention the same thing twice; I therefore first mention two things seen and then indicate something else, namely equality. Is there any reason to report the argument for holding that there is otherness?
KATHERINE: No, none. We all hold that there is a distinction between two sticks seen and equality. Presumably we all agree with Plato in this: the sticks are objects of perception, and equality, an object of thought.
RECORDER: Indeed. Let us grant Plato or the Socrates of his dialogue something further. Suppose one says,

17

"That is a poor imitation or a poor copy." One implies
that one has knowledge of an original. So sight of a
poor copy implies knowledge of its original. Similarly, suppose someone sees something and thinks that what
he sees wants to be like something else but is not able
to be. Sight of a defective copy implies knowledge of
its original.

KATHERINE: So perception presupposes knowledge and
knowledge is therefore prior. I grasp how the argument
would go for the prior existence of a mind. But how
does the argument bear upon our attempt to secure a
distinction between perception and thought?

RECORDER: It seems to me that the argument rests upon
the assumption that in seeing two sticks which are
equal one sees their defective copy of equality.

ALEXANDER: Perhaps you can help us understand the assumption. It is certainly possible to see a house and
thereby see several things: for example, a window and
a door. Do you mean that when I see two sticks which
are not really equal, I thereby see four things: two
sticks, defect and equality?

RECORDER: Something like that. You see two sticks,
defect and a copy of equality.

KATHERINE: Julian, are you serious? I would like to
get our voyage underway. Do we really need to take so
much of your tradition aboard?

ALEXANDER: Julian states an assumption we should be
clear about. You represent Plato as holding that we do
not see equality itself.

RECORDER: Such forms are grasped, thought or known;
they are not perceived. But copies or instances of
them can be objects of perception. And I don't think
such an assumption is peculiar to Plato. Aristotle
holds that particular forms can be seen, and modern
philosophers hold that instances of such universals as
colors and shapes can be seen.

ALEXANDER: We should certainly consider whether we can
keep your assumption in our account of perception. But
even if we do, I wonder whether the conclusion of the
argument you reported really arises. I mean the conclusion which Katherine stated when she said, "So perception presupposes knowledge and knowledge is therefore prior." You seemed to assent to a point which I
made in a previous discussion, namely that one can see
something without either knowing that one sees or knowing what one sees. So if one could see either defect
or equality, one could do so without knowledge of the
fact or of the nature of what is seen.

RECORDER: I assent to the original point and follow
your use of it.

ALEXANDER: Then perhaps you are willing again to consider how to answer this question: there are two possibilities for accounting for the origin of a presupposition; the first is seeing a copy, and the second, thinking that one sees a copy; Which possibility is the right one?
RECORDER: We can obviously rule out the first possibility. For if I can see a copy and not know what I see, then it is not seeing a copy which presupposes knowledge of an original.
ALEXANDER: Then knowledge is presupposed not for seeing a copy but for thinking that it is a copy which one can see. For such a thought presupposes that a copy is a copy of an original. So Plato does not show that we cannot perceive as we do without prior knowledge; the truth is rather that we cannot perceive and think as we do without prior knowledge. It is nevertheless open to us to say, as I have been saying, that we perceive before we think and, second, that we begin to acquire knowledge as we begin to think.
RECORDER: I am still not persuaded to deny my belief that to perceive is to be in thought.
ALEXANDER: I have heard you say that a perception is an hypothesis.
RECORDER: Can we consider my belief?
ALEXANDER: Of course. But perhaps not now; let us consider it after we have at hand an account of sameness and otherness.
RECORDER: Fine.
ALEXANDER: I hope that I speak at least for the Chancellor and myself when I say that I have secured a distinction between acts and achievements of the second level and acts and achievements of the third level of mind. In light of the distinction an observation was made: the continued execution of one act of thought is challenged only by some achievement of thought or by the execution of another act but not by perception. To say so is not to make perception irrelevant. For by seeing well enough for this and that, hearing well enough for this and that, for example, we sufficiently improve our positions to make the construction, the mastery and the use of our framework possible.
CHANCELLOR: So we are in need of an account of the building up of our framework in order to account for knowledge of the truth.
KATHERINE: Before Professor Alexander gives such an account, I wish to make sure I grasp the significance of our recent discussion. I take it our goal has been a satisfactory statement of a distinction between perceiving and thinking. It has been assumed that we do

19

not examine acts and achievements of perception for truth or falsity. I am neither right nor wrong in looking at something; seeing something is neither true nor false.

ALEXANDER: So much we have assumed.

RECORDER: Would you say of deception what you say of falsity?

ALEXANDER: Yes. I can be deceived in thinking something; I am not deceived in seeing something.

RECORDER: But in his first meditation Descartes writes that it is sometimes proved to him that senses are deceptive. For example, when he dreams he sits before his fire when in fact he lies in bed, he is deceived.

ALEXANDER: Deceived in dreaming?

RECORDER: Descartes argues--or writes--as though deception arises in dreams and in hallucinations.

ALEXANDER: It is evident that the word "deception" is used in exercising the office of criticism. Further, it is a principle of criticism that we criticize people for doing or saying things--which doing or saying is under control. Can we agree to say that the allowance that there is an exercise of power is a necessary condition for just criticism?

RECORDER: Yes.

ALEXANDER: Then if one is deceived, mistaken or wrong, one is so in some action for the execution of which one is responsible.

RECORDER: So much follows.

ALEXANDER: Are you responsible for your dreams?

RECORDER: It is not in my power to dream as I would wish.

ALEXANDER: And reporting a dream?

RECORDER: The conduct of such an act of language is within my power.

ALEXANDER: Suppose you say to us: "Last night I dreamt that I came to Edmonton to participate in conversations about the foundations of an academy. I dreamt that I would again see William Alexander." Would it be appropriate for me to respond, "And you were right. You were in Edmonton; you were about to meet me again after several years."

RECORDER: It would be absurd to examine my dream for truth or falsity.

ALEXANDER: Then can dreaming be an object of deception and error?

RECORDER: No.

KATHERINE: The reason why we do not examine acts and achievements of perception for truth or falsity must be different from the reason why we do not examine a dream for truth or falsity. The latter fails a basic princi-

ple of criticism. But looking and listening are within
our power. We nevertheless do not say that one is
right or wrong in looking at something or in listening
to something. Why are acts of perception inappropriate
objects of criticism for truth or falsity?
ALEXANDER: The question can be answered after we have
at hand definitions of truth and falsity.
KEITH: I'm afraid that there is a question which I
would like to put. You said a while ago that your
first epistemological thesis is that to reach the third
level we must master acts and actions of the world of
communication. I take it that an implication of the
thesis is that we must master and use a language in order to reach knowledge of the truth. When you used the
word "must", I took it that use of language is necessary for reaching achievements of disclosure and knowledge. Was I right in formulating such assumptions?
ALEXANDER: Yes.
KEITH: Then surely your first thesis has two parts.
The first is that mastery and use of a framework is
sufficient for reaching achievements of disclosure and
knowledge; the second is that use is also necessary.
ALEXANDER: Necessary for us.
KEITH: Yes, yes: for us.
ALEXANDER: I do not propose to argue that it is not
possible for anyone or for any kind of being to reach
knowledge without effecting the kind of means which we
effect when we speak, write or think a language. I
mean rather to account for the means which we can and
must employ in order to reach knowledge of the truth.
CHANCELLOR: I very well see that you are anxious to
turn to an account of the foundations of a framework.
We do have leisure, and so we need not rush ourselves.
ALEXANDER: We have leisure. Your Premier is obviously
devoted to education. A wealthy province can afford
leisure for the planning of a new academy.
CHANCELLOR: Well, yes, thank you. I hope so. Should
Julian publish his record, the same thought would by
now have occurred to its reader as has occurred to me.
Karl Popper distinguishes among three worlds. In a recent book, written with John Eccles,--I mean The Self
and Its Brain--Popper distinguishes among World 1,
World 2 and World 3. First, there is the physical
world: the universe of physical entities. Second,
there is the world of mental states and dispositions.
And third, there is the world of the contents of
thought and of the products of the human mind. Are
your and his systems of distinctions near enough to
warrant discussion?
ALEXANDER: Do you fear confusion?

CHANCELLOR: Someone might think you've simply taken over his distinctions and then try to follow the rest of our conversation in light of his thought.
ALEXANDER: Then let us by all means take pains to obviate misunderstanding. The three worlds of my system are worlds of events, actions and achievements; the questions When and How long are appropriate. Objects of actions are not thereby classified. But by means of "World 3" Popper classifies, for example, stories, problems and theories. Further, it is evidently Popper's intention to classify things that are real. I have not introduced so ambitious an undertaking.
CHANCELLOR: Let us pause for coffee before we continue.
(5.1)
RECORDER: (putting down my pen and turning to Alexander) Before we stop, I would like to have my puzzlement resolved. Keith put a question to you a moment ago; surely your answer goes too far.
ALEXANDER: What do you mean?
RECORDER: You acceded to Keith's two-part summary of your thesis: first, use of a framework is sufficient for reaching achievements of disclosure and knowledge; second, use is necessary. I have followed your work for over a decade; it is not like you to admit oversimplification.
ALEXANDER: We have now made a beginning. I don't want either to bore Katherine or to perplex the Chancellor.
CHANCELLOR: We can stand an accurate summary, if we were to be misled by a simple one.
ALEXANDER: Some things are independently sufficient for other things, and some things are dependently sufficient. A full cause is by itself sufficient for its effect. On the other hand, if you say of a player playing a certain game, "He's playing well enough to win," you need not mean that he is playing well enough to win by himself; for in fact winning depends upon several players playing well enough. Let us accordingly distinguish between saying that one thing is adequate in its own way for another and saying that one thing is adequate by itself for another.
RECORDER: I see. So the first part of your thesis is that use of a framework is sufficient in its own way for reaching achievements of disclosure and knowledge; second, use is necessary or, conversely, the achievements depend upon use.
ALEXANDER: Right.
RECORDER: Perhaps now I have my record straight.

PART II

ALEXANDER: Earlier this morning I distinguished three levels of mind and three worlds of action.

KATHERINE: I take no satisfaction in your accounts of the two trios of distinctions. Philosophers are apt to make distinctions without carrying us along with them. I sometimes suspect that your desire for innovation is greater than that for utility.

KEITH: She doesn't mean to sound disrespectful; she's hiding her own embarrassment.

ALEXANDER: What do you mean?

KEITH: When we were undergraduates, we presumed to sort ourselves out philosophically. I became a part-time nominalist and idealist; Katherine became a materialist.

CHANCELLOR: (turning to Alexander) A part-time nominalist and idealist? Is that the sort of thing I should permit on my campus?

ALEXANDER: Do you know what it is to be that sort of thing?

CHANCELLOR: I'm not entirely sure.

ALEXANDER: What were you then, Keith?

KEITH: As a nominalist I held that the only things that exist are particulars; as an idealist I held that the only things that are real are spirits or minds and their ideas.

KATHERINE: And I more or less agreed with Keith about nominalism. I disagreed about idealism and recommended materialism in its place, arguing that only the physical world is real. So when Keith said that I was embarrassed, he was suggesting something right: I did think back on my education; I felt a twinge of nostalgia, thinking how I would have reacted to your distinctions a few years ago. Now I find your account of them inadequate; then I would have found it quaint.

ALEXANDER: I would like to have Katherine state and defend materialism and to have Keith state and defend idealism. But we are not yet ready to have you do so. We must first command accounts of two families of notions: the first of sameness and otherness and the second of combination and separation.

RECORDER: There is surely a little you can do now to secure the distinctions which you drew a few minutes ago.

ALEXANDER: I drew one distinction between perception and thought.

KATHERINE: I'm satisfied with your statement and defense of the distinction.

RECORDER: But I am not.

ALEXANDER: I will hear your worries after we have discussed sameness and otherness. I drew another distinction between a natural and a social world and still another between either of them and a communicative world.
KATHERINE: I would be satisfied if you can secure a
distinction between the natural and the communicative
worlds.
ALEXANDER: A premiss of otherness can be argued in the
following way. We say that to make a sound is to complete an action of the level of nature; we also say
that uttering or pronouncing a word is to complete an
act of the level of communication. But an act of the
second is not the same as any act of the first level.
For the word which you utter I can write down; if the
word which you uttered is a sound, I would also be able
to write down and read the sound. It is, however, absurd to say so. The possibility is therefore to be rejected that a word is a sound. Further, when I make a
sound and thereby utter the word "the", you can inquire
whether I made a loud or soft sound; the word "the", of
course, is neither loud nor soft. So to utter or pro-
nounce a word is not the same as making a sound. Having argued for a premiss of otherness between a level
of nature and one of communication let us put the question what the relation is between them. It will be
granted on all sides that it is possible for one to
make a sound without uttering a word. We can therefore
grant a premiss of independence of natural from communicative acts with respect to actuality. But the relation of independence is not necessarily symmetrical.
And so we require a third premiss: uttering a word depends upon natural action with respect to potentiality.
For it is not possible for one to utter a word without
making a sound or to write a word without moving one's
body.
    I hope we make a plausible start by setting before
ourselves three premisses. The first is a premiss of
dualism: there is an order of nature; there is a human
order. It is wrong to say that they are one and the
same. The second is a premiss of the independence of
nature with respect to actuality, and the third is a
premiss of dependence of speech with respect to power
or potentiality. It is therefore also wrong to say
that the order of nature and the human order are independent of one another, each running, as it were, parallel to the other.
RECORDER: In setting forth your premisses of a distinction, of independence and of dependence you contradict an established principle of metaphysics which I
have written here in my record. It is said that what

24

is distinct is separable. You mark a distinction; it
follows that God can create the one without the other.
So if writing a word is distinct from any instance of
bodily movement, it is possible for a word to be written without any bodily movement. But since the inference is to be rejected, so is the supposition of a distinction.
ALEXANDER: Use of the principle that what is distinct
is separable leads you to reject the supposition that
there is a distinction. But since there is a distinction between writing a word and bodily movement, we
confront an argument reductio ad impossibile. We properly resolve the argument not by giving up either the
supposition of a distinction or that of a relation of
dependence but rather by abandoning the principle that
what is distinct is separable. It should be replaced
by its contradictory, namely that some things which are
distinct stand in a relation of dependence.
CHANCELLOR: It is surely a part of sound metaphysics
to say that some things which are distinct stand in a
relation of dependence.
ALEXANDER: Then I can complete my summary of certain
consequences of this morning's conversation--conse-
quences relevant to our present conversation. By exercising control in subordinating one thing to another
and in coordinating two things we can win a position
adequate for certain achievements. Of such achievements it is my task to give an account: in particular
to account for the possibility of achieving clarity of
speech and of mind. It is my task to account for the
possibility of making clear, of revealing, of saying,
of coming to be clear or of knowing a number of things,
in particular How, Who and What. I shall have occasion
to emphasize the possibility of making clear and of
being clear how we continue and also what, for example,
something is or what its color or length is.
(0.1)
CHANCELLOR: Before you begin, I have a complaint to
make against two of your three premisses. It seems to
me you concede too much ground to materialism.
RECORDER: We'll hear an argument against materialism
this evening.
CHANCELLOR: I know. What ground is conceded in the
morning it may be too late in the evening to recover.
(turning to Alexander) You mentioned three premisses.
The first makes a distinction between the natural and
the human worlds. So much I am persuaded of. The second, you say, is a premiss of the independence of nature with respect to actuality. I suppose I don't understand the premiss. But I would see more clearly

what I don't like about the premiss if I knew whether independence excludes causality.

ALEXANDER: We shall doubtless discuss causality this evening.

CHANCELLOR: It would be useful to have a definition at hand now.

ALEXANDER: Fine. A cause is a range of factors each one sufficient in its own way for an effect, each one necessary and jointly sufficient by themselves for the effect. Since "necessary for" and "depending upon" indicate the same relation but the one converts the terms of the other, it follows from my statement of the definition that an effect depends upon each factor.

CHANCELLOR: I find the definition acceptable. Did you mean to have the second premiss say that the human world is no part of the cause of the natural world?

ALEXANDER: Yes. According to the second premiss the natural world gives support but is not supported.

CHANCELLOR: You seem to allow that when a lawgiver lays down a law, he helps create a social world.

ALEXANDER: Indeed.

CHANCELLOR: Suppose he is speaking when he lays down the law. A certain sound is made. Suppose in fact that the lawgiver has such a booming voice that as he makes sound, he breaks a window. Is the breaking of a window an event of the natural world?

ALEXANDER: Yes.

CHANCELLOR: Does that event depend upon making sound?

ALEXANDER: Yes.

CHANCELLOR: And does making sound in turn depend upon the lawgiver laying down a law?

ALEXANDER: Yes.

CHANCELLOR: Doesn't it follow that laying down a law at a particular time is part of the cause of the window breaking?

ALEXANDER: So much does follow.

CHANCELLOR: Then can all of nature be independent of every part of the human world?

ALEXANDER: No.

CHANCELLOR: Are we still to employ your second premiss when we do our most serious thinking about relations between the two worlds?

(There was a pause after the Chancellor put his question. I was surprised to find Alexander at a loss; I was surprised, in fact, to find one of his views refuted.)

ALEXANDER: I think you are right to refute my second premiss. It must surely be given up in favor of some premiss which sets forth relations of reciprocal causality between the two worlds. Let us consider this

evening how to state such a premiss.
CHANCELLOR: Fine.
ALEXANDER: I would like to have us adopt a creation
myth concerning our conceptual framework.
CHANCELLOR: Not a very scientific thing to do.
ALEXANDER: Having a plausible myth at hand will prove
adequate for our purposes.
CHANCELLOR: I hope so.
(1)
ALEXANDER: Let us assume that the world of completing
acts of language is reached: not only grunting or
groaning in complaining or in warning, for example, but
also uttering a word in complaining or in warning.
Upon the basis of my assumption we consider both the
act of utterance and also the achievement of making
clear, for example, what the word is which is uttered.
RECORDER: You imply a distinction between acts and
achievements: uttering a word is an act and making
plain what the word is, is an achievement.
ALEXANDER: Yes. The first is an act of speaking; the
second, an achievement of communication. Let us consider our resources for reaching achievements of communication. There is a primary distinction between two
kinds of resources of uttering or writing a word. The
first is uttering a word at a certain time or with a
certain speed; the second is uttering a word with a
certain intonation. With respect to the first possibility we contrast saying, "The table is red" and saying, "Is the table red." It may further be observed
that when one utters a word, one has an opportunity to
exercise coordinated control both in the natural and in
the social world. One can control the volume of voice
and also utter words in accord with a procedure or a
practice. With respect to the second possibility mentioned we contrast writing, "The table is red" and
writing, "The table is RED."
     Let us further consider a genus of times and ways
control of which provides a basis for achievements of
clarity. I distinguish two species of the genus; the
distinction is based upon a corresponding distinction
between two kinds of achievements. Of the first kind
is the achievement of making clear, for example, that
one is uttering a word or that one is putting a question. Of the second kind is the achievement of making
clear, for example, what the word is which one utters
or what the question is which is put.
RECORDER: So on the one hand we have disclosing or
saying what is done or achieved; on the other, disclosing or saying, for example, what this is or what its
color or length is.

ALEXANDER: Yes.
RECORDER: You evidently wish us not to confuse a disclosure of our own activity and achievements with a disclosure of the nature of things.
ALEXANDER: In light of the distinctions now drawn I advance the Principle of Distinguishable Resources. The first plank of it is that when we allow a distinction between the two kinds of achievements, we can also allow a distinction between two species of times and ways of utterance. For example, since we can distinguish between making it evident that one is speaking and making clear what words one speaks, we can also distinguish between certain times and modes which are together sufficient, on the side of speaking, for making it evident that one is speaking and certain times and modes which are together sufficient for making evident what words are spoken. The second plank is that we do not reach two distinct achievements by using the same resource at the same time.
RECORDER: Can you clarify the first plank?
ALEXANDER: Suppose someone puts a question when he says, "Is the table red?" He controls word-order and intonation simply in putting a question; he thereby makes it evident to us that he is putting a question. He follows a pattern of timing and intonation which belongs to the first species; its use and control we call a resource or a kind of resource. If there is to be another achievement of making clear what the question is, there must be a distinguishable kind of resource. Clearly there is such a thing; for he can give certain words clear pronounciation.
RECORDER: You accordingly claim that we can distinguish a certain mode of pronounciation from sustaining a pattern appropriate to putting a question.
ALEXANDER: Yes. For I can properly articulate a word whether in the course of putting a question or issuing a command.
RECORDER: And what about the second plank of the Principle?
ALEXANDER: According to the second one the resource drawn upon to make clear what word is uttered is not sufficient to reveal what one is doing. Suppose I say, "I ask you whether the table is red." I utter the word "ask" in order to make it evident that it is a question...
RECORDER: You hesitate.
ALEXANDER: Additional support is necessary for us to know whether it is a question which is put, reported, suggested or rejected. Other support is necessary for us to know whether the person speaking gives an example

28

or whether he is being ironical.

RECORDER: Your statement of a distinction between the kind of resource adequate for disclosing a word and the kind of resource of time and of modes of intonation admits of a consequence. It is that there is a further distinction between meaning and force. Philosophers distinguish three questions regarding meaning: what someone means when he utters a sentence; what someone means by an expression, and what a word means. Let us ignore the middle question.

ALEXANDER: The first question can arise when we wish to inquire to what end someone speaks; one may wish to have him try again to make himself clear; we may well wish to know what he intends to do or to say. To answer the third question dictionaries are written.

RECORDER: Indeed. Some philosophers interconnect their accounts of act and meaning.

ALEXANDER: Let us distinguish saying what a word means from saying what all one must be able to say or to do in order to allow that one does know the meaning of a word. I make the distinction in order to prevent you from thinking that a statement of the acts which can be performed by uttering a given word is a part of the statement of the meaning of the word. One may wish to base an account of the acquisition and the change of meaning upon one of acts both social and communicative. It is wrong, however, to proceed as if to derive knowledge of the act from that of meaning. Let us suppose that someone is performing in a room to which we have no access. A second person acts as intermediary. He tells us what the words are which the first person utters; he utters them as if he were giving dictation. From his retelling we are to tell what the dominant act is which the first person initiates, continues and completes. I claim that although we well know the words and their meanings, we are not put in a position adequate for telling what the dominant act is.

RECORDER: But suppose the following words are quoted to us: "I claim that...."

ALEXANDER: Remember we do not know whether he is reading from a letter, reciting a play or sending something up. For setting aside such possibilities we are too far removed from the context of performance.

RECORDER: And so you argue that from the resource sufficient for clarity of vocabulary alone we cannot infer the dominant act of language.

ALEXANDER: Yes. And since the given resource is not sufficient, neither is knowledge of the meaning of the words sufficient for knowing what the dominant act is.

RECORDER: You have been explicating and defending the

two planks of the Principle of Distinguishable Resources. According to the first there is a distinction
between two kinds of resource: the first is of times
and modes sufficient to make clear what act of language
one performs, for example putting a question; the second is of times and modes sufficient to make clear, for
example, what the question is which is put. According
to the second, two distinct achievements--making clear
that a question is put and saying what the question is
--are reached by using distinct resources. According
to your recent discussion it is not enough, saying,
"ask", to make clear that one is asking something.
(2)
ALEXANDER: Let us turn next to an account of uses of
words essential to our examples. There are four groups
of words for us to consider: demonstratives, T-expressions, O-words and U- and A-expressions. Let us adopt
a creation myth, by changing a myth of our tradition.
Let us say that Adam and Eve have lived in society for
some time. It was laid down in the last part of our
discussion that society precedes the evolution of language. So Adam, Eve, their children, friends, acquain-
tances and enemies did not first form a community by
speaking with one another. There was no original con-
tract. You understand me.
RECORDER: Yes, yes. I'm writing as fast as you're
speaking. (turning to the Chancellor) Will teaching
his myth be obligatory in my department?
CHANCELLOR: No. Mr. Alexander, do continue.
ALEXANDER: People first mastered patterns of timing
and intonation of my first species: patterns sufficient
to make it evident that a warning is given, that help
is being called for or that an order is given. For
making so much clear it is not necessary to coin an expression such as "warn", "help" or "order". At last
the time came when words were coined. Achievements
were first reached of disclosing what is done. There
are, in particular, certain actions whose mastery is
necessary for the creation and the maintenance of society. One day Adam ordered someone to do something.
Their society was far enough developed to make certain
instances of clarity possible: the person can follow
Adam without Adam having to say who is giving the order
and without having to say that he is giving an order;
so much is already clear. But since Adam means to order the person to do what he can only anticipate having
him do, it becomes necessary for Adam to make clear to
the person what it is that he is ordered to do. To
that end he coins the verb "to fish". Under some such
call to reaching certain objectives many other verbs

are coined.

Our community of people are still without means for saying Who and What (beyond what actions are executed either in the natural, the social or the communicative worlds). So let us consider the coinage and use of a demonstrative word, for example the word "this". It can be granted that simply in showing someone something I do not make clear either that that is what I am doing or what it is that is being shown. But I can make clear what I am showing you by subordinating the utterance of the word "this" to the act of showing you something. For in showing you something I coordinate moving my arms and uttering a word; thus do I account for subordination and coordination on the side of action. With respect to achievements I say that making plain what the word is which is uttered is subordinate to making plain what is being shown, namely this. Lest you misunderstand the force of what I am saying I will append a distinction between making clear what I am showing you and saying what this is. To achieve the first, clear utterance of a demonstrative word can be sufficient; to achieve the second so much is not sufficient. But for either achievement showing someone something is not sufficient. When I say that I can show you what I have in my hand, I mean, therefore, that I can show you the thing which I have in my hand. I do not mean that I can show you what it is. Showing would then not be an action but an achievement of communication.

KEITH: I allow that by pronouncing a word in a certain way one can succeed in making evident what the word is which is pronounced. I must still ask you how it is possible further to reach the achievement of making clear what is shown.

ALEXANDER: An additional achievement is managed because one subordinates uttering a word to showing someone something. In a corresponding way the achievement of making evident what the word is whose utterance is thus subordinated becomes support for making evident what it is to the showing of which utterance of the word is subordinated.

KEITH: So by thus uttering the word "this" you make plain what you are showing us. You do not SAY what this is.

ALEXANDER: Indeed not. To do so we must allow the existence of what I call T-expressions. But we are now in a position to lay down guidelines for accounting for their coinage.

CHANCELLOR: Before you do so, I wish to be sure I have the spirit of your discussion. It has been customary for people who think about language to say that words are building blocks, capable of combination and separation.

ALEXANDER: Over the years there has been a shift in my thought from a substance centered towards an act and achievement-centered philosophy. The linguistic counterpart of the shift is one from an emphasis upon words and their relations to an emphasis upon the utterance, the thinking and the writing of words and the relations between and among acts of utterance, thought and writing.

CHANCELLOR: So the focus of your discussion is upon acts of utterance and the achievements which the acts support.

ALEXANDER: Yes.

CHANCELLOR: The immediate achievement of uttering the word "this" is making plain what the word is which is uttered; that achievement supports another: making clear What. Even the second achievement is not much.

ALEXANDER: Indeed, it is not much. The coordination of simple achievements supports the reaching of complex achievements. And with respect to action it is not enough simply to say, "this"; if you mean to support a conceptual hierarchy, you must do more. You join a community and participate in certain institutions; within a certain institution you join certain activities. In particular, you point to something or show me something and utter the word "this". You may now have assembled support sufficient for continuing.

CHANCELLOR: I understand. You said a moment ago that we are in a position to have guidelines for accounting for the coinage and the utterance of T-expressions. (3)

ALEXANDER: Yes. The first guideline to remember is that the second achievement of uttering a T-expression such as "a pen" is to say What; the second guideline to remember is that to complete certain tasks which subordinate uttering the words "a pen" it is necessary to coordinate their utterance and some other act of utterance.

KEITH: Do you mean to imply that it would not be enough merely to point to something and to utter the words "a pen"?

ALEXANDER: Yes.

KEITH: Then in the sense in which I reach a higher achievement when I both point to something and utter the word "this" I do not reach a comparable achievement when I both point to something and utter the words "a table".

ALEXANDER: Indeed. You do not succeed in saying what

you are pointing to simply by pointing to something and by uttering the words "a table". By doing some thinking on our own, of course, we may take it that you are pointing to a table.

KEITH: So the act of pointing to something is a third act in addition to uttering a T-expression and a second act of utterance.

ALEXANDER: Yes. To make perfectly plain to you what we have in mind when we speak of a T-expression let us imagine Adam completing a family of natural acts; he brings our attention to bear upon that at which he is looking when he says, "This." He continues in order to say what this is, saying "is T."

RECORDER: We're to understand that "T" can stand for "a pen", "a book", "water" or "gold".

ALEXANDER: Yes. The third class of words I call O-words.

RECORDER: Before you discuss them, I wish to make sure I have the point of your last two discussions of demonstratives and T-expressions. The first achievement of uttering or writing a word is making known what the word is which is uttered or written.

ALEXANDER: Right.

RECORDER: The second achievement of the first class of words is making clear What, Who, When or Where. I can reach the second achievement saying, "This", "I", "Now" or "Here".

ALEXANDER: Right.

RECORDER: The second achievement of the second class of words is saying What. I take it that second achievements are sometimes coordinated.

ALEXANDER: You now anticipate our discussion of assertion.

CHANCELLOR: Perhaps you should turn to the third class of words.

(The Porter knocked at our door and entered, pushing his tray in front of him.)

PORTER: How are things going? (He looks around. Katherine looks up and smiles.)

KATHERINE: Fine. Now we've got a myth on our hands.

PORTER: A myth? That's not scientific.

KATHERINE: An evolutionary myth.

PORTER: At school we were told that evolution is science and creation, a myth.

KATHERINE: There are two ways a philosopher can go. He can suppose our conceptual framework tries to match a reality which is contemporaneous with it. Suppose the framework were a photograph of you. I have both before me at the same time: I look from your photograph to you in order to tell whether there is a sufficiently

strong likeness. You understand me?
PORTER: (still pouring coffee) I suppose so.
KATHERINE: The philosopher of the first way has no
urgent need of history; indeed, he would prefer to
match timeless entities: propositions and facts, for
example. The second philosopher can suppose our conceptual framework is a rational instrument whose use
aims at certain achievements. Its construction and use
are grounded in a community; as a community evolves and
develops so does its framework.
PORTER: But how does the question of its construction
and evolution become a philosophical question? Why
would I come to your academy and study philosophy in
order to get an answer?
KATHERINE: I suppose it's an assumption of the second
way that a philosopher desires to understand the use of
high ranking conceptual instruments; he fears confusion
and error concerning their employment.
PORTER: Is such understanding not possible without an
account of the construction and the evolution of what
you call a conceptual framework?
KATHERINE: It is not possible.
PORTER: Can you make me see why not? Along the first
way a philosopher is busy matching. So of course he
must account for two things: a photograph or a copy and
an original, as you say. Your second philosopher is
equally busy.
KATHERINE: Yes. The first is busy comparing. On his
best day the things compared are contemporaneous or
timeless. The second is busy criticizing. On his best
day the things examined are successive. The first philosopher arms himself in the house of sameness and
otherness; his principal question is whether two things
compared are the same. The second philosopher arms
himself in the house of defect, sufficiency and excess;
his principal question is whether means taken are sufficient for a certain end.
PORTER: I still don't see why a myth is part of the
second way.
KATHERINE: An account of the second way needs a plausible story of institution and of the laying foundations; the second way then needs to make sense of following.
PORTER: Never mind. I'll be back at 10:00. You evidently have a long day before you.
(4)
ALEXANDER: By "O-words" we have in mind such pairs of
words as "long" and "short" and "hot" and "cold". The
symbol "O" was originally lifted from the word "opposite".

34

RECORDER: Your O-words have been of great service to philosophers. Locke would say, I believe, that "cold" names a simple idea.
ALEXANDER: To say so is to over-characterize O-words. I would have you take to heart a principle about the use of O-words. The first achievement of using an O-word, of course, is making clear what the word is; the second achievement is not saying what is before us or saying what its length or color is. The word "long" is not uttered in giving support for the achievement of saying what idea is in the mind. Further, the second achievement of using "long" is not disclosing a length.
CHANCELLOR: Perhaps you should explain your principle.
ALEXANDER: Suppose one says, "The child is becoming taller." The word "tall" is an O-word. Suppose, contrary to my principle, that the word is the name of a quality, in particular that the word means the same as "four feet". It would follow that when one says, "The child is becoming taller," one means, "The child is becoming more four feet." Following a method which will be laid out when we discuss sameness and otherness I inquire what the two subordinate sentences are which can be extracted from the sentence "The child is becoming more four feet." I answer: first, "He is four feet now" and, second, "He was four feet then."
But one cannot mean to assert that the height which he has now is the height which he had then. It is therefore not possible to subordinate and coordinate the two sentences towards making the desired remark. It follows that the initial premiss is wrong, namely that "tall" is the name of a quality. My principle is accordingly defended that it is possible to remark that a child is becoming taller without saying how tall when one utters the word "tall".
KATHERINE: Despite the explanation and the illustration of your principle I still fail to follow. You argue from the supposition that the word "tall" is the name of a height. So when one says, "The child is becoming taller," one would mean that the child is becoming more four feet. Why do you use the word "more" in saying what would be meant?
ALEXANDER: I mean to suppose that we treat the word "tall" as we do the expression "four feet"; for we do say that four feet is a height. The expression "er" remains. I have further assumed that the expression belongs to the family of expressions indicating sameness and otherness; "er" indicates otherness.
KATHERINE: Could we not allow that tall is a height, as we do allow that four feet is a height, and mean rather that the child is becoming of a greater height?

ALEXANDER: But "great" and "small" are O-words as well; they are not A-words of a U-system.
KATHERINE: I can express myself in another way: he is coming to be of another height.
ALEXANDER: Do you mean that he is coming to be of another four feet?
KATHERINE: Why do you put that question to me?
ALEXANDER: Because a pair of O-words and their U-word, in this case "tall", "short" and "height" behave in similar ways; I mean to distinguish their uses from that of the A-expression "four feet"; for it is the A-expression which we use to disclose a height or a length.
KATHERINE: I see. So I should try to make tolerable sense of saying, "The child is coming to be of another four feet" or of saying, "The child is becoming more four feet."
ALEXANDER: I would say so.
KATHERINE: I cannot.
ALEXANDER: Then are you satisfied that I have disproved the assumption that the word "tall" is the name of a quality?
KATHERINE: Yes.
ALEXANDER: Another problem arises if one makes the assumption. Suppose one does assume that long is a quality as we do hold that 60 degrees is a temperature. One says at one time that this tape is long, that it is getting longer and now that it is long. One would have to concede that one uses "long" in an ambiguous way. For one utters the word to disclose different qualities. Further, one is open to the question, "And through how many qualities has the tape moved?"
KATHERINE: But suppose in an analogous way I say that a column of mercury shows a degree, that it is rising and now that it shows a degree. The word "high" would be in the same position you place "long" in. Further, one is open to the question, "And through how many degrees has the column risen?"
ALEXANDER: Indeed. We can answer your question; we, after all, did the calibrating. But with respect to my example there are philosophers who argue that there is no way of finding out through how many qualities the tape has moved as it was becoming longer.
KATHERINE: Is your point that Zeno's paradoxes have not been solved?
ALEXANDER: No. I mean to argue rather that it is a particular account of the use of O-words which invites having difficulties formulated. My account does not admit the formulation of them.
    Having already stated a principle, namely that the

utterance of an O-word does not support making evident,
for example, what is before us or what its length is,
I propose to give our positive account. The first
achievement of using the word "long", for example, is
making evident what the word is; the second is making
evident what is being said in the course of laying down
or taking a path to which there can be a parallel path.
There can therefore be disagreement as to what to say--
not, however, as to what the length is of the object
before us. So the use of O-words helps provide a foundation for another kind of achievement.
(4.1)
CHANCELLOR: I'm not sure I know the point of your discussing a vocabulary that includes such words as "hot"
and "cold". I know very well that you mean to promote
a view of a hierarchy of acts; acts, in turn, are sometimes necessary and sufficient for certain achievements.
ALEXANDER: In order to make some things clear I depend
upon certain examples, saying "The water is hot" or
"The table is long." Further, it is the practice of
philosophers to consider simple acts and achievements
presupposed for reaching the kind of knowledge of traditional interest to philosophy. I would say, finally,
that things can go wrong even with an inquiry that con-
siders simples. Perhaps I can give you an example of
what I mean if Julian is willing to read aloud a part
from George Berkeley's first dialogue between Hylas and
Philonous.
(He opened a book and showed me from what place he
wished me to read.)
RECORDER:
    PHILONOUS: Heat therefore, if it be allowed a real
    being, must exist without the mind.
    HYLAS: It must.
    PHILONOUS: Tell me, Hylas, is this real existence
    equally compatible to all degrees of heat, which we
    perceive: or is there any reason why we should at-
    tribute it to some, and deny it others? And if
    there be, pray let me know that reason.
    HYLAS: Whatever degree of heat we perceive by
    sense, we may be sure the same exists in the object
    that occasions it.
    PHILONOUS: What, the greatest as well as the
    least?
    HYLAS: I tell you, the reason is plainly the same
    in respect of both: they are both perceived by
    sense; nay, the greater degree of heat is more sen-
    sibly perceived; and consequently, if there is any
    difference, we are more certain of its real exis-

37

tence than we can be of the reality of a lesser
degree.
PHILONOUS: But is not the most vehement and in-
tense degree of heat a very great pain?
HYLAS: No one can deny it.
PHILONOUS: And is any unperceiving thing capable
of pain or pleasure?
HYLAS: No certainly.
ALEXANDER: I think you can stop. Things go from bad
to worse. (turning to the Chancellor) Berkeley uses
the word "heat" as if its use were adequate to accomplish a certain sort of thing.
CHANCELLOR: Of course: to reach the achievement of
saying what is perceived. I'm sure he would say the
same about the use of the word "hot". Suppose I plunge
my hand into water. I say, "It feels hot."
ALEXANDER: We would certainly complain if we were in
want of vocabulary suitable for saying what the objects
of actions and achievements are. Suppose I reach out
my hand, meaning to touch something. We don't go as
far as we would wish to go, using only the words "some"
and "thing".
CHANCELLOR: No one would say you had gone as far as
one would wish.
ALEXANDER: Suppose I meant to realize my wish of saying what it is I can touch. Would you offer the word
"heat"?
CHANCELLOR: No. But no one is talking about touching
heat. We're concerned with perceiving heat.
ALEXANDER: Perceiving heat?
CHANCELLOR: Yes, yes.
ALEXANDER: Perceiving is either an action such as
looking at something or touching something or it is an
achievement such as seeing something.
CHANCELLOR: Feeling hot is obviously not an action.
The words have the ring of passivity about them.
ALEXANDER: I'm sure I don't know what feeling hot is;
I'm sure I know what it is not: neither an action nor
an achievement.
CHANCELLOR: Indeed. The word "hot" neither tells one
what the object of an action is nor tells one what the
object of an achievement is. Perhaps we should distinguish perceiving and feeling. Would it help to do so?
ALEXANDER: Certainly we should, if we mean to distinguish acts and achievements of mind from states of the
soul.
CHANCELLOR: If we use the distinction, would we be
closer to saying what is accomplished when I say, "It
feels hot"?
ALEXANDER: I'm not able to go beyond what I have al-

ready said to you: by putting your hand in the water and by being affected you are in a position suitable for making a comment about the water. Use of the word "hot" makes evident what to say. I fear there is no further secret in the use of such words.
CHANCELLOR: And I fear I am not so easily won over. Suppose I assert, "This room is too hot to sit in." I leave. Have I not given an explanation as to why I leave?
ALEXANDER: Yes, I suppose so.
CHANCELLOR: But surely there cannot be means excessive for one end without there being means sufficient for another end. It follows the room is hot enough for leaving. Leaving, we can say, is an effect: an effect which depends upon a certain cause. Part of that cause must be the room being hot to a particular degree. It must therefore be proper to say that the room being hot is a real event, helping to form the cause of a real effect. So the word "hot" must reveal to us a property which, together with this room compose that event.
KATHERINE: So just as we sit in this room so in part we must be sitting in heat. Is that what you mean?
ALEXANDER: No. He means that my account of what I call O-words is wrong. He means that the word reveals a property which helps play a causal role; it can therefore be an object of our experience. (turning to the Chancellor) Do I have you wrong?
CHANCELLOR: No. You look at me with astonishment. Have I said something absurd?
ALEXANDER: I don't know. You've said several things and implied several things. Tell me: Do you mean to say that every explanation is a causal explanation?
CHANCELLOR: Why do you ask?
ALEXANDER: You implied, a moment ago, that when you say, "This room is too hot to sit in," you explain why you leave. You then laid down a premiss which I do not feel fit to criticize: if there are means excessive for one end, those means are sufficient for another end. So since the room is too hot to remain in, it is hot enough for leaving. It seems to me that you then reason by means of a very powerful instrument of reason.
CHANCELLOR: I was not aware of having in my hands any such instrument.
KATHERINE: Since I don't know what Bill is referring to, I wasn't aware of any such thing either.
CHANCELLOR: What instrument do you mean?
ALEXANDER: I mean the premiss that whenever there is sufficiency of some means for an end, the emergence or the continuance of the end depends upon the existence of the means. Let's abbreviate a statement of the pre-

miss by saying that a statement of sufficiency usually implies dependency. The abbreviated statement helps us see that use of the premiss carries us from the category of defect, sufficiency and excess to the category of dependence and independence.

KATHERINE: I've never heard the premiss articulated before. Mind you, I don't find it surprising. When I first took up the study of logic, I was told that the words "If ..., then ..." suggest the dependence of one event or state of affairs upon another. It is granted that the if-clause states something sufficient for something else. I think it is thought to follow that the second depends upon the first.

KEITH: But no good logician thinks that what is sufficient is therefore also necessary. And to say that the first of two things is necessary for the second is simply to say that the second depends upon the first. So although it is true that the room is warm enough to sit in with comfort, it does not follow that sitting in the room with comfort depends upon the room having a certain degree of heat. If there is a causal relation within view of our example, it is between sitting in the room and believing or saying that the room is warm enough.

CHANCELLOR: I accept the consequence of your criticism of the premiss.

KEITH: Then you have not done enough to move us to give up Alexander's account.

CHANCELLOR: But now I wonder whether the account is worth having.

KATHERINE: Have we wasted your time so early this morning?

ALEXANDER: (ignoring Katherine's question) What do you mean?

CHANCELLOR: Can anything really be real which does not play a causal role? I don't think the scientific mind has time for something that is neither part of a cause nor yet part of an effect. According to your account the use of the words "hot", "cold" and "heat" is not adequate for disclosing a cause or an effect. I take it that so much can also be said about the following triads of words: long, short, length; light, dark, color, and near, far and distance. The employment of such words is not adequate for disclosing objects of perception or causes and effects. You grant their use is adequate for disclosing certain objects of using conceptual resources. Not much of a grant! You can imagine a conversation between us short on philosophy. I say, "A warm day." You reply, "Yeah, it really is."

KATHERINE: Not a brilliant conversation. Not even

Socrates could dump it into the lap of philosophy.
CHANCELLOR: I still have something on my mind. According to Alexander's account, when I utter the word
"warm", I do not succeed in disclosing what it is I
have perceptual experience of. I do not mention any
part of either a cause or an effect. I contribute only
to an understanding of what is to be said in the context of daily life.
ALEXANDER: You've come to the bottom of the foundation
of our conceptual framework.
KATHERINE: He expected to see pylons, driven deep into
nature, supporting our framework. (looking at the
Chancellor and smiling, but expressing a certain sympathy) How little you must feel at home, trying to sit
down in Bill's account of pragmatism.
RECORDER: (looking at the Chancellor) If you were
sympathetic with Bill's position, you would also be
sympathetic with Democritus: by convention is sweet; by
convention, bitter; by convention, hot; by convention,
cold; by convention, color.
KATHERINE: Don't forget the wonderful conclusion: "In
truth are atoms and the void."
ALEXANDER: I'm not sure how much I can help you. I
wonder, though, how serious you are when you say that
nothing is real which does not play a causal role. Are
you serious?
CHANCELLOR: Lord knows you know that I am not a philosopher. Perhaps I vent anger against metaphysics. I
would like to stand with people of science.
ALEXANDER: We will have occasion today to discuss
causality. I hope I'm not wide of our best road when I
say that a cause is a range of factors each one necessary for an effect, each one adequate in its own way
for an effect and which are together sufficient for an
effect. Thus do some of us define causality.
CHANCELLOR: The definition is fine with me.
ALEXANDER: In giving it I mentioned a causal relation,
namely that of dependence of an effect upon a cause or,
conversely, that of the necessity of a cause for an
effect. Are you willing to say that a cause is one
thing and its effect another?
CHANCELLOR: Yes. Your distinction I respected when I
say that to be real is to be either a cause or an effect.
ALEXANDER: Is the relation of dependence a third
thing, distinct from or other than either a cause or an
effect?
CHANCELLOR: I wish I were not involved in this argument. It is very early in the morning. I ought to
have kept my view to myself.

KATHERINE: Exposure is not over-exposure.
RECORDER: You can't give up the argument now. I'm
taking notes.
CHANCELLOR: I wish you hadn't learned short-hand. All
right. I'll answer the question. If there were no
such thing as the relation of dependence, there would
be no causation. For then everything would be separate
and independent. But I will not say that the relation
is a third thing, something other than either a cause
or an effect. I would then have to alter my definition
of reality. So the relation is either part of a cause
or part of an effect.
ALEXANDER: Do you happen to have any idea which it is?
CHANCELLOR: You do force me to take a stand, don't
you? I'll say, "part of the cause."
ALEXANDER: I believe the cause of the top of this
table maintaining its position in space is a range of
things including several legs, their strength and disposition. According to your view the range also includes the relation of dependence. So the table top
in part depends upon dependence. Just now, when I uttered the two words "depends" and "dependence", did I
indicate two things or one thing only?
CHANCELLOR: One thing alone: part of the cause.
ALEXANDER: Now tell me: Do you think one can mention
a part of a whole when one means to mention a relation
between that whole and something else?
(The Chancellor paused--I thought a long time. He
looked at Alexander and smiled.)
CHANCELLOR: The argument has become too difficult for
me to prosecute. (turning to Katherine) Perhaps you
know how to answer.
KATHERINE: I haven't a clue.
ALEXANDER: Perhaps we can take up the argument at a
later time.
CHANCELLOR: Fine.
(5)
RECORDER: You said you were going to mention four
classes of expressions. We have now discussed the demonstrative "this", the expression "a table" and the ad-
jectives "hot" and "cold". The fourth class of expressions you call U- and A-expressions.
CHANCELLOR: What do the letters stand for?
ALEXANDER: "U" stands for "universal" and "A", for
"answering expression". By a U-word we understand, for
example, "length" and "color". Remember that uttering
a U-word makes it possible to put a certain kind of
What-question, for example, what the length is of something or what its color is. And by an A-expression we
understand such expressions as are uttered or written

in answering a U-question, for example, "one foot", "two feet", "red" and "blue".
RECORDER: Your argument about O-words shows that there is a distinction between the use of a pair of O-words and their U-word on the one hand, and, on the other, their A-expressions.
ALEXANDER: Yes. T- and A-expressions support second achievements: saying What in the first case and, in the second, revealing a U.
CHANCELLOR: Revealing a U? You mean, for example, revealing a number, a color, a length or a name.
ALEXANDER: Yes.
CHANCELLOR: Do universals exist?
ALEXANDER: Can one reveal or disclose and yet reveal nothing?
CHANCELLOR: You must disclose something.
ALEXANDER: Something that is or something that is not?
CHANCELLOR: Something that is.
ALEXANDER: Then since, by uttering a U-word, I sometimes do enough to disclose a universal, universals exist.
KATHERINE: (looking at the Chancellor with some sympathy) I know how you feel. I was once an avid nominalist, don't you know: denying the existence of universals. I have made my peace with Bill's persistent effort to help me find the Mean: some position between two extreme positions.
CHANCELLOR: What do you mean?
KATHERINE: Let us play God, wondering what it would be either to create a world in which there are particulars and no universals or to create a world in which there are universals and no particulars.
KEITH: Well, in the first world one would perceive without knowing and in the second one would know without perceiving.
KATHERINE: You have too often played God. I'm speaking with the Chancellor. You can imagine that in the first world there are substances: objects and masses. I suspect that you, as a scientist, would feel at home in the first world.
CHANCELLOR: I should say rather that as a nominalist I would feel at home. Some scientists, after all, are Platonists.
KATHERINE: Of course. I didn't mean to abuse your colleagues.
CHANCELLOR: You must have had some point saying that God's plans for two such worlds would be extreme. Did you mean that each plan is defective or excessive for creating a world which we can make sense of?
KATHERINE: Yes.

CHANCELLOR: Why would a world of universality be defective or excessive?
KATHERINE: There would be space but nothing which occupies it; places but nothing at them; durations but
nothing which lasts them, and times but nothing happening at them. I would say such a world would be defective. Wouldn't you?
CHANCELLOR: Lord knows I didn't think up such a world.
KEITH: Could God have placed any people in it?
KATHERINE: No, of course not. For there isn't anything at a place or anything which is of a certain
quantity.
KEITH: What about minds without bodies?
KATHERINE: Wouldn't you like that? Well, there would
be no thinking either at or for a time. Further, there
would be only one of us, as it were, a species. Consider: when I point to Julian and assert, "That is a
person," I point to a particular thing and make clear
to what I point, saying, "that." Now that thing would
not exist in our first extreme world.
RECORDER: I wouldn't want to, either.
KATHERINE: No one is consulting either your desires or
your aversions, Julian. Let me carry on: in addition
to making clear to what I point I also say what that
is, saying, "a person." Now saying What, is an
achievement: its object is a universal. To know that
universal is to know what that particular thing is.
The universal would exist in our first world; Julian
would not. But since I know the same universal when I
know what you are, what you are and what you are, there
would be only one universal and none of us. You see
what I mean.
CHANCELLOR: I've heard enough of the first world. I
agree with you, Katherine; it would be defective. Any
world too little to support the communication of scientists is absolutely defective. Let's turn to the plan
for a world of particularity. Very clever people have
tried to make it appear inhabitable.
KATHERINE: Indeed. Both Keith and I, when we first
met at college, argued that we do in fact live in such
a world. But over the years Professor Alexander has
convinced me that even that world is too little.
RECORDER: But not me.
KATHERINE: Not Julian. Through his anglo-saxon veins
runs not blood but nominalism.
CHANCELLOR: What would the defect of that world be a
defect of in particular?
KATHERINE: Of thought and knowledge. We recently accounted for the use of such O-words as "many" and
"few"; we understand how their use can serve the making

of comparisons, saying, for example, "There are as many
books here as there are there." I can also say, "The
two piles are of the same number." Suppose I know that
number. We would not have the knowledge I have, were
there no universals, for example the number 5. That
number is a universal and not a particular: it is not
at a place; it does not occupy space. It does not happen at a time nor last for a time. Should God have
created the second world, have placed us in it and yet
not have made it possible for us to know how many books
are in each of two piles?
KEITH: Don't answer. She wants to go on. The question was entirely rhetorical.
KATHERINE: In the first world we tried to imagine
times without particular events. Try now to imagine
events without times. Things happen but not at or for
a time; there are bodies but none occupying space. Can
you imagine it?
CHANCELLOR: I don't think you mean to invite me to
exercise the faculty of imagination. I suspect your
point is other: God would not know what He is doing,
planning either such world. Let me try to understand
you: God would reason defectively either when He
thinks, "Times and places, but no events or bodies" or
when He thinks, "Events and bodies, but no times or
places." Do I understand you?
KATHERINE: Yes, yes. Go on.
CHANCELLOR: Go on? Go on where?
KATHERINE: You know how to articulate a certain metaphysical insight.
CHANCELLOR: No, I don't. You over-estimate me.
KATHERINE: You do it, then, Keith. You're our budding
metaphysician.
KEITH: Well, I'll try. (He paused, looking at
Alexander and appeared to me to be nervous.) Thinking
the reality of universals mutually depends upon thinking the reality of particulars. We do not say that
particulars and universals depend one upon the other
for their reality. Our metaphysical position does not
restrict God's creating, as it were, but His conceptual
planning. The mind does not have conceptual resources
adequate for making clear what it would be to plan to
create the first and the second worlds.
CHANCELLOR: Perhaps I'll ask you, later in the day, to
deliver your insight to me in some detail. I think I
understand that the two extreme positions are not adequate. We're to believe in the existence and the reality both of particulars and of universals.
RECORDER: If both particulars and universals exist and
if there is a distinction between them, then one of

four metaphysical positions must be right. I base the
inference upon the premiss that if there is otherness,
then there is either dependence or independence. The
first of the four would be that universals depend upon
particulars for their existence; the second, that particulars depend upon universals. The third is that
there is mutual dependence, and the fourth, finally,
that there is independence between the two kinds of
things.
ALEXANDER: There will be an opportunity this afternoon
to consider the positions.
RECORDER: Fine.
ALEXANDER: Having completed a partial survey of vocabulary essential to our examples I can turn to our next
objective: an account of our framework sufficient to
support simple assertion and negation. My first example is, "This table is long"; the second example, "This
table is six feet long."
CHANCELLOR: Before you begin, I ask you why an account
of such examples is relevant to giving an account of
the possibility of speaking the truth.
(6)
ALEXANDER: We proceed according to the following position. There are two stages which we pass either in
coming to make a disclosure as to a matter of fact or
in making an assertion. The first stage is one of instigation; the second, one of use. The first stage has
three steps. The first is taken by selecting an example, a paradigm or a standard.
CHANCELLOR: Of course. One must begin by taking a
stand in the natural or in the social world.
ALEXANDER: The second step is reached having laid down
a path of language with respect to the example, the
paradigm or the standard selected. For example, I lay
down what to say in order to say what the color of this
is, saying, "This is red."
CHANCELLOR: So at the second step one can both coin a
word and subordinate its coinage to instituting its utterance.
ALEXANDER: Yes.
KEITH: And can a member of our mythical community pass
from the first to the second stage?
ALEXANDER. Yes. For suppose that Adam does coin the
word "red" and institute its utterance when he says,
"This is red." It is possible for a follower to pass
to the second stage by saying the word after Adam; a
member of the community can follow Adam.
KEITH: And can the question arise of proceeding correctly?
ALEXANDER: Of course. But now you anticipate subse-

46

quent discussion. The third step of the first stage is reached by creating a potential basis the realization of which is sufficient for continuance. For example, Adam lays down the premiss "Whatever other object has the same color as this object is red." When he utters the words "whatever other object has the same color as this object", he creates a potential basis for continuance. You can effect realization by making application; you make application by asserting that that object has the same color as this one. By making application you can follow Adam. Indeed, by applying and following the premiss you reach the second stage; for you make complete use of it.

RECORDER: So the first stage is one of creation and instigation; the second stage is one of use.

ALEXANDER: Yes.

RECORDER: I understand your accounts of the first two steps. The Premier reached the first step when he selected this man as Chancellor. An assembly reaches the second step when it lays down what to say in order to say of what weight or length a scales or a ruler is.

ALEXANDER: Indeed.

RECORDER: But I do not have an adequate grasp of your account of the third step.

ALEXANDER: There will be an opportunity to consider it at a later time. My concern, at the moment, is to help you to an understanding of the first two steps of the first stage.

CHANCELLOR: So much we do understand.

RECORDER: Do we?

CHANCELLOR: (looking surprised and turning to Julian) Have I not responded appropriately?

RECORDER: All metaphysical systems face two principal alternatives. The first is that our conceptual framework stands in certain critical relationships either to a divine system of thought or to the structure of the natural world. According to the first alternative the ground of truth lies outside our framework; moments of genuine authority lie apart from it. The second alternative is that with respect to certain critical questions our conceptual framework is autonomous. Authority is exercised in creating the framework.

The two alternatives have been taken by great philosophers: the first by Plato and by Platonists, and the second by Confucius and by Confucians. The choice of a kind of metaphysical system adjusts the subsequent burden of philosophical proof. Choosing the first kind leads to an emphasis upon the relations between system and ground and showing how the relations can be demonstrated; choosing the second kind leads to an emphasis upon acts of authority and acts of following. Consider further the second case; for I think you will find that it is Alexander's.

A philosopher who makes the second choice is bound to adopt either a creation myth or a myth of restitution and further instigation. Confucius looks back to the Sage-king Wu; in "The Rectification of Terms" Hsüntze writes, "When the Kings had regulated names, when they had fixed terms and so distinguished realities, and when this principle was carried out and hence their will was everywhere known, they were careful to lead the people and so the people were unified." Such philosophers mean to keep alive a moment of authority; for their myths are kept close at hand for purposes of reform.

It is my opinion that our friend here (pointing to Alexander) is of the second school. The backbone of his system is an account of two kinds of action: instigating, first, and, second, applying and following.

ALEXANDER: Julian is right to place my efforts along side those of the second school. I hope you can join me in dividing our time: between trying to understand but to refute the first school and trying to account for and to defend the interests of the second school. (7)

CHANCELLOR: Of course. There is a second matter which I should perhaps express. You have the vice scholars sometimes have: you speak as if those listening have pencils at hand, writing everything down. I am not a student. Though I would like to join you in the pursuit of philosophical wisdom, I have little patience for the classification of vocabulary. I don't mean to offend you; I hope you understand me. I suppose I know well enough what demonstrative expressions are. By "T-expression" do you mean thing-words?

ALEXANDER: More or less.

CHANCELLOR: And by "O-words" "opposites"?

ALEXANDER: Yes.

CHANCELLOR: And I suppose there's no mystery about U-and A-expressions: "U" stands for a universal and "A" for an answering expression. Is there anything more to your abbreviations?

ALEXANDER: Not much more.

CHANCELLOR: Why have you burdened us with the use of such abbreviations?

ALEXANDER: Some years ago we met at a session of a summer institute.

CHANCELLOR: I know. Julian made a record of that session.

ALEXANDER: We came to think it important to account

48

both for a distinction between particular things and
movements, on the one hand, and, on the other, universals and also for a distinction between the use of expressions which help make clear what particular things
and movements are before us and the use of expressions
which disclose universals. For example, this chair is
a particular object; its shape, color and weight are
universals. We were also concerned to account for the
use of the expressions "this" and "chair", on the one
hand, and, on the other, "white" and "20 pounds".
     Part of the reason why we thought so much important
is that influential philosophers sometimes do not adequately account for particulars and universals. With
respect to universals, for example, we formulated the
thesis that nothing both is and has a U: nothing both
is and has a color; nothing both is and has a time;
nothing both is and has a duration.
RECORDER: Many students read St. Augustine's Confes-
sions: in Book XI he asks what time is. According to
the sort of diagnosis that Alexander has taught us to
give, Augustine writes as though a time has a time and
a duration has a duration. We accordingly criticize
his thinking and convict it on a charge of confusion.
For example, he asks whether time can be long or short.
He continues somewhat in the following way. The present time, which alone we found worthy to be called
long, is contracted to hardly the space of a single
day. But not even a single day is present in its to-
tality. It is completed in twenty-four hours of night
and day.
CHANCELLOR: I very well see what you mean. Augustine
writes as though he were writing not of times and durations but rather of the running of a race.
RECORDER: In such a state of confusion he argues a
commonplace among students first learning philosophy:
past and future time is not real; the present moment
alone is real. But his argument is defective; for it
rests upon a mistaken assumption: namely that a duration comes to be, endures and passes away.
CHANCELLOR: Your example does convince me that we require a statement of a distinction between motion and
time. How would such a statement help one with the
problems which must have led Augustine into speculation
about the nature of time?
RECORDER: You remember how Genesis opens: "In the beginning God created the heaven and the earth."
Augustine imagines someone asking, "What was God doing
before He made heaven and earth?" Augustine argues
from the assumption that God created time. Since there
was no time before heaven and earth, it is pointless to

49

ask what God did then; there was no "then".
CHANCELLOR: But if you're right, Augustine no longer
has an answer to the Trouble-maker's question. For
times and durations, you say, are universals. A universal neither begins, continues nor ends; it does not
change. It is therefore not created.
KATHERINE: Let me take over the role of the Trouble-
maker; you know I never could stand so-called medieval
thought. Keith, you play Augustine. I suspect you
would like to have lived in the high Middle Ages.
KEITH: Fine.
KATHERINE: You grant that God created the heaven and
the earth at a time; it took Him one day, let's say, to
do so. With respect to the end of the first day we
ask: "What was He doing two days ago?"
KEITH: The question still makes no sense. When there
is neither motion nor action, there is no time. For
although time and motion are distinct, time depends for
its existence upon motion or action.
CHANCELLOR: A few minutes ago (II.5) we mentioned six
metaphysical positions about particulars and universals; we eliminated two extreme positions. I suppose
I see that your attention to the classification and the
use of language makes it possible to avoid certain con-
fusions. But such attention is not by itself adequate
to resolve the sort of metaphysical puzzle which St.
Augustine evidently had before his mind. (He turned
and looked at Alexander) Has Keith given us a formula
for resolving Augustine's puzzle?
ALEXANDER: You mean the formula that although time and
motion are distinct, time depends for its existence
upon motion or action?
CHANCELLOR: Yes.
RECORDER: Keith's formula belongs to the position
sometimes called that of immanent realism: universals
depend upon particulars.
CHANCELLOR: I've heard enough classification for the
moment. I want to know whether Keith has taken a firm
stand. Is his ground too, like Augustine's, slipping
away?
ALEXANDER: Well, let us see. (turning to Keith) You
say there would be no time, were there no motion.
Would you also say, not only on your own but also on
Augustine's behalf, that the world started?
KEITH: Yes.
ALEXANDER: You have joined me, I believe, in the use
of a certain metaphor: there is a city of concepts. On
a hill, slightly elevated above the others, sits the
reigning house--that of defect, sufficiency and excess.
Along the main street are located three principal but

minor houses: sameness and otherness, combination and separation, and dependence and independence.
KATHERINE: We may tire of the metaphor, Bill, but we will never never never forget it.
ALEXANDER: (not turning to acknowledge Katherine's remark) Do you know to which house the word "start" belongs? We are relentless borrowers of three concepts: those of beginning, of continuing and of ending. Is it not true?
KEITH: It is true; I grant it. To start? What is it to start, to continue and to finish? Let me think. Perhaps you'll let me change my mind by this afternoon when we discuss the family of sameness and otherness; but at the moment I'm inclined to say that "start" and "finish" belong to the genus of sameness and that "continue" belongs to that of otherness. For to say that it has started to rain is to say that there is an earliest time at which there is rain. To say that it has stopped raining is to say that there is a latest time at which there is rain. And to say that it continues to rain is to say that there are earlier and later times at which there is rain.
ALEXANDER: Let us let your explications stand. Since the world began, there is an earliest time at which there is motion. Suppose God accepts both your explication of beginning and your formula of immanent realism. He contemplates the creation of the world. If the world is to start, there must exist a time at which it starts; there must in fact be motion earlier than which there is no more world. For by your analogy, since it has started to rain, there must be raining earlier than which there is no more rain. But since time depends upon motion for its existence, there is no time until there is motion. Therefore, there exists no time AT WHICH the world starts. It follows further that the world does not start.
KATHERINE: So God is relieved of the job of creation.
RECORDER: Then God would have to create time and motion together.
ALEXANDER: What does "together" mean?
RECORDER: "At the same time."
ALEXANDER: Now you offend against a plank of what we used to call our U-Thesis: that no U has a U; in particular, that no time has a time. For you now suggest that a time would have a time.
RECORDER: Yes, yes, I see. Such metaphysics has been dropped on a charge of defect. (turning to the Chancellor) So you see, there is a puzzle.
CHANCELLOR: I see that your philosophy of language coupled with Keith's immanent realism is not powerful

51

enough to resolve the puzzle.

KATHERINE: We started out this morning with six positions regarding particulars and universals. Two fell
early; another's down. Three to go.

ALEXANDER: We can discuss the others as we go along.
(7.1)

KATHERINE: (turning to the Chancellor) You were evidently bored by our classification of vocabulary. Even
I find that sort of thing tiring. Do we too much attend to language to pursue philosophical wisdom?

CHANCELLOR: I have no wish to accuse you of excess.

KATHERINE: But you're thinking it. You find us in
love with words.

CHANCELLOR: I was once persuaded by reading Berkeley
that the abuse of language can raise a learned dust.
(Upon hearing the Chancellor mention Berkeley I went to
a shelf and secured a copy of his Principles of Human
Knowledge.)

RECORDER: I think the Chancellor has the end of the
introduction in mind--I mean the introduction to his
Principles:

>...In vain do we extend our view into the heavens,
>and pry into the entrails of the earth, in vain do
>we consult the writings of learned men, and trace
>the dark footsteps of antiquity; we need only draw
>the curtain of words, to behold the fairest tree of
>knowledge, whose fruit is excellent, and within the
>reach of our hand.

KATHERINE: What an extraordinary passage! Does he
mean that one can reach knowledge without the use of a
language or of any conceptual framework?

RECORDER: You have the privilege of belonging to a
tradition which thinks, from time to time since Plato,
that certain things can make known to us what they are;
so much they can make known without the help of language. Such things you can take naked into view, as
Berkeley says. Plato and Augustine could also have recommended the exercise to you. You perhaps remember
how Plato's remarkable dialogue Cratylus ends.
Socrates gives two reasons why we ought not finally
rely upon language for our knowledge. First, the giver
of the first names had knowledge of the things which he
named. But since he had knowledge before he gave
names, he could not have acquired the knowledge from
names. Therefore, knowledge is prior and independent.
Second, there may be inconsistency. For resolving the
inconsistency there must be another standard which,
without employing names, will make clear which of the
two is right. This must be a standard which shows the
truth of things.

KATHERINE: Some time ago (II.6) we were nursing along a creation myth. In the context of telling ourselves that myth I don't find Plato's first reason convincing. Adam sets a precedent for the use of the expression "a tree". Prior to setting the precedent he may well know what he is pointing to, namely that; prior to setting the precedent he does not know what that is. It is Plato's philosophy, my friend, and not ours that is burdened by the question "How, if he didn't then know what that is, could he get its name right?"
CHANCELLOR: You ought not lecture Julian on a point of history. He placed us between two great alternatives: either there is a ground of truth, existing naturally apart from our framework of language, or there is a foundation of truth, laid down by our first community in creating a framework. It seems to me that Julian meant to contrast Plato and Hsüntze by means of the question which you say burdens Plato's but not your philosophy.
KATHERINE: I don't doubt that it was Julian's remarks that stirred me to my own thoughts. Someone who writes as Plato does in his Cratylus, as Augustine does in his dialogue On the Teacher or as Berkeley does, concluding his introduction, writes as though one could set the ediface of language aside, see for oneself what things are and then perhaps reform and replace language, having freed one's intelligence from the constraints of bewitchment. Someone who writes as Julian represents Hsüntze writes as though one can find one's way back to the wisdom of sage-kings who set precedents and laid down paths of language. In light of that wisdom reform can be undertaken. Do I have everything wrong, Julian?
RECORDER: (I was in fact listening to Katherine with some admiration.) No, no. Your comments seem to me to be just.
CHANCELLOR: Would you expect a different kind of purification and reform in Europe than in China?
RECORDER: I don't know.
CHANCELLOR: (turning to Katherine) When a philosopher thinks he has set language aside, does anything terrible happen?
RECORDER: (Before Katherine could answer the Chancellor's question, the door opened and our Porter pushed his tray into the room. Katherine smiled and said hello, both protecting herself from the Chancellor's question and making Keith jealous, I believe. He served coffee according to protocol. When he came to Katherine, she said:)
KATHERINE: Would you like to know what we've done the last hour?

PORTER: I suppose so. Though I don't mean to imply
that you've convinced me philosophy is worth studying.
KATHERINE: We discussed causation a little. The Chancellor said at some point that whatever exists and is
real plays a causal role.
PORTER: You sound like the manager of this hotel: the
only real thing here is either someone who serves or is
served.
KATHERINE: There we have it: to be real is to act or
to be acted upon.
PORTER: Do you believe that? (He asked, astonished
and looking at Katherine.)
KATHERINE: I don't know what reality is.
PORTER: It would be nice to know.
KATHERINE: Indeed. If you were to spill coffee on my
dress, we'd all say that was real. We were discussing
universals and particulars during the last hour. I
suppose everyone allows that objects of perception play
causal roles. But universals don't.
PORTER: What is a universal?
KATHERINE: It's best to try to pick up philosophy by
means of examples: the number one is a universal. You
wouldn't want to say that the number one is the cause
of anything.
PORTER: No, I wouldn't.
KATHERINE: If you say, "There's one book here," you
don't employ the word "one" in giving a causal explanation of anything.
PORTER: I shouldn't think so.
KATHERINE: But isn't the number one real?
PORTER: Of course.
CHANCELLOR: You lead the boy on too easily.
RECORDER: Indeed. Aristotle would say that the number
one or unity is the formal cause of your knowledge of
how many books lie here.
KATHERINE: I'm not asking Aristotle.
CHANCELLOR: In any case the number one is an idea or a
concept. I don't know whether an idea or a concept is
a cause; I can assure you that a concept is an effect:
an effect of mastering the use of the numerals. To be
a number is to be the effect of mastering a certain
part of our linguistic framework. Or have I misunderstood your pragmatism?
ALEXANDER: The effect of mastering a certain part of
our framework is either knowing something or increased
power to know; the effect is not the thing known. So
a concept is an effect if by "concept" you mean "conceiving" but not "what is conceived." We know certain
universals; since a universal is neither a cause nor an
effect, it is not the cause of knowledge.

PORTER: (moving towards the door) I'll be back at
11:00. Call me if you find out what reality is.
KATHERINE: Of course we will.
KEITH: Before you turn to a discussion of laying down
and taking a path of language, I wish to make sure I
have your distinction between acts and achievements.
There is a distinction and a relation of dependence between an act and an achievement. I also have in mind
certain examples: seeing something is an achievement of
perception; knowing something is an achievement of
mind.
ALEXANDER: There are two classes of achievements: some
are reached or managed at a time; others endure. In
the first case, for example, one wins a race; in the
second case one sees or knows and still sees or knows
the same thing. Winning a race, let us say, is a mo-
mentary achievement; seeing something and knowing something are enduring achievements.
KEITH: There is an interesting difference between seeing and knowing. It would not be said that I still see
someone, if I were not looking; it would be said that I
still know something, if I am not thinking.
ALEXANDER: Your remark helps emphasize a point made in
the first part of our discussion, namely that there are
differences between acts and achievements of perception
and acts and achievements of thought.

PART III

(1)
ALEXANDER: I distinguished two stages of our ascent to
knowledge of the truth. The first is a stage of institution and the second, one of use. There is a corresponding distinction between two kinds of acts of language: the first I call laying down a path, and the
second, taking a path. Suppose a member of our mythical first community has given birth to a child; it is
brought to Adam for naming. For Adam to give the child
a name is for Adam to lay down a path; for another to
call the child by name is for him to take a path.
RECORDER: I'm not sure whether I understand you in
your distinction between laying down and taking a path
of language.
ALEXANDER: To make differences clear I depend upon a
statement of a difference between acts and achievements.
RECORDER: About so much we are clear; I have it in my
record.
ALEXANDER: Good. In taking a path I complete every
relevant act; in creating a path I do not execute every
relevant act. I do reach certain achievements. Further, an act which I omit to do, if done, makes it possible to apply or to follow rather than to lay down a
path.
RECORDER: I do not understand.
ALEXANDER: Remember the following motto. Whenever I
speak of laying down a path, ask wherein there is omitted action. I will give you an example. Someone says,
"The bird is building a nest"; someone else says, "The
bird builds nests." The first person takes and the
second lays down a path. For the first person points
to something and makes clear to us what he is pointing
to when he says, "The bird." The second person does
not point to anything; he does say What; but the act
which supports the second achievement of saying What,
is not coordinated with an act such as pointing to
something.
KATHERINE: Let me further test the distinction. Suppose I turn to Julian and give him advice when I say,
"You should write down the words 'Part One'." Do I
then lay down or take a path?
ALEXANDER: You lay down a path. For you advise him as
to what to do without its being done. You do make it
possible for him to apply and follow your advice. For
him to follow you is for him to do it.
KATHERINE: So to advise or to command is, as you say,
to create a path. To take advice or to obey a command

is to take a path.
ALEXANDER: I wish to have you say so.
RECORDER: I take your point that there must be insti-
tution before there can be application and following.
But I have a further worry. Can a path which has been
taken in turn be followed? Suppose, for example, that
I claim that the Premier is in Edmonton. You would
say, I believe, that to make a claim is to take rather
than to lay down a path.
ALEXANDER: I would.
RECORDER: And can another person follow me?
ALEXANDER: Of course. For he can quote you.
RECORDER: Then we can follow not only paths laid down
but also paths taken.
ALEXANDER: Yes.
CHANCELLOR: I suppose philosophers resist having their
distinctions put in a blunt and simple way. Perhaps
you will say whether I do your distinction an injustice
when I say that there is a distinction between creating
and using instruments of reason. The first kind of act
you call laying down a path, and the second, taking a
path. Further, there are two modes of using an instrument of reason: applying and following. When I pass a
law, I lay down a path; I take a path when I apply the
law to someone and follow it with respect to him.
ALEXANDER: You do the distinction no injustice. Since
you in fact present it in an adequate way, let us turn
to the consideration of an example of a simple assertion.
RECORDER: I'm still not satisfied.
KATHERINE: Julian, you're never satisfied.
RECORDER: In our time there are three phases of philosophy: rebellion against tradition, in particular
against the Cartesian tradition; second, the story-
telling phase of ordinary language philosophy, and
third, a systematic phase--the building of systems.
KATHERINE: And I'll bet you tinkered with the middle
phase and turned to the history of philosophy.
RECORDER: In the middle phase we resist having ordinary words turned into instruments whose use is forced
into technical labor.
KATHERINE: Come to the point, Julian!
RECORDER: I'm not denying that there is a distinction
between giving a name and calling someone by name and
between giving and taking advice. I resist allowing
a philosopher think he has an adequate and general way
of making such distinctions. He ought not readily
think he has a statement of a distinction which can be
universally applied.
KATHERINE: He would lose his humility, wouldn't he?

58

RECORDER: (Although I was annoyed with Katherine, I
didn't say a thing to her. I looked at Alexander and
continued:) Bill gave us a motto and thereby invited
us to think that he has a general statement of his distinction: whenever one speaks of laying down a path,
ask wherein there is omitted action. Now suppose I
stand at a window lecturing a child on the habits of
birds. I say, "The bird builds nests." On behalf of
the example Bill claims that one does not refer to anything. Therefore, although one manages the achievement
of saying What, one does not manage the achievement of
saying to what one is referring when one utters the
word "bird". But suppose I do point and refer to a
bird. Does it follow that I am not laying down a path?
ALEXANDER: No. You might interrupt yourself and say,
"The bird--for example that bird--builds nests." But
you would not say, "The bird--I mean that bird--builds
nests." In the second case you would not be laying
down a path.
RECORDER: I agree. But in the first case I both lay
down a path and also point to and refer to something.
Do you agree?
ALEXANDER: Yes.
RECORDER: Then I do not omit action.
ALEXANDER: But you do. You make future action possible without performing it. You make it possible for
your pupil to apply and follow your premiss. When he
refers to a bird and continues, "So that bird too must
build nests," he does not inquire whether you meant
that bird.
RECORDER: Perhaps we should go on.
(2)
ALEXANDER: I shall take it for granted that we command
a distinction between laying down and taking a path.
Let us turn to an example of a simple assertion. Someone says, "This table is long." Pointing to and speaking about something one first utters the demonstrative
word "this" and then the T-word "table"; by such means
one manages two achievements: making clear what is
pointed to and saying What. The two achievements are
parts of a complex achievement, namely saying what this
is.
KEITH: Can we criticize the person for how he proceeds?
ALEXANDER: Yes. You can accuse him of not having suc-
ceeded in saying what this is and of being wrong in his
use of "table". But let us not yet consider modes of
criticism. The person speaking goes on to utter the
word "is". In saying "is" we depend upon several contrasts: is/are, is/was and is/be. Let us set aside a

59

question of number. What are we to mean by "tense"?
(3)
KEITH: Tense is any one of the different forms in the
conjugation of a verb which indicate the different
times (past, present or future) at which the action or
state denoted by it is viewed as happening or existing.
ALEXANDER: When you say that a tense indicates differ-
ent times at which an action takes place, would anyone
take you to mean that it indicates the date of some ac-
tion?
KEITH: Good heavens, no!
ALEXANDER: Do you mean that it indicates at what time
something takes place?
KEITH: Let me think.
ALEXANDER: Do you mean that it indicates when some-
thing takes place?
KEITH: I'm not sure what to say.
ALEXANDER: When I say, "He came to town," do I make
superfluous either asking, "At what time?" or asking,
"When did he come?"
KEITH: No.
ALEXANDER: Can your definition be right?
KEITH: No, it cannot be right. What then are we to
mean by "tense"? What does tense indicate?
ALEXANDER: That one thing is or potentially is before
another, at the same time as another or after another.
To reveal the present tense is to make it evident that
one thing is or is potentially at the same time as an-
other; to reveal the past tense is to make it evident
that one thing is or is potentially earlier than or
before another, and to reveal the future tense is to
make it evident that one thing is or is potentially
later than or after another.
KEITH: So it is your definition that tense is a species of sameness or of otherness with respect to time.
ALEXANDER: Yes.
KEITH: To give a tense is to indicate sameness or
otherness of time.
ALEXANDER: Yes.
KEITH: It seems to me that your definition is not complete. Surely we need to know what the terms are of a
path of sameness or otherness.
ALEXANDER: Saying what the terms are is not part of
the definition. Inquiring what they are is part of a
method which applies and follows the definition. You
are right that we should make the inquiry; why we
should will become clear this afternoon when we discuss
sameness and otherness. Let us now simply assume that
we require knowing what arises or potentially arises
at the same time as or at another time than what.

KEITH: What are the two terms?
ALEXANDER: Remember that there are two possibilities.
The first is of potentiality, and the second, of actuality. In our example the terms of a path of sameness
are actual. The first is a dominating act of language,
namely making an assertion.
KEITH: And the second?
ALEXANDER: It must be something changeable and so
timeable about this table. Whatever it is, it must be
statable without first saying what is being asserted
about the table. Otherwise, a part would not be a part
of its whole.
KEITH: So what would you say?
ALEXANDER: The second term is the table's being of a
certain length. I accordingly account for the present
tense with respect to our example by saying that the
time at which one makes a certain assertion is the same
as the time at which the table is of a certain length;
by making the assertion one reveals an identity of
time.
(4)
ALEXANDER: We have been considering the utterance of
the first three words of my example, "This table is
long." Having considered the tense of "is" let us consider the verb "be".
KEITH: Metaphysical theories are examined for their
accounts of being. It can be no small matter to say
what it is to be.
KATHERINE: Logicians have tamed the word "be", showing
us its three distinct senses: that of predication, that
of identity and that of existence. With respect to the
first I take it we follow Aristotle, saying that "is"
is a copula, joining subject- and predicate-expres-
sions.
CHANCELLOR: What is your account, Mr. Alexander?
ALEXANDER: You will hear me make much of the four
great families: that of sameness and otherness, that of
dependence and independence, that of combination and
separation and that of defect, sufficiency and excess.
Let us not assign work appropriate to one family to another.
CHANCELLOR: Your introductory comment leads me to suspect that the word "be" is either an instrument for
identifying, an instrument for combining or an instrument for indicating sufficiency.
ALEXANDER: The word "be" indicates sufficiency; being
is a kind of sufficiency. This afternoon I will consider the family of defect, sufficiency and excess in
detail. I anticipate that consideration by saying that
when there is a claim of sufficiency, there are two

61

subordinate questions. The first is of what there is
enough; the second, to or for what there is enough. In
answering the first one indicates the subject of sufficiency; in answering the second, the objective.
CHANCELLOR: Then according to your definition of being
when you remark that this table is long, you indicate
sufficiency of a subject for an objective. What is the
subject and what is the objective?
ALEXANDER: The subject is coordinating acts of utterance in making the remark; the objective is making
clear what to say. I can answer your question in general by saying that I indicate sufficiency of a mode of
continuance for reaching a certain achievement of language.
CHANCELLOR: Quite extraordinary! I dare say I am not
the person to question you. Katherine and Keith have
been trained in philosophy. They must know how to
bring appropriate criticism to bear.
KEITH: Katherine, I think you should conduct an investigation; you made suggestions for accounting for the
uses of the word "be".
KATHERINE: (turning to Alexander) Do you mean that to
assert that this table is long is immediately to assert
sufficiency?
ALEXANDER: Yes.
KATHERINE: So to make any such assertion is to assert
that I employ means sufficient for reaching an end. It
is implied that by employing certain means I attempt a
certain end. Is so much a fair presentation of your
view?
ALEXANDER: Yes.
KATHERINE: I don't know how further to examine your
view. A sustained examination is too difficult for me.
I think it would be more useful to contrast your view
and the view on which I was educated. Perhaps you
should then accept the burden of examining my view. If
you refute mine, I am prepared to make a serious effort
at understanding yours.
CHANCELLOR: I think Katherine makes a reasonable and
fair suggestion.
RECORDER: I do, too.
ALEXANDER: Very well. Remind us of your own view.
KATHERINE: In the sentence "This table is long" the
word "be" is a copula which joins the subject-expres-
sion "this table" with the predicate-expression "long".
Further, the word stands for a relation of combination,
if the sentence is true, between an object and a property.
ALEXANDER: What is the immediate object of the assertion?

KATHERINE: One asserts a connection between a substance and a property; one shows or exhibits a connection between expressions.
ALEXANDER: I fear I don't understand you. You
wouldn't want to say, "I asserted this table."
KATHERINE: Of course not. It would be absurd to say
so. A table is not the same kind of thing as a connection.
ALEXANDER: Indeed not. But I wonder whether you really mean to say that a connection is the immediate object of assertion.
KATHERINE: What else would I mean when I say, "One asserts a connection between a substance and a property"?
ALEXANDER: For all I know you might mean, "One asserts
that there is a connection between a substance and a
property." Or do you mean to differentiate and contrast the following: "I assert a connection" and "I assert that there is a connection"?
KATHERINE: I did not mean to differentiate and contrast them.
ALEXANDER: Is to say the one to say the other?
KATHERINE: No.
ALEXANDER: Suppose I put this pencil together with
this book. Do you know what it means to answer this
question: "Can you assert that connection?"
KATHERINE: It would mean, "Can you assert that there
is a connection?"
ALEXANDER: Then when you say, "One asserts a connection," do you not really mean that one asserts that
there is a connection?
KATHERINE: Yes, perhaps I do.
ALEXANDER: Now tell me. When I say, "There is a con-
nection," do I twice indicate a connection, once saying, "there is" and once saying, "a connection"?
KATHERINE: I don't know.
ALEXANDER: If I did, I would be saying that one as-
serts that a connection a connection.
KATHERINE: Am I really talking nonsense when I present
and try to defend the view on which I was educated?
ALEXANDER: I think it does lead to nonsense to say
that "there is" and "a connection" both indicate a connection.
KATHERINE: Clearly the meaning of the first is not the
same as that of the second.
ALEXANDER: Then the immediate object of assertion is
not a connection.
KATHERINE: I very well grasp that so much follows.
RECORDER: Then we are returned to the foundation of
our tradition. We can say with Parmenides and Plato
that "be" indicates being and that the immediate object

63

of assertion is being. Professor Alexander's view is
still unproved that being is a kind of sufficiency.
ALEXANDER: Katherine made a suggestion. If I have refuted her view, then she should be prepared to make a
serious effort at understanding mine.
KATHERINE: You have refuted mine; I am prepared to
make the effort.
ALEXANDER: Then let me continue with my account. We
have so far considered the uses of the words "This table is." One then goes on to utter the O-word "long";
he so utters it that he reaches the first achievement
of making evident what the word is. That achievement
is part of the chief achievement of making the assertion, namely saying what to say. One can utter the
word "long" in such a way as to express surprise; but
by thus controlling the mode of utterance one does not
make clear what one's feelings are; one rather expresses them.
RECORDER: And so we depend upon making a contrast: one
says, "long" rather than "short" or "long" rather than
"light".
ALEXANDER: Yes.
RECORDER: Have you now accounted for one possibility
of simple assertion?
ALEXANDER: Yes.
RECORDER: Then we have reached an important juncture.
(5)
ALEXANDER: Indeed, we have. I have given the account
not in terms of unity or combination but in terms of
the sufficiency of a subject for an objective. A subordinate account of effecting a subject has been given:
an account in terms of the subordination, the coordination and the continuance of acts of language. I strike
a principal coordination between uttering the words
"this table" and uttering the word "long". The word
"be" indicates sufficiency asserted of the coordination
for reaching a certain achievement. The subordinate
account of effecting a subject is given in applying and
following our Thesis of Subordination, Coordination and
Continuance.
CHANCELLOR: And you offer your Thesis of Continuance
in place of our traditional account of combining and
separating expressions in acts of assertion.
ALEXANDER: Yes.
CHANCELLOR: Do you wish to encourage Mr. Ingram to
turn the family of combination and separation out of
doors, seeking friendship elsewhere for the pursuit of
epistemology and metaphysics?
ALEXANDER: No, not at all. All four great families,
that of defect, sufficiency and excess, that of same-

ness and otherness, that of combination and separation and that of dependence and independence, have philosophical work to do. A good administrator knows what kind of person to employ for a certain kind of work. Similarly, a wise philosopher knows what paths of language to employ for a certain kind of account.

The notion of coordination is a complex notion having as parts a notion of combination and a notion of mutual dependence for reaching certain objectives. So our question is not whether we have use of the family of combination and separation in conducting our inquiries. Our question is what those things are between which there is combination or mutual dependence and, in particular, coordination. I answer: acts of language and achievements of communication.

RECORDER: So your disagreement with an aristotelian arises here: he speaks of combining the word "this" with the word "table". You deny him not his use of a notion of combination but rather his account of the terms of combination.

ALEXANDER: Yes.

CHANCELLOR: I recognize that there is a shift from an account which relates expressions to an account which relates acts of utterance. Is the shift important for metaphysics and epistemology?

ALEXANDER: Yes. The shift is important both for metaphysics and for epistemology. It is a supreme principle of metaphysics that universals are neither in space nor in time.

KATHERINE: (turning to Julian) Julian, you better write that principle down.

RECORDER: I'm writing it down.

ALEXANDER: Since words are universals, words are neither in space nor in time. But a path of combination or separation is a path whose taking implies spatiality or temporality with respect to the terms of combination or separation. It follows that words are not terms of combination or separation: they are neither together nor apart. So the shift from an account which relates expressions to an account which relates acts of utterance is important for metaphysics.

CHANCELLOR: And why is the shift important for epistemology?

ALEXANDER: Of epistemological criticism there are subjects said to be sufficient for knowledge. But to effect a subject is to act. So the subject of criticism is action. How my answer to your question is to be taken will become clear this afternoon.

CHANCELLOR: Fine. Then let us turn to the second example.

ALEXANDER: A second example of assertion is saying, "This table is six feet long." We have considered the uses of all words of my sentence excepting that of the expression "six feet". The expression is an A-expression of the U-system length. Let us suppose that authority has prepared ground for us by laying down what to say in order to say what a number is, what a unit is and what a length is. We are indeed accustomed already to saying that one is a number, ..., that six is a number, that foot is a unit, that one foot is a length, ...and that six feet is a length. We come to the institution of such U-systems of expressions.

RECORDER: What is it that is instituted: an expression or its use?

ALEXANDER: To speak with care appropriate to metaphysics say this: the utterance of an expression is subordinated to an act of institution. Such institution is accomplished, of course, only by developing a skill and by creating standards and paradigms. Since we contrast speaking of a standard with speaking of laying down a procedure, we distinguish two steps of the stage of institution: selecting a standard or an example and laying down a path of language with respect to it.

Let us pretend to assume authority: we select this table as a standard for measuring length. An absurd assumption, I know; you will extract the right point from it. We further lay down a path of language by ruling that we say, "six feet" in order to say what its length is. The dominant act is laying down a path; its dominant achievement is making evident how to continue in order to follow.

RECORDER: So after Adam has laid down what to say, followers know how to continue.

ALEXANDER: Yes. When it is originally said, "This table is six feet long," a path of language is laid down. We now know not only what to say to reveal a length but also what to say to reveal its length. So enough is done both to create an instrument of the stage of instigation and to use it at the stage of use.

RECORDER: We have considered the second example. The third is saying, "It is not six feet long." I presume you will now take us along the route of negation.

(7)

CHANCELLOR: Before we turn from assertion to negation, let us look over the part of our conversation now completed. We know from our discussion that there are two kinds of acts of assertion: one is of instances of laying down a path and the other, instances of taking a path. I presume both examples of our discussion are examples of laying down a path. In both cases one proceeds by uttering the word "is", first saying, "This table is long" and then saying, "This table is six feet long."

Mr. Alexander laid down a definition of being: being is a kind of sufficiency of a subject for an objective. It follows that both instances of assertion are instances of asserting sufficiency. You have said that there are subjects and objectives of two kinds: those of actuality and those of potentiality. Am I right in assuming that one can lay down one path of sufficiency whose subject is actual and that one can lay down another path of sufficiency whose subject is potential?

ALEXANDER: Yes.

CHANCELLOR: If there is a subject of actuality, there must be a corresponding objective of actuality. If I actually marshal resources said to be adequate when I assert, "This table is long," then they are said to be adequate for actually making clear what to say. Can my inference be retained as part of your philosophical framework?

ALEXANDER: Yes. You understand me perfectly. Continue with your summary.

CHANCELLOR: What I have said about the first example can also be said about the second. But it is also possible to lay down a path and thereby create a subject of potentiality.

ALEXANDER: Indeed. Can the Premier found an academy without making it possible to train and educate students?

CHANCELLOR: He cannot. So in founding an academy he creates a subject of potentiality, namely making it possible to train and to educate students. Since there is a potential subject, there must be a corresponding objective of potentiality.

ALEXANDER: Indeed. The Premier founds the academy in order to make it possible for students to become educated and to acquire knowledge of the truth. Making it possible to become educated is an objective of potentiality.

CHANCELLOR: I am happy to have you confirm me in my use of my own inference. There is a final part of my review. You have given us an account of assertion which makes possible a unified account of the criticism of assertion. Since an assertion is immediately an assertion of sufficiency, the general question of criticism is whether there is sufficiency of subject for objective. This morning you stated the three steps of your method. (I.2) First, inquire as to the dominant

objective of a given act. So if I am now to follow the
first step, I would say that towards answering the general question of criticism the first question is what
the objective is for which a subject is said to be adequate. Answering the question requires a division of
cases: into those of objectives of potentiality and into those of objectives of actuality. Have I correctly
followed the first step of your method?
ALEXANDER: Yes.
CHANCELLOR: As I remember, you stated the second step
of your method in this way: Inquire whether, and if so,
how our notions of beginning, continuing, developing
and completing apply and also our notions of subordination and coordination. If I am now to follow the second step, I would say that our second question is what
the subject is, said to be adequate for its objective.
Answering the question again requires a division of
cases into those of potentiality and those of actuality.
ALEXANDER: You have also correctly followed the second
step. Suppose, having completed your criticism, you
deny sufficiency. You should further inquire whether
a subject is defective or excessive for its objective.
The principal use of the Principle of Distinguishable
Resources is in examining for defect. On the other
hand, we examine for inconsistency in order to examine
for excess. But now I anticipate a subsequent discussion.
(8)
ALEXANDER: Let us apply our discussion of assertion to
a law of continuance. The law I have in mind is commonly called modus ponens. Suppose that the Chancellor
lays down a premiss, saying, "If the Premier is in the
province, then he is in Edmonton." Suppose further
that Julian then asserts, "The Premier is in the province." According to the law of modus ponens enough has
been done to support a further mode of continuance, for
example concluding, "So the Premier must be in Edmonton."
RECORDER: The law is familiar to us; I can't imagine
anyone wishing to dispute it.
KEITH: There can be disagreement as to how it should
be formulated.
RECORDER: Of course. (turning to Alexander) You as-
sented to the Chancellor's summary when he said that
assertion is immediately assertion of sufficiency. It
follows that to lay down a path is immediately to lay
down a path of sufficiency. So when you call modus
ponens a law of continuance, I take it you mean that it
is a law of adequacy for modes of continuance.

68

KATHERINE: Won't Julian make a meticulous head of department?
ALEXANDER: We ought not ridicule a philosopher when he means to put his record perfectly in order.
RECORDER: May I pursue my line of questioning?
ALEXANDER: Of course.
RECORDER: If modus ponens is a law of adequacy for modes of continuance, then it is nothing but a law of applying and following certain paths of language. We were imagining that the Chancellor lays down a premiss when he says, "If the Premier is in the province, then he is in Edmonton." According to the remarks we account for the use of the premiss in two parts: applying and following. One applies the premiss by meeting the condition laid down; one meets the condition by asserting that the Premier is in the province. I take it the word "if" indicates that one lays down a condition.
KEITH: And what about the word "then"?
ALEXANDER: The word "then" indicates sufficiency: sufficiency of thus meeting the condition for following the premiss.
RECORDER: One follows in subordination to concluding, "So he must be in Edmonton." Now it seems to me that to apply and follow the premiss as I have is one and the same thing as proceeding according to the law of modus ponens. So I would say modus ponens is nothing but a rule whereby one correctly uses certain paths of language.
KEITH: If Julian is right, then an account of modus ponens rests upon one of laying down paths of language, one of applying and following them and one of doing so correctly. Such an account of modus ponens would not rest upon an account of truth.
KATHERINE: But don't logicians explicate modus ponens partly in terms of truth? As I remember, they say something like this: if "p" is true and if "If p, then q" is true, then "q" is true.
ALEXANDER: The question whether an instrument of reason is correctly used can be, and should be, answered independently of answering the question whether a consequence of use is true.
KATHERINE: But it is assumed by logicians that the meaning of a word such as "then" can be given in terms of truth-conditions.
ALEXANDER: Such an assumption is not right. An account of the meaning of "then" does not rest upon an account of the truth of any part of asserting, "If p, then q." Further, a test of the entire assertion by asserting "p", inferring "q" and denying "q" presupposes

and does not illuminate the meaning of "then". For a test is only fairly run when we allow that the assertion of "p" is enough to infer, "q"; since the possibility of such an allowance is prior to the judgment of a fair test, our understanding of the meaning and the use of "then" does not depend upon an account of the result of running a proposed test. We should accordingly distinguish the question whether there is sufficiency of a subject for following from the question whether there is sufficiency of applying and following for an objective of using a certain instrument of reason.

KATHERINE: Then would you say that in the first instance logic is concerned with the correct use of instruments of reason?

ALEXANDER: Yes.

KATHERINE: And that such a concern should be distinguished from one as to whether the consequences of correct use are true?

ALEXANDER: Yes. We will have an opportunity later today to discuss the consequences of the distinction. Perhaps we should turn to negation before we stop for lunch.

RECORDER: Is it too late to make a final remark?

ALEXANDER: No.

(9)

RECORDER: I want to make sure I can place you in my record.

ALEXANDER: Do make your remark.

RECORDER: You must find my company tedious; you know I'm a compulsive note taker.

KATHERINE: Julian, we understand you in your desire to maintain a tidy record.

RECORDER: When I make a record of one view, I like to make clear what its alternative is. Who's up and who's down--don't you like to know such things about the history of philosophy?

KATHERINE: Not especially. But I'm sure the Chancellor means to have historians in his academy.

KEITH: And I'm interested.

RECORDER: (turning to Alexander) Let me see whether I have an adequate account of part of your Thesis of Continuance. I say, "This table is six feet long." I first mention a substance and subsequently disclose a length. Now a length is a universal and not a substance. So I don't mention the same thing twice first saying, "this table" and then saying, "six feet."

ALEXANDER: Indeed, you do not mention the same thing twice.

RECORDER: As I was listening to you speak, I suspected

that you mean to set forth an alternative to nominalism. For an essential part of nominalism is the view that in nature there is nothing universal; everything is particular. It is also part of nominalism to hold that when one says, "This table is six feet," one does not mention something in addition to and distinct from whatever one first mentioned when one said, "this table." I suspect a serious nominalist would say that the second expression helps explicate the meaning of the first one.

ALEXANDER: I do mean to provide an alternative to nominalism.

RECORDER: In light of my summary of part of your metaphysical view I would like to have us define the epistemological orientation of your neo-pragmatism. You know that people like me like to put questions about the object of knowledge both with respect to nature and with respect to the knower. When I disclose the length of this table, saying, "This table is six feet long," I myself manage, according to your account, a complex achievement of knowledge; I both know what is referred to and also know a length. There is a question whose answering divides philosophers. I want to have your position recorded in my record of our conversation.

ALEXANDER: What is the question?

KATHERINE: Lord, yes, Julian; let us hear the question.

RECORDER: Is the thing which one knows, knowing a length, the same thing which the table has? Now depending upon whether one says Yes or No, one holds a realist theory of knowledge or a representationalist theory of knowledge. How do you answer?

ALEXANDER: When I know the length of the table, I know that length which the table actually has. Let us not yet settle the question what "has" means.

RECORDER: Fine. Let us consider the knower. Is the thing which one knows the same either as the achievement of knowing or as the mind of the knower?

ALEXANDER: No. The object of knowledge is not the same as either the achievement of knowing or as the mind of the knower. Both you and I know the length of this table, but although we both know the same thing, we did not manage the same achievement of knowledge. Similarly, two minds can reach knowledge of the same thing.

RECORDER: So there is knowledge of a universal had by a distinct substance and grasped by a distinct mind. I doubtless put your view in a clumsy way; do I misrepresent it?

ALEXANDER: No, I don't think so.

71

RECORDER: It leads, don't you know?, to an impossibility.
ALEXANDER: How?
RECORDER: There is a premiss which no one has seen fit
to give up; it is that whatever is distinct is combined
or separate.
ALEXANDER: I anticipate discussing its use in metaphysics this afternoon.
RECORDER: Fine. Its use is an established part of the
western practice of metaphysics. Since the universal
grasped is distinct from the substance which has it,
the universal is either combined with or separate from
that substance. Further, since the universal grasped
is distinct from the mind of the knower, the universal
is either combined with or separate from that mind. If
the universal were separate from the mind, the mind
would not know the universal; knowledge would accordingly be impossible. But there is knowledge of universals. Therefore, a universal is combined with a mind.
Any universal actually grasped is also combined with or
separate from a certain substance. If combined, then
mind and matter are also combined and linked. For if
A is combined with B and B with C, then A and C are
also combined. But if the universal and the substance
are separate, what one knows would not be the length
of this table, such a thing not being knowable. But
there is knowledge of universals, according to your
position. Therefore, mind and matter are combined and
linked. But if combined and linked, they must be
things of the same kind: either both immaterial and unextended or both material and extended. So either
there is no such knowledge as you claim or, if there
is, one of two monistic positions must be right: either
idealism or materialism.
CHANCELLOR: (looking surprised and turning to
Alexander) Good heavens, if Julian is right, your
project seems to me to be in a rather bad way.
KATHERINE: One ought to have known better than to expect to get through Bill's schedule in one day. Do
you think your government would put us up in this hotel
for another day?
ALEXANDER: I don't think we'll require another day.
We do need the afternoon.
KEITH: (still looking perplexed) I'm sure we're all
willing to wait to see how you will answer Julian's
argument. The argument marvellously captures the moves
our tradition has made. But wouldn't it do to replace
the family of combination and separation by the family
of dependence and independence?
RECORDER: We can't dismiss the family of combination

and separation because its employment makes our going rough. It has a permanent place in our metaphysics. Logic helps secure its place. For predication is understood in terms of combination. Even so, making the replacement which you recommend doesn't help Bill's project; indeed, it would make most of this morning's conversation irrelevant to a real account of the acquisition of knowledge.

KEITH: What do you mean?

RECORDER: The acquisition of knowledge depends upon the use of a conceptual framework; the foundation of the framework is laid by means of action he calls laying down paths of language. So his account deserves to be called a conventionalist account.

KEITH: Of course. But how does such an account become irrelevant to what you call a real account of the acquisition of knowledge?

RECORDER: Let us again go through my argument, making the replacement you recommend. Since the universal grasped is distinct from the substance which has it, the universal is either dependent upon or independent of that substance for its existence. Further, since the universal grasped is distinct from the mind of the knower, the universal is either dependent upon or independent of that mind for its existence. If the universal were dependent upon your mind for its existence, then if you did not know it, there would be no universal for me to know. But there is; therefore, it is not dependent upon any particular mind for its existence. So it is independent. Further, if the universal were dependent upon this substance, then if this substance were destroyed, so would the universal be. But it is possible for another substance to have the same length. Therefore, it is not dependent upon any particular substance for its existence. So it is independent both of minds and of matter. An account of our creativity in constructing a framework is therefore irrelevant to an account of acquiring knowledge of independent universals.

KATHERINE: If Julian's arguments are conclusive, I frankly don't see the point of continuing. Mind you, I don't want to miss the Premier's banquet. But perhaps we could have it for lunch and go home. Julian's arguments come to this: either there is no knowledge or Bill's project is on the wrong track for discovering it.

CHANCELLOR: We would look like fools if we quit now. Should I say to the Premier, "We should certainly have an academy but not a department of philosophy. Philosophy is too hard to get along with"? (He pauses and turns to Alexander.) You say nothing.

ALEXANDER: Philosophy causes perplexity; a solution is worth nothing to him who does not know the pull of philosophical perplexity. Katherine was joking when she suggested we stop.

CHANCELLOR: (turning to Katherine and smiling) Were you joking?

KATHERINE: Not entirely. After I took my first degree in philosophy, I gave up its formal study. I found it too perplexing and too discouraging--for me, you understand.

CHANCELLOR: Of course.

KATHERINE: I still think no education is complete without a study of philosophy. I agree with something I've heard Bill say before: philosophy is the chief watch over the office of criticism.

CHANCELLOR: Perhaps I haven't taken enough philosophy in to feel its indigestability. I think I see a way out of our perplexity. Our difficulty is due in part to the use of a metaphysical premiss in the mode of modus ponens. Such instruments are double handled. We can surely employ the premiss that whatever is distinct is combined or separate and conclude that minds and the objects of knowledge are not distinct.

RECORDER: Drawing that conclusion would unite you with Aristotle.

CHANCELLOR: It can be no disgrace to join Aristotle's company.

RECORDER: Aristotle adopts his own position partly in light of a problem which he discusses in De Anima (III.4). If thinking is a passive affection, then if mind is simple and impassible and has nothing in common with anything else, how can it come to think at all? For interaction between two factors is held to require a precedent community of nature between the factors. In light of such a problem Aristotle adopts his own position: actual knowledge is identical with its object.

KATHERINE: Julian, do you know the date?

RECORDER: Yes, of course. It is November 8, 1978.

KATHERINE: You can't expect us to take Aristotle's position seriously. I don't become a length when I know the length of this table. Even you become absurd but not absurdity when you propose an absurd position. There is only one way out of the difficulties your arguments cause us. You originally asked Bill whether the thing which one knows, knowing a length, is the same thing which the table has. Your arguments show that a realist theory of knowledge is not adequate. So let us join modern philosophers and endorse a representationalist theory of knowledge. One immediately knows an idea, a notion or a concept.

RECORDER: I would rather have Aristotle's than your company. I would like to have lived in an age when three things were widely held to be true. First, objects of knowledge are the same as natures of things; second, our minds are adequate for such knowledge, and third, we all share in the agent intellect. So there would be a common world, common knowledge and a communal mind. In such an age solipsism, skepticism and agnosticism would have a small claim on our attention.

CHANCELLOR: Since you have recently come to our Province, Mr. Ingram, I can assure you that you do not live in such an age. We live in an age whose cultural and intellectual defects or excesses include solipsism, skepticism and agnosticism. (turning to Alexander) Do you intend to address yourself to Ingram's arguments?

ALEXANDER: Yes, but only after we have discussed the two monistic positions mentioned (VIII.18). Our conversation should proceed a ways further before I reply to his arguments.

CHANCELLOR: Then we will wait until this evening to hear your reply.

RECORDER: (Shortly after the Chancellor spoke, the Porter entered the room. He asked us whether we wished anything to drink before lunch, which we could expect to find served at noon.)

PORTER: (looking at Katherine) Have you found out yet what reality is?

KATHERINE: No, not yet. I think reality will be served up after dinner. But we know what being is.

KEITH: With a capital "B" (he said, trying to join in.)

RECORDER: You do us an injustice. Say: we know what the near object of assertion is.

KATHERINE: If you were to lift up your trolley, you would demonstrate....

PORTER: Demonstrate?

KATHERINE: Yes, demonstrate not strength, you understand, but the adequacy of your strength for lifting up the trolley. They want you to say this: the near object of demonstration is adequacy. As it is with acting so it is with speaking. To assert is to assert the adequacy of certain means for a certain end.

PORTER: What are the ends of assertion?

KATHERINE: Philosophy can hardly answer that question.

PORTER: Then whatever is the use of philosophy?

KATHERINE: It can help you get straight what it is to assert and, further, help you sort out and sharpen tools used for the criticism and the evaluation of assertion.

75

PORTER: I think I get enough criticism here and at home.   I don't want to go to your academy only to be criticized all over again.   I'll be back in an hour. (He leaves.)

PART IV

(1)

ALEXANDER: Let us turn to negation. There are several acts which we perform and of which we should be able to give an account: in the social world we may prevent, attack and take action against; in the communicative world we may deny, reject and set aside. By initiating, continuing and completing such acts we can manage certain achievements; I shall account for the possibility of such achievements by giving you the planks of the Thesis of Negation. The first plank is that there are expressions whose use can be subordinated to making evident what act one performs.

RECORDER: Can you say something further in order to make evident what the rationale is of the first plank of your thesis?

ALEXANDER: Perhaps you would follow me through the following piece of reasoning. When parallel routes of language emerge with similar patterns of time and intonation, it is necessary to coin and institute expressions by means of which it is possible to make clear that one is, for example, denying something rather than affirming something; it must be possible to make clear that one is rejecting something rather than accepting something. So according to the first plank there must be resources adequate to make clear how one proceeds.

RECORDER: I have no difficulty with the first plank. You say that there are some words, such as "no" and "not", whose first achievement of making clear what the words are can support a second: disclosing an action. When I say, "No", I make evident how I continue, namely that I reject something or issue a denial. I would further suggest to you that uttering the word "not" is not itself part of issuing a denial.

KATHERINE: I don't agree with you. I would say, on the contrary, that uttering the word "not" may be part of issuing a denial. Further, making evident that a certain act is attempted depends upon the continuance or the completion of the act in question.

RECORDER: I disagree. I accept the general premiss laid down earlier that every achievement depends upon the continuance or the completion of some act, action or activity. There must therefore be some actual basis, if I may so express myself. But I reject the suggestion that the basis of the disclosure must be the act disclosed. Surely I can announce that I am about to issue a denial; to utter the word "deny" would not then be part of issuing a denial but rather a part of announcing my intention to issue a denial.

KATHERINE: I agree with what you have said. I did not say that uttering such a word as "not" must be part of denying; I said that uttering such a word may be part of such an act.

RECORDER: But I am arguing that uttering such a word is never part of issuing a denial. When I say, "I claim that the Premier is in Edmonton," I disclose to you the fact that I make a claim; uttering the word "claim", however, is no part of doing so. Further, I fail to see how uttering the word "claim" can ever be part of making the claim or how uttering the word "deny" can ever be part of issuing a denial. Although the disclosure of what path one has set upon depends upon taking some path, the second is no segment of the first. To utter the words "I am telling them a story" is no more to tell them a story than uttering the words "And that was the news" is to bring to a conclusion the reporting of the news.

ALEXANDER: Perhaps I can help you resolve your dis-agreement. Suppose that Katherine says to me, "You arrived in Edmonton two days ago." I reply by saying, "No, I didn't." Do you wish to say, Julian, that ut-tering the word "not" is no part of issuing a denial?

RECORDER: Yes.

ALEXANDER: You remember we distinguish two species of times and modes of utterance. We all agree to say that I use resources of the second kind in order to support making evident what I do. You would be right to insist that I do not employ such resources simply in issuing a denial. But it would be wrong to say that utterance of the word with such and such an intonation and timing is no part of issuing a denial. For I control an in-stance of timing and modality of the first species in issuing the denial; I control an instance of timing and modality of the second species in order to make clear what the word is which I utter, saying, "not"; the sec-ond achievement of control is revealing an action, namely denial.

CHANCELLOR: We are satisfied with your statement of the first plank of your thesis. What is the second?

ALEXANDER: The second is that saying or making evident What--what it is, for example, against the claiming of which the speaker takes a stand--is coordinate with making clear what act is either set upon, asked for or rejected. Let me put the second plank in another way. In the last part of our conversation we somewhat worked out the thesis that to assert is to assert sufficiency. Now just as the immediate object of assertion is suffi-ciency so the immediate object of negation is suffi-ciency. So according to the second plank the uses of

"not" and "is" are coordinate: the use of "not" supports a disclosure of action and the use of "is" supports a disclosure of the object of the action.
KEITH: The Principle of Distinguishable Resources and your Thesis of Negation together give rise to a consequence which interests me. Does it not follow that use of the word "not" can support one of two coordinate achievements but not both?
ALEXANDER: It does follow.
KEITH: I can give care to controlling the utterance of the word "not" either in order to make evident that I reject something or in order to make evident what it is the suggestion of which I do reject, but not in order to achieve both.
ALEXANDER: So much does follow.
KEITH: Now you said that the word "not" is employed to make evident that I reject something, for example. It therefore follows that uttering such a negative particle provides no basis for disclosing the content of the suggestion rejected.
ALEXANDER: Such a consequence arises, as you infer. Have you cause to reject it?
KEITH: None I can think of at the moment.
ALEXANDER: Then let me complete my presentation of the thesis by taking up the example suggested some time ago: "This table is not six feet long." According to our method the first question to be answered is what the dominating act is to the completion of which utterance of the words of the sentence is subordinated. Since there are several possibilities, we are at liberty to make a decision. So let us say that we subordinate uttering the words to issuing a denial. Suppose that A and B are in the company of those discussing the table which they take someone to have purchased. They come to saying what the length is of the table. I accordingly wish to have us understand that the object of their inquiry is coming to know and to point out what its length is. Since there is such an objective of inquiry, there must exist not only parallel routes of continuance but also alternate routes. There is therefore footing in the conduct of the inquiry for disagreement. Indeed, the conversation can develop in the following way. A says, "The table is six feet long." B then issues a denial.
KEITH: You have today encouraged us to respect a distinction between act and object. We accordingly account for coordinate achievements: making plain what act is performed and making plain what the object is of the act. So just as A asserts sufficiency when he says, "The table is six feet long," B denies suffi-

ciency when he says, "It is not six feet long."
RECORDER: I am not of a mind to affirm Keith's remark.
I think that B denies either the length of the table or
what A says it is.
KEITH: Even I can see that it will not do to say, "He
denies the length." Whatever would one mean, Julian,
saying that one denies a universal?
RECORDER: Sorry, perhaps you're right. The first alternative I gave is no good.
KEITH: And what do you mean by "or what A says it is"?
RECORDER: I think I meant that B denies A's claim as
to what the length is. I argue from the observation
that to deny is to take action against someone or something; to complete any such action, of course, is to
depend upon such power as we have and to exercise such
skill as we have mastered.
KEITH: I don't find anything wrong with your second
alternative.
ALEXANDER: Then are there two objects of denial: sufficiency and a claim?
RECORDER: If both of us are right, there must be. We
do say, "He denied the charge." It seems to me that
one implies that a charge is the object of denial.
ALEXANDER: Can two people on separate occasions bring
the same charge against someone?
RECORDER: Yes.
ALEXANDER: And two people make the same claim?
RECORDER: Yes.
ALEXANDER: According to our usual procedures would we
not be inclined to say that charges and claims are universals?
RECORDER: Yes.
ALEXANDER: But you acceded to Keith's suggestion that
universals are not objects of denial.
RECORDER: I remember.
ALEXANDER: Have you now changed your mind?
RECORDER: No. I do want to express myself slightly
differently. The object of a denial is not a claim or
a charge as a universal. The object of a denial is
rather the making of a claim or the bringing of a
charge. Strictly speaking we oppose action: just as I
oppose someone building a fence along a certain bound-
ary so I reject the making of a certain assertion.
ALEXANDER: To make an assertion on a particular occasion is to effect, let us say, a particular event. Although it is possible again to make the same claim, it
is not possible again to effect the same event; such
particulars do not recur. You understand me?
RECORDER: Yes.
ALEXANDER: How can you attack or oppose something past

80

and done?
RECORDER: Are you serious?
ALEXANDER: I think so. You before moved Keith to wonder and astonishment with your suggestion of denying
universals; you now move me with your suggestion of
denying particulars. I wonder what in the world one is
saying when one utters the words "I deny a particular
event already passed."
RECORDER: I confess that I had not so far looked into
my thoughts. I suppose it is absurd either to say that
one denies universals or to say that one denies particulars. We are then left with your own alternative: one
denies sufficiency. But what does it mean to say, "I
deny the charge"?
ALEXANDER: One immediately denies the sufficiency of
grounds or evidence for sustaining the charge.
(2)
KATHERINE: I would like to put a question. Would you
say, Mr. Alexander, that doubting is an act parallel to
rejecting and denying?
ALEXANDER: Yes.
KATHERINE: And do you also mean to account for the
possibility of doubt?
ALEXANDER: Yes.
KATHERINE: Then how many kinds of possibilities are
there? I'm sure that Julian would like to write the
number down.
ALEXANDER: I don't know. There are at least two
kinds; further, the second kind admits of a division.
Regarding the first I would say that one performs the
act of doubt simply and directly out of one's position
and predicament. By looking about me I reject the idea
that there is an elephant in the room.
KATHERINE: So as there is an original situation in
which one instigates there is one in which one rejects,
refuses, sets aside, turns away and pushes from one.
ALEXANDER: Yes.
KATHERINE: And what is the second kind?
ALEXANDER: Rejection in light of one of two considerations. The first is that there is inadequate support
for taking the path of language in question; the second
is that taking the path can or does conflict with another path which one is committed to taking. Due to
inadequacy of support in the first case or, in the second, due to conflict and inconsistency one gives up and
rejects the proposed path.
KATHERINE: So there are at least two ways in which one
has room to be a skeptic: rejecting a path because of
insufficiency of support and rejecting a path because
of commitment to an alternate path.

ALEXANDER: Yes. In the first case we say, "The number one is not just" and, in the second, "This table is not red."
KATHERINE: Thank you. I think I see in what ways there is room for doubt.
(3)
ALEXANDER: After we completed an account of assertion, I formulated the law of modus ponens. Having now presented my Thesis of Negation we have an opportunity to formulate two triadic laws. The first is that any subject is defective, sufficient or excessive for any objective. For example, it is either too dim, bright enough or too bright to read a book in this room. A given object is either too short, long enough or too long to be measured.

Consider a further example relevant to our discussion of negation. Suppose that someone claims sufficiency of a subject for an objective. Since there are objects alternative to sufficiency, namely defect and excess, negation is possible. For were there no alternative to sufficiency, there would be nothing for which to criticize the original claim. But since there are two alternatives to sufficiency, it is open to deny sufficiency either in favor of criticizing for defect or in favor of criticizing for excess. Further, since there are three alternatives, negation of one of them is not itself sufficient for determining an alternative. An act of negation and one of providing an alternative are therefore distinct acts; further, there is continuity between them.

By means of the first triadic law and my account of negation a second law can be inferred. It is that no subject is defective, sufficient and excessive for the same objective; further, no subject is any two of the three for the same objective. Suppose we match a subject and an objective: taking a certain path of language and reaching a certain achievement. It follows that the subordinate action of effecting the subject is not both sufficient and excessive, for example. But suppose the subject is both sufficient and excessive. It would not then be possible to deny sufficiency in favor of arguing excess. But since there is a distinction between denying sufficiency and providing an alternative and doing so with continuity, the given subject is not both sufficient and excessive. So it is evident that the second law follows from the first by means of my account of negation. The second triadic law is meant to replace Aristotle's law of non-contradiction.
RECORDER: Aristotle states his law in Metaphysics

Gamma: the same attribute cannot at the same time belong and not belong to the same subject and in the same respect. I do not grasp how to put his law in your sort of way.

ALEXANDER: To accommodate his account of metaphysics let us suppose that what I call a subject is two things reaching a point on a continuum of nearness and farness. It follows that they are not both too far away and near enough for combination. If they are near enough for combination, then they are neither too far away nor too near. And since, according to Aristotle, to assert to be combined what is combined is to speak the truth, the assertion that they are combined is not also false.

RECORDER: But Aristotle thinks that to denying the truth of an assertion there is no alternative in addition to claiming falsity.

ALEXANDER: Indeed. For in accounting for truth and falsity he mentions a duality: combination and separation. So he naturally does not see the nature of things supporting triadic laws.

RECORDER: And according to your account one is not justified in inferring the falsity of an assertion from the denial of its truth.

ALEXANDER: Right. Why one is not so justified will become clear this afternoon when we consider the family of defect, sufficiency and excess.

RECORDER: I would like to hear that discussion before I put another question.

ALEXANDER: Fine.

(3.1)

KATHERINE: You must all be very keen on lunch.

ALEXANDER: What do you mean?

KATHERINE: Like sheep your students follow along behind your first triadic law of continuance, or whatever you call it. You did say, "Any subject is defective, sufficient or excessive for ANY objective", didn't you?

ALEXANDER: Yes.

KATHERINE: Any objective?

ALEXANDER: Yes, any objective.

KATHERINE: Then I suppose most things are sufficient for most other things. For example, this cup of coffee is hot enough for me to prove the Pythagorean theorem. And so much follows from use of your law. For it is evident that the coffee is neither too cold nor too hot to prove the theorem. Right?

ALEXANDER: Right.

KATHERINE: So it follows that it is warm enough. (She pauses while Keith laughs.) The law is ridiculous enough to laugh--or is it too ridiculous? How come

you're not laughing, Julian?
RECORDER: One person laughing is one enough.
KATHERINE: Come now, Julian; that's not amusing.
RECORDER: (turning to Alexander) What do you say?
ALEXANDER: My attempt to formulate a law may of course
be ridiculous. There is one notion which I have not
employed to help make it so.
KATHERINE: Which notion do you mean?
ALEXANDER: That of dependence. My notion of sufficiency does not include that of dependence. So when I
assert, "This cup of coffee is hot enough for me to
prove the Pythagorean theorem," I do not mean that my
proving the theorem depends upon the coffee having a
certain temperature. The assertion is therefore not
offered as an instrument for explaining why I do or do
not prove the theorem. I hope it does not sound odd
because you misunderstand its intention.
KEITH: There now, Katherine: Do you misunderstand it?
KATHERINE: I don't know. You know I always gasp for
time to think.
KEITH: While you're gasping, I would like somewhat to
explore the metaphysical use of the first triadic law.
We know that some philosophers have held a view of universal harmony.
RECORDER: Leibniz, to mention the cleverest of them.
KEITH: I take it that harmony is a kind of sufficiency. Let us take as an objective conserving the
universe. By means of the first law it follows that
everything that exists is sufficient in its own way for
conserving the universe. For if anything at all, for
example, the position of this table, were either defective or excessive for conserving the universe, it would
follow that the universe is not conserved. There is
therefore a harmony of all things.
RECORDER: Leibniz holds an analogous view about the
harmony of monads. They exist in a framework of mutual
interrelation. We may fail to see it, Leibniz remarks,
because our senses lead us to judge superficially. In
reality, because of the interconnection of things, the
entire universe, with all of its parts, would be wholly
different and would have been another world altogether
from its very commencement, if the least thing in it
happened otherwise than it has.
KATHERINE: Good Lord, what an extraordinary view! A
moment ago Keith said that the position of the table is
adequate for conserving the universe. Can Leibniz be
saying that if the position had been other, the universe would have been other?
RECORDER: I think so.
KEITH: Leibniz's view is not mine. A subject of ade-

quacy can change within room provided by the umbrella
of adequacy or, for that matter, by the umbrellas of
defect and excess. There are several positions each
adequate for preserving the universe. Suppose several
children are keeping an equilibrium, sitting on a tee-
tertotter. One child can fidget a little, still occupying a position adequate in its own way for keeping
the equilibrium.
(Katherine was listening to Keith, nodding assent. No
one thought to object. I looked up once, but kept
writing, keeping my own balance.)
KATHERINE: Let me see whether I've got you straight.
Suppose a certain subject is adequate for a certain objective. It is possible that the subject can change or
vary, remaining adequate. Otherness, therefore, does
not imply either defect or excess; it follows further
that otherness does not imply an objective other than
the original one. Have I got you right?
KEITH: Yes.
KATHERINE: What a relief! People can change jobs
without upsetting universal harmony. It seems to me we
are spared a piece of absurd Leibnizian metaphysics,
namely that we would be living in another universe, had
this table, a moment ago, been there rather than here.
CHANCELLOR: None of you encourage me to speak up. I
sometimes suspect you don't like men of science dab-
bling in philosophy.
KATHERINE: Nonsense! You know we like you. You may
be able to find jobs for us when we are otherwise un-
employable.
ALEXANDER: What do you wish to say?
CHANCELLOR: I think the universe is eternal. There is
only one; further, we do not one moment live in this
universe and another moment live in a universe other
than this one. We can nevertheless say that this universe changes. Please don't ask me to argue for my
view; nor do I want you to examine it--at least not
this morning. Can you give me the satisfaction of supposing it true?
KATHERINE: Until lunch. Even during lunch.
(4)
CHANCELLOR: Before we stop for lunch, let us consider
this morning's conversation in a summary way. You have
accounted for the possibility of laying foundations
sufficient for building up a framework of speech and
thought. You have naturally restricted yourself to
considering certain elementary examples. In accounting
for the institution of a T-expression such as "a table"
and of an A-expression such as "six feet" you give us
an example of philosophy by reference to which we can

85

continue. I am still short of help for considering
certain philosophical issues.
ALEXANDER: Can you say what issues you mean?
CHANCELLOR: I would like to try. Suppose Adam lays
down what to say in order to say what the length is of
this table, saying, "It is six feet." At the lowest
level of the framework he utters the expression "six
feet"; its first achievement is revealing what expression is uttered. The first issue which concerns me is
a metaphysical one. Is there a distinction between the
expression uttered and the uttering of an expression?
ALEXANDER: Yes, there is a distinction. I hope you
are not tempted by idealism into holding that an expression is nothing but an act of utterance. Proof
that there is a distinction can be given in the following way. After Adam has coined the expression "six
feet", I can utter the same expression; I do not again
perform the same act which he performed. For he institutes and I follow. There is therefore a distinction
between the expression coined and the coining of an expression.
CHANCELLOR: I am persuaded of the answer which you
give to my first question. The second issue is epistemological. Suppose Adam lays foundations upon the
basis of which a framework can be built up and extended. Such work he does when he says, "One is a number."
There is still too little room, I take it, for doubt.
ALEXANDER: In laying such foundations there is too
little room for doubt.
CHANCELLOR: I wish to make quite sure I know the argument.
ALEXANDER: This afternoon you will learn that truth
and falsity belong neither to the family of sameness
and otherness nor to the family of combination and separation but to the family of defect, sufficiency and
excess. Our philosophical tradition has thought the
notions of truth and falsity through in terms of the
first two families. We would have you, in your academy, think truth and falsity through in terms of defect, sufficiency and excess. To do so remember that
when there is a question of defect, sufficiency and excess, there are two subordinate questions: first one of
objective, namely to or for what there is too little,
enough or too much. Remember too that objectives are
of two kinds: one kind is of potentiality and another
kind is of actuality. Truth is sufficiency of act for
an objective of actuality; falsity is excess of act for
an objective of actuality, and exiguousness is defect
of act for an objective of actuality. With so much in
mind consider the possibility of doubt when Adam says,

"One is a number." At the lowest level of our framework words are uttered.
CHANCELLOR: Surely a skeptic can ask whether words are
so uttered that first achievements are reached.
ALEXANDER: It is not fitting that we should presume to
answer every question which a skeptical philosopher can
raise. Even when we do make an effort at answering, we
need to know something of what moves him to questioning. For example, does he apply and follow a general
method or does he question and argue as certain oppor-
tunities present themselves? In the second case there
is nothing that need trouble us when a critic asks upon
a particular occasion whether someone so utters certain
words that he makes clear what the words are which he
utters. But in the first case something troubling can
arise. For a critic may be proceeding according to a
general method: asking whether anyone ever does succeed
in making clear what he is saying.
CHANCELLOR: Let us suppose the first case; I very well
see that we would not otherwise feel called upon to
respond to his challenge.
ALEXANDER: When he lays out the source of his doubt in
a general way, he becomes an enemy in his own house.
RECORDER: Plato makes a similar complaint against
those who hold that whatever is distinct is separate.
He has the Stranger say (<u>Sophist</u> 252c) that in referring to anything they cannot help using the words
"being", "apart", "from the others" and "by itself".
They cannot refrain from connecting such expressions in
their statements and so need not wait for others to refute them; the foe is in their own household.
ALEXANDER: Can a critic both say he wonders whether
anyone ever succeeds in making clear what the words are
which he utters and also say that he has made clear
what the object is of his wonder?
CHANCELLOR: There would be inconsistency.
ALEXANDER: So the allowance of intelligible and consistent doubt presupposes that there is a foundation of
our framework: a foundation sufficiently strong for
first achievements.
CHANCELLOR: Indeed. A skeptical philosopher depends
upon so much footing.
ALEXANDER: At a higher level of our framework a path
of language is laid down; its objective is one of actuality, for example to make clear what to say. Such objectives are of reaching second achievements. For the
reason I have given it would still not be coherent for
a serious skeptic to say he wonders whether any such
achievement is ever reached. Further, such objectives
are not objectives of truth or falsity. When Adam

names a child and lays down what to say to say what the name is of the child, it is not appropriate to inquire whether Adam, at the moment of institution, got the child's name right.

CHANCELLOR: Indeed. It would not be appropriate to ask whether what Adam says is true or false.

ALEXANDER: In laying down a path Adam creates both a subject of potentiality and an objective of potentiality. The subject is making it possible to apply and follow; the objective is making it possible to reach an achievement. He accordingly creates a subject whose actualization is a subject of truth or falsity; there is not any such actualization yet. There is therefore too little a basis for serious skepticism.

CHANCELLOR: So before there are subjects of truth, there are objectives of actuality. Such objectives are posterior to objectives of potentiality. They arise, in turn, along with the institution of paths of language.

ALEXANDER: Yes.

CHANCELLOR: Then the proper question of a serious skeptic is not whether there is a foundation of our framework with one or two floors in it; his question is how many more floors of higher achievements are built upon the first few floors.

ALEXANDER: Yes.

CHANCELLOR: Suppose we do cease to think through truth and falsity in terms of sameness and otherness and so too cease to contemplate truth in terms of a correspondence between our framework and the ground which its foundation rests upon outside it. Suppose we train ourselves to think through truth and falsity in terms of sufficiency and excess. The supreme question of truth is not whether the framework reflects, represents or corresponds to the part of the world which lies outside it; the question is rather whether the use of lower levels in working at a level is sufficient for objectives of actuality appropriate to the given level. A question of truth or falsity is therefore a question whose terms are internal to our framework.

ALEXANDER: I would like not to insist upon more precision in your summary than is appropriate to your own objectives of administering an academy. But certain things, mis-stated, can lead to misunderstanding. A question of truth is a question of sufficiency whose subjects are internal to our framework; but its objectives are not internal to any use of a framework. It is true that for reaching knowledge we depend upon use of the framework; actually reaching knowledge is no part of its use.

CHANCELLOR: Thank you.
RECORDER: (looking first at the Chancellor and then at Alexander) You have entranced the Chancellor and smuggled perplexity out of the room.
ALEXANDER: Perplexity?
RECORDER: One of the great skeptical questions of modern philosophy has been neglected.
ALEXANDER: Which question do you mean?
RECORDER: Whether I know and, if I do, how I know that there are other minds.
ALEXANDER: I have assumed we are conversing.
RECORDER: We are conversing; I'm keeping a record of our conversation.
ALEXANDER: Do I now converse with a body?
KATHERINE: (laughing) Some body! Bachelors in middle age begin to look as if they need kneading from the outside and inflaming from the inside. Only the love of another can do the former, and only desire the latter.
RECORDER: You sound like your friend, launching a personal attack upon me because of my defense of skepticism. You can't taunt into existence a good argument nor yet laugh real perplexity away. Not all of western philosophy is vigorous dialogue; some of it is profound meditation.
ALEXANDER: Is philosophy not critical and reflective?
RECORDER: It is critical and reflective.
ALEXANDER: The Chancellor asked me this morning (I.1) upon what I would have him reflect as we take up our study. I would have you reflect upon means we have, sometimes thought to be sufficient, for achievements of knowledge.
RECORDER: I have reflected upon such means.
ALEXANDER: Then guide yourself in the following kind of meditation: the means I employ for reflection and meditation I evidently have from others. For it is evident to me that I have not made up my own language. I speak, think and write the language of others. It sometimes happens that certain things are made clear to me. It accordingly sometimes happens that communal achievements are reached. The full cause of such achievements includes both action and effort made by another and action and effort made by me. So much implies the existence of at least two people one of whom is speaking and the other listening. Therefore, if there is a skeptical question, it is not whether there are others who have made it possible for me to speak, think and write a language; it is whether I am a person who has a place in their world.
CHANCELLOR: But you do. Would you like to be chancel-

lor?

ALEXANDER: No, I think you should be. Can't you take
seriously my offer of a skeptical question about my own
existence?

CHANCELLOR: No. Can you?

ALEXANDER: No.

KATHERINE: Before we stop for lunch, I would like to
make a remark. Something is gradually dawning upon me
which moves me to astonishment. Due to the genius of
ancient Greek philosophy...

RECORDER: (interrupting) Thank you for the admission,
Katherine.

KATHERINE: Due to Aristotle, I suppose, western philosophers have taken hold of a doctrine of the mean.
Had we met this morning to discuss moral philosophy,
no one would have been surprised to hear you lay out an
account of defect, sufficiency and excess. But it blew
me away to hear you say that being is a kind of sufficiency. I just didn't know how serious you were. I
now see you do mean to apply an account of defect, sufficiency and excess to metaphysics and epistemology.

Now I think it was a great and good thing for
thinkers to have formulated a doctrine of the mean.
Confucius said, "The superior man exemplifies the mean;
the inferior man acts contrary to the mean. Perfect is
the mean. In practicing the ordinary virtues and in
the exercise of care in ordinary conversation, when
there is deficiency, the superior man never fails to
make further effort, and when there is excess, never
dares to go to the limit." I think Aristotle would
very well have understood Confucius, don't you?

RECORDER: Yes.

KATHERINE: But it is one thing to apply a doctrine of
the mean to ethical matters; it is quite another to
apply it to metaphysics and epistemology. So I very
much look forward to our discussions this afternoon.

ALEXANDER: I'm glad to hear you say so.

CHANCELLOR: Let us stop for lunch. (The Porter enters
and invites us to follow him to a dining hall.)

PART V

ALEXANDER: We passed part of the morning accounting for certain ways of building up a conceptual framework. There are additions which we should discuss this afternoon. The additions are the resources of four families of instruments whose employment makes conceptual activity possible. The four houses are universally accessible: the full exercise of human intelligence requires access to all of them. The reigning family, as you know, is that of defect, sufficiency and excess. The first of the minor categories is that of sameness and otherness; the second, that of combination and separation, and the third, that of dependence and independence.
KATHERINE: So having finished lunch you propose to take us on a tour of a town of concepts organized by family.
(1)
ALEXANDER: We'll start the tour by visiting the house of sameness and otherness.
KEITH: I shall presume upon the role of a metaphysician and put a question right off: What are sameness and otherness?
ALEXANDER: Abstract objects. You know that we acknowledge the existence of abstract objects and of universals. There are two categories of abstract objects: defect, sufficiency and excess and sameness and otherness.
      Having acknowledged the existence of certain abstract objects let us consider vocabulary whose use is sufficient for indicating species of sameness and otherness.
RECORDER: Your account is short on metaphysics and will doubtless be long on the philosophy of language. (turning to the Chancellor) Have you noticed how quickly he turns from the one to the other?
CHANCELLOR: I don't understand you.
RECORDER: Metaphysics is a treasury of accounts of abstract objects. It's a thin and ailing discipline that has nothing more to say in addition to "Well, such objects do exist." Some philosophers have written treatises on abstract objects, their existence and their relations to other things. It pains me to realize to what extent the philosophy of language has taken over the role of metaphysics. So much would be justified if nominalism and idealism were justified--particularly linguistic idealism.
ALEXANDER: But you know I think both nominalism and idealism excessive or defective. Nor do I mean to

slight metaphysics. I have some hope that Keith will
prosper as a metaphysician. I have supposed that there
will be an opportunity this evening to define existence
or reality. If you would otherwise think me unserious,
I'll state my definition now and then again (VIII.11).
RECORDER: You should do so. We'll then have time to
think about it before this evening.
ALEXANDER: The statement relies upon tools on loan
from the major category: existence or reality is sufficiency of means for objective. For example, I assert,
"Atoms exist." We know from a discussion this morning
that the near object of assertion is the sufficiency of
the use of the words "atoms" and "exist" for a certain
objective. Let us not now concern ourselves with answering the question what that objective is. The remote object of a subordinate path is the sufficiency of
the use of the word "atom" for certain objectives appropriate to natural science. The means of the remote
object are potential: my assertion accordingly promises
resources, part of which is the use of "atom", adequate
for explaining out of what certain things are composed.
RECORDER: What is it, then, to assert that sameness
exists?
ALEXANDER: The near object of assertion is the adequacy of your act of uttering the sentence "Sameness
exists" for the objective at hand. The remote object
is the adequacy of the use of the words "the same" for
certain objectives. We are accordingly led to ask what
the objectives are of identifying or of differentiating. But before we consider such objectives, let us
consider the construction of paths of sameness or
otherness.
KEITH: You understand then, Julian, that Bill is not
arbitrarily short on metaphysics. The proper practice
of philosophy leads smartishly from metaphysics to the
philosophy of language.
RECORDER: Very smartishly. There is not even time to
ask what the relations are between sameness and other
things. We move straight on to consider our power to
construct certain paths and to indicate what path is
either laid down or taken.
ALEXANDER: But it is not as if I mean to neglect to do
something which exists to be done. There is no such
thing to do. There are no relations between sameness
and other things. Sameness does not depend upon anything else; it is not combined with or separate from
anything else. It is therefore appropriate that we
turn to our vocabulary whose use is adequate to indicate what path it is whose construction is of further
interest to us.

RECORDER: I place no obstruction in your way. Do continue.
ALEXANDER: A survey of the linguistic landscape of the
family reveals two pairs of species of expressions. In
the first species of the first pair is the expression
"the" and "the same"; in the second species, the expression "other than". Suppose Keith says, "Julian is
the person who came;" Katherine disagrees, saying,
"Julian is someone other than a person who came." In
the first species of the second pair is the expression
"only"; in the second species, the expression "other in
addition to". Suppose Keith says, "Only one person
came;" Katherine disagrees, saying, "Another came in
addition to that person." Let us call the first species of the first pair identity; the second, otherness,
and let us call the first species of the second pair
uniqueness, and the second, addition. Let us turn now
to constructing paths of the family.
KATHERINE: I'm not sure I could classify any expression proposed to me. For example, what about "as as"
and "-er than"? Where do they go?
ALEXANDER: The first indicates a kind of identity and
the second, a kind of otherness. Notice that in many
cases there are alternate routes before us: "You are as
tall as Keith is" and "You and Keith have the same
height." The same kind of identity is indicated first
by means of the words "as as" and then by means of the
expression "the same".
KATHERINE: And what about other expressions such as
"similar" and "dissimilar" and "like" and "unlike"?
ALEXANDER: When there is similarity, there is identity; when there is dissimilarity, there is otherness.
KATHERINE: I suppose I see my way. Perhaps we should
have your account of laying down or taking paths of the
family.
ALEXANDER: You understand then that my concern now is
with a creation of a community of people. Remember
that our creation myth is not of a path: it is not of
sameness and otherness. Such things are not created;
they are eternal. Our creation myth is rather of means
adequate for laying down or taking a path.
     With a certain complexity already achieved there
are created distinct ways along which the community can
continue to speak and to think. As soon as there are
parallel paths it becomes necessary for there to be resources adequate for making evident what path of language one lays down or takes. Resources for making
clear what path one takes are provided with the possibility of uttering expressions of our three pairs of
expressions. It is accordingly the first plank of our

Thesis of Sameness and Otherness that the utterance of
such words has a role to play with the emergence of
certain complex modes of continuance, namely to disclose what the path is along which there is continuance. The second plank is that the minimal complexity
which is necessary to make possible the gainful employment of the words is that of coordination among three
achievements reached or understood, say X, Y and Z. We
satisfy the second plank of the Thesis by allowing that
there is a minor path from X to Y and also that there
is a second minor path from Z to Y. We thereby satisfy
the condition of minimal complexity of two supporting
paths which one coordinates and subordinates in laying
down or taking a subordinate path of sameness or otherness. The third plank is that there is a third
achievement, Y, which is common to both; due to coordination, of course, it may not be reached twice.
RECORDER: Let us see whether I have followed you. According to the first plank you place a speaker under
obligation to signpost the major trail; this he must do
in order to make clear which of parallel paths he is
laying down or taking.
ALEXANDER: Yes. He can do so by controlling the timing and the modality of uttering the words "er than" or
"as as".
RECORDER: According to the second plank you place the
speaker under obligation to coordinate or to have understood three achievements. And according to the
third, there must be something held in common by two
minor paths.
ALEXANDER: Yes.
KATHERINE: I would be happy for an example.
ALEXANDER: Suppose I point to something and remark,
"This is the desk which I used early this morning."
Making clear what it is to which I point, is the first
relevant achievement; saying What, is the second, and
the third is revealing an act of use.
KATHERINE: According to your account you strike a coordination in order to provide support for taking the
major path, a path indicated, I take it, by the words
"the which". You take the first minor path in saying,
"This is a desk." You thereby coordinate two of the
three relevant achievements. You take the second minor
path in saying, "I used a desk early this morning."
You thereby coordinate two of the three relevant
achievements. Using the words "a desk" in order to say
What, is the basis of the common achievement.
ALEXANDER: Yes. You seem to have grasped the account.
Perhaps we are ready to have it examined.
KEITH: One more example. See whether I can talk it

through correctly. I assert, "This table is as long as that one is." According to our recent discussion I immediately assert sufficiency; thus is the word "is" accounted for. I effect a subject asserted to be sufficient by taking a path of sameness; the path is indicated by means of the words "as as"; thus are those two words accounted for. I effect one minor trail by coordinating the use of the words "this table" and "long"; I effect another minor trail by coordinating the use of the words "that one" and "long". Due to subordination a second use of "long" is omitted. Have I correctly applied and followed your Thesis?

ALEXANDER: Yes.

RECORDER: Are you willing to have the Thesis examined?

ALEXANDER: Of course.

(2)

RECORDER: I was educated on a different thesis; according to my thesis identity is a relation. According to your thesis identity is an object. You would then have us put aside the question what kind of object it is and take up another question: what it is to assert the sufficiency of laying down or taking a path of sameness or otherness. But according to my thesis I can answer your discarded question: identity is a relation between anything and itself. For we assert that each thing is the thing which it is and not another thing. If my thesis is right, yours cannot be. For suppose my thesis is right. And with respect to yours let us again consider the example, "This is the table which you used early this morning." You take one route when you say "the" and another when you say "other". Can you leave the minor paths intact and now take a path of sameness and now a path of otherness?

ALEXANDER: Yes.

RECORDER: And in both cases talk sense even if in one case you speak truly and in one case falsely?

ALEXANDER: Yes.

RECORDER: Are minor paths sufficient for a path of sameness also sufficient for a path of otherness?

ALEXANDER: Yes.

RECORDER: Always?

ALEXANDER: Yes.

RECORDER: Then consider my example: "Something is the same thing as itself." According to your answer to my question one would talk sense whether one said, "Something is the same thing as itself" or said, "Something is a different thing than itself." How, I ask you, can one merely take alternate routes when in the one case one utters a truth of reason and in the other one contradicts oneself?

ALEXANDER: To contradict oneself is not necessarily
not to talk sense.
RECORDER: But I think one does not talk good sense
when one says, "Something is other than itself."
Therefore, minor paths sufficient for taking a path of
sameness are not sufficient for taking a path of otherness. But your thesis predicts double use of the same
base; but the prediction is false. So your thesis must
not be right.
ALEXANDER: An assumption of your argument is that
there are minor paths sufficient for taking a path of
sameness when one says, "Something is the same thing as
itself." To meet the first plank of my thesis one
makes clear upon what path the mind moves.
RECORDER: So much is done when one uses the words "the
same as".
ALEXANDER: According to the second plank there must be
a certain complexity provided by two supporting minor
paths, giving us three achievements. What are they?
RECORDER: I take the first when I say, "Something is a
thing"; I take the second when I say, "Something is a
thing."
ALEXANDER: But you give us only two: that of using the
word "some", and that of using the words "a thing".
You have not yet done enough to support taking a path
of sameness sufficient for the objective of an assertion. There are no minor paths sufficient either for
taking a path of sameness or for taking one of otherness. So you have not shown that use of the thesis
leads to a false prediction.
RECORDER: But the cost of saving your thesis is very
high: you would reject the law of self-identity.
ALEXANDER: Yes. I have in fact shown why the law is
defective.
RECORDER: I cannot agree. Logicians and mathemati-
cians make liberal use of the law of self-identity when
they write, for example, "1 = 1." I would rather count
it a defect of our conversation that we cannot account
for it than a defect of the law that it doesn't say
enough.
ALEXANDER: I can apply the thesis somewhat differently
than I have with respect to the minor paths of writing,
"1 = 1." The first is that I here write a number; the
second, that I there write a number. The question
which calls for the major path is whether at both
places or at both times I have written the same number.
Our earlier demands are met: the minor paths are distinct; to each there is an alternative. So I have no
objection to raise against writing the formula "1 = 1."
In light of my account of it I think we should say that

96

I write it not in using the law of self-identity but rather in using the principle of repeatability. For let us suppose that Adam institutes the use of a T-expression, for example "a tree". He points to something and lays down what to say, saying, "That is a tree." If the path which he lays down is to be followed, it is necessary for another to be able again to utter the same word.

RECORDER: The principle is as essential for building a framework as it is for establishing an institute. I think I see how your account of sameness and otherness leads you to replace the law of self-identity by the principle of repeatability. I'm sure that a defender of the law would also want to embrace your principle. Indeed, he can claim that self-identity as a property of things supports your principle.

ALEXANDER: He can make the claim; he can hardly support it. For according to your thesis both a word and a tree are equally self-identical. It is therefore not that property which makes it possible for us to repeat the one but not the other.

RECORDER: Suppose that a pupil is doing a mathematical problem. He finally writes, "1 = 1." Is doing so part of doing mathematics?

ALEXANDER: No. By virtue of issuing an instance of the principle of repeatability he has reached a point so basic that it lies beneath mathematical practice. Accordingly he has finished his problem by virtue of following procedures which make it possible to pass to the principle of repeatability.

RECORDER: My attempt to examine your thesis has evidently not led to its refutation; nor has it led to my satisfaction. I must feel as Katherine did when she said she didn't know how further to examine your view of assertion. I wish to follow her. If you refute my thesis about identity, I am prepared to make a serious effort at understanding yours.

(3)

ALEXANDER: Fine. Let us examine your thesis. It is that identity is a relation which a thing has to itself. In light of what example shall we examine your thesis?

RECORDER: I assert, "Cicero is Tully." The example is useful in another way. Katherine claimed on behalf of contemporary logicians that there is an "is" of identity. We have it in my example.

ALEXANDER: Let us proceed according to our method. What is the immediate object of your assertion?

RECORDER: Identity. Since identity is a relation between a thing and itself, one asserts a relation, in

the example at hand, between a person and himself.
ALEXANDER: Is to assert a relation one and the same
thing as asserting that there is a relation?
RECORDER: I don't think you need to teach me the same
lesson you taught Katherine. I accept a consequence of
our discussion of assertion: to assert is immediately
to assert sufficiency.
ALEXANDER: And not identity?
RECORDER: Not immediately.
ALEXANDER: What then is the subject said to be suffi-
cient?
RECORDER: Taking a path of identity.
ALEXANDER: And the objective?
RECORDER: Making clear who Tully is.
ALEXANDER: Let us further consider the action of ef-
fecting a subject. According to your definition, to
indicate identity is to indicate a relation which a
thing has to itself. Is to indicate the relation which
Cicero has to himself enough to say who Tully is?
RECORDER: No.
ALEXANDER: Is to indicate the relation which Tully has
to himself enough to say who Tully is?
RECORDER: No.
ALEXANDER: Then how can your account be one of means
sufficient for such ends?
RECORDER: I think you now cavil with me and refuse to
take my thesis seriously. When I assert that Cicero is
Tully, I mean to assert that Cicero and Tully are names
of the same man.
ALEXANDER: Doubtless you and I would mean as much; I
fear your thesis doesn't. The first minor trail of the
assertion is, "Cicero is a name of a man;" the second,
"Tully is a name of a man." When your thesis uses the
words "the same," it indicates a relation which some
man has to himself. Thus to use the definition of the
thesis is to fall short of saying who Tully is. In order to correct the defect it is sufficient to give up
the definition that sameness is a relation. Sameness
is not a universal. Your definition would make of
identity too complex a thing. In point of fact sameness and otherness are simple objects of modes of continuance. In order to effect a subject of assertable
sufficiency it is necessary to do more than merely utter the words "the same" or "other".
RECORDER: It is obvious that it is necessary to do
more. No one makes an assertion when he says, "The
same."
ALEXANDER: If sameness were a torso, it would have two
legs so that the whole can stand. But now I sound as
if I were talking about sameness rather than about

modes of continuousness whose objects sameness and
otherness are. If taking a path of sameness were a
torso, it would have two legs so that the motion of the
whole is sufficient for its objective. Immediately in
question is the use of a common term; its use is essential to erecting a path of sameness or otherness.
RECORDER: I think you have given cause for me to reject my thesis and to adopt yours. It is not easy to
give up such a thesis. It has never occurred to me
that an alternative is possible. In a lecture on identity Martin Heidegger says, "Sameness implies the relation of with, that is, a mediation, a connection, a
synthesis: the unification into a unity. This is why
throughout the history of Western thought identity appears as unity."
ALEXANDER: When you become head of a department of
philosophy in the Chancellor's academy, I hope you encourage someone to consider what consequences would
arise from a systematic account of differences between
concepts of sameness and concepts of connection.
RECORDER: I'm sure such a study would be useful.
CHANCELLOR: Why don't you do it, Julian? I wouldn't
like to have you spend all your time at administration.
ALEXANDER: I would like to extend somewhat my Thesis
of Sameness and Otherness.
CHANCELLOR: Fine.
(3.1)
KEITH: I want to make a suggestion before we turn to
the second and the third of the minor families of concepts. I suggest we slightly modify and shorten Bill's
account of the use of terms drawn from the category of
sameness and otherness. For our purposes it would do
to say that there are two pairs of species. The first
pair concerns identity and otherness. Its terms are,
on the side of identity, "the" and "the same" and, on
the side of otherness, "other than". The second pair
concerns uniqueness and addition. Its terms are,
first, "only" and, second, "more in addition".
KATHERINE: Where do you mean to house "as as"?
KEITH: In the species of identity. I'm sure, viewing
our ends, no harm is done.
KATHERINE: Then you would house "-er than" in the
species of otherness.
KEITH: Yes.
KATHERINE: I'm willing to play along.
KEITH: I hope I can state part of Bill's account in
the following way. Laying down or taking a path of
sameness or otherness depends upon a presupposition.
An appropriate presupposition has two parts; they share
a common term.

ALEXANDER: Your abbreviated account sounds all right
to me.
KEITH: I'm interested in the logical relations among
statements of the four classes. Let "I" stand for a
sentence of identity; "O", for one of otherness; "U",
for one of uniqueness, and "A", for one of addition.
Suppose I display the four cases in this way:

sameness	otherness
I	O
U	A

     A number of things seem to me to be certain.
First, it is true either that I or that O and also true
either that U or that A. Surely there must be either
identity or otherness; there must be either uniqueness
or addition. Second, if one of a pair is true, the
other is false. It would be absurd to suppose, in a
given case, that there is both identity and otherness
or that there is both uniqueness and addition. For
example, if there is only one table before us, there
are not more than one.
KATHERINE: You're just looking from side to side
across your diagram. But take a vertical glance.
Don't logicians define uniqueness in terms of identity?
KEITH: Some do.
KATHERINE: Then can't we say that if U, then I? It
therefore follows that if not-I, then not-U. But the
negation of I is O; the negation of U is A. Therefore,
it follows that if O, then A.
RECORDER: Isn't that nice: Keith provides us with hor-
izontal truths and Katherine with vertical truths.
KEITH: I fail to see why we deserve Julian's contempt:
Is it contemptible to state the obvious?
RECORDER: I didn't mean to sound contemptuous.
KEITH: I would have thought that my first premiss is
as secure as Bill's first triadic law. Whatever A is
and whatever B is, A and B are either the same or
other. Has anyone thought to deny it?
RECORDER: I don't have a record of a serious denial.
Aristotle certainly affirms your premiss.
KATHERINE: I find it equally obvious that if there is
uniqueness, there is identity. For example, if Julian
is the only person who is keeping a record, then Julian
is the person who is keeping a record.
RECORDER: I don't see my way to denying that premiss.
But you inferred another, namely that if there is
otherness, then there is addition. If that premiss is

right, then whenever there is comparability, there is computability. So much causes me unease.
KATHERINE: Why?
RECORDER: I take it that Bach is a greater composer than Irving Berlin. The assumption is one of otherness. By your premiss something else follows: Bach has the greatness which Berlin has and more in addition.
KATHERINE: Whatever do you mean?
RECORDER: Is the notion of accumulation clear to you?
KATHERINE: I suppose so. Here is a book; I take another one in addition to this one.
RECORDER: Particulars accumulate, given certain modes of combination. Books can be placed together, as you say. Events accumulate too. You can add another session to a certain meeting. Substances and masses accumulate. But universals do not amass and accumulate. The number one doesn't get bigger.
KATHERINE: Heaven forbid! Why don't you come to the point, Julian? It's not like you to pretend to be a great metaphysician.
RECORDER: Either musical greatness is a universal or a particular capable of accumulation. If it is a universal, then the inference which your premiss generates makes no sense.
KATHERINE: You mean the inference "Bach has the greatness which Berlin has and more in addition."
RECORDER: Yes. But if greatness is a particular capable of accumulation, then the assertion which applies your premiss makes no sense. I mean the original comparison according to which Bach is a greater composer than Berlin is.
KATHERINE: I'm still not sure I understand you.
RECORDER: Consider these two books. I make a comparison by asserting, "This one is thicker than that one." We say that thickness is a universal. It would therefore be defective or excessive to infer, "This book has an additional thickness." It is not an original thickness which has grown. We say rather that this book has more pages; additional pages were added to other pages in making this book.
KATHERINE: I understand.
RECORDER: I don't think you do. For your premiss begins with a comparison with respect to a universal and ends with addition with respect to some mode of combination. It begins with a comparison with respect to a universal, for example width or thickness, and ends with addition with respect to a mode of combination. But we do not combine thicknesses; we combine pages.
KATHERINE: You'll have to give me time to figure out whether I should abandon my original premiss. Should

it go, I do have an alternative premiss. It is that if there is otherness, there is addition but with respect to an associated mode of combination. Your example suggested the premiss to me a moment ago: if this book is thicker than that one, then this book has these pages and some more in addition. It acquired more pages, as it were. One can count the additional pages to find out how much thicker this one is than that one. You see what I mean.

RECORDER: I suppose so. How do you mean to discover what the associated mode of combination is?

KATHERINE: We first apply Bill's thesis of sameness and otherness: decompose a sentence of otherness and discover the presuppositions or the minor paths. Then look around for a sensible mode of combination. I say, "Bach is greater than Berlin." The first minor path is "Bach is great." It's no good tinkering with the concept of greatness. It doesn't accumulate, as you say. But you can get a bigger and bigger pile of compositions. We can say, "Here's another one in addition to those." So put his compositions together. My new premiss asserts that such a thing is possible. Further, we can measure how big a pile we have. Since we can measure in numbers and units, we can measure the piles scientifically and come, finally, to the making of a scientific comparison.

RECORDER: And is it meant to follow that our original comparison is or is not justified?

KATHERINE: So much I'm not claiming. I'm only asserting that if the original comparison is justified, it is possible to follow such a procedure as I've suggested.

KEITH: Julian and Katherine look as if they're satisfied as to what should be said about the premiss that otherness implies addition. I'm not. Katherine's original argument has perplexed me. We all seem to stand by its beginning, namely the premiss that if there is uniqueness, there is identity. Consider again Katherine's example. Let "U" stand for "Julian is the only person who is keeping a record" and let "I" stand for "Julian is the person who is keeping a record." I take it Katherine's argument can be laid out in the following way:

(1) if U, then I
(2) so if not-I, then not-U
(3) but if O, then not-I
(4) and if not-U, then A
(5) therefore, if O, then A.

The second step follows from the first by contraposition. The third and the fourth are due to my laws: if there is otherness, there is not identity, and if

102

there is not uniqueness, there is addition. So by transitivity the fifth follows from the first. With respect to our example what actually follows is that if Julian is someone other than a person who is keeping a record, then there is someone else in addition to Julian who is keeping a record. But let us suppose that there is only one person who is keeping a record. Further, let us suppose that Julian is someone other than a person who is keeping a record. By the final step and modus ponens it follows that someone else in addition to Julian is keeping a record. A presupposition of the inference contradicts certain assumptions. There is therefore defect or excess somewhere in the argument.

RECORDER: (I made a copy of Keith's argument and looked up to study Katherine's face.) You originally made up the argument, Katherine. Do you see how to take flight from the puzzlement Keith sees in it?

KATHERINE: (looking at the piece of paper Keith had been writing on) No, I don't think so. Logicians have established step one. Only an optimistic fool would give it up. Step two is taken by following a well established procedure.

KEITH: The third and fourth have impeccable credentials.

KATHERINE: I agree. (pause) Well, you've got me. I don't know how to resolve the argument.

RECORDER: We can all live with a little puzzlement.

KATHERINE: And the puzzlement at hand is not excessive?

RECORDER: Is it?

KATHERINE: I don't know. (turning to Alexander) Is it?

ALEXANDER: I think it is. Let's try to resolve the puzzle somewhat later this afternoon. (VII.6)

KATHERINE: Fine.

(4)

ALEXANDER: Identifying and differentiating are two kinds of action human intelligence depends upon for science and philosophy. Having accounted for the subordinate actions of laying down or taking paths of sameness and otherness let us consider bridgework which carries intelligence from paths of the family to its wider community. Let us consider laws of the sufficiency of a path of otherness or sameness for continuance. I suspect it would be easier for us to begin with an elementary example than with the law of the indiscernibility of identicals.

Suppose that Adam means to make counting possible. His community has the O-words "many" and "few" under employment; the U-word "number" is also at hand. Adam

103

has ordered his chief wordsmith to coin a set of A-expressions to fill out a U-system. He gathers about himself his linguistic council and lays down what to say in order to say how many objects he has in his hand, saying, "One." He thereby institutes the use of the A-word "one". The council grants that one is a number.

There exists a law of sufficiency whose subject is taking a path of otherness: I mean "other in addition to". The first condition concerns laying down a path of otherness. One can do so by saying, "If there are more objects in my hand by one than there are in Adam's hand." If the first condition of the law is met, we pass on to the second condition, namely, "If there is one object in Adam's hand." If both conditions are met, one follows the law either by instituting an A-expression for saying how many objects there are in my hand or by using the expression "two", already instituted. In either case the law is a law of sufficiency for continuance.

RECORDER: So use of the law carries him who uses it from two instances of meeting a condition to a mode of continuance. Meeting the first condition presupposes uses of a certain kind of expression. Can you help me with a statement of the presupposition?

ALEXANDER: Perhaps we can identify the kind by identifying pairs of a question and an answer. The question is: More by one what?

RECORDER: So the following pairs are all right: More by one what? By one foot. More by one what? By one minute. Further, it makes sense to say that the room is lighter than it was by one degree and that the water is warmer by one degree. But the following pairs are not all right: Brighter by one what? By one color. More by one what? By one opinion.

ALEXANDER: You seem to have an adequate grasp on the implications of meeting the first condition of the law.

RECORDER: Meeting the second condition presupposes that we have taken step two of the first stage of institution: for example, we can say of a paradigm how many, of what length, of what duration, of what degree brightness or of what degree temperature. Upon thus applying the law we can follow it; for it promises resources adequate either for creation or for use. In one of two ways we continue.

ALEXANDER: There is a law which is essential to the continuance of thought. The law is a law of sufficiency of potentiality for potential continuance. The condition of the law is a condition of sufficiency whose subject is laying down a path of sameness; the consequence of the law is a consequence of sufficiency whose subject is realized by him who applies and follows the law.

KEITH: If you had now spoken Arabic, I would not have understood less.

RECORDER: Nor I. And I make the record. Perhaps you can give us an example.

ALEXANDER: I can apply and follow the law of continuance in this way: if this table and the paradigm have the same color, then if the color of the paradigm is brown, then this table is brown. I explicate the law thus: taking a path of sameness is sufficient for continuing; such continuing is potential; a certain assertion is sufficient for actually continuing as to the color of this table. So meeting two conditions is sufficient to make full use of the law, concluding of this table that it is brown.

KEITH: We used to call your law of continuance half of Leibniz's law: if A is identical with B, then A and B have the same properties. Your law of sufficiency for continuance is also called the principle of the indiscernibility of identicals.

KATHERINE: And is false.

KEITH: False?

KATHERINE: False. Consider. Suppose you do know what the color is of the paradigm to which Professor Alexander was referring. But suppose you had never seen this table nor had been told anything about it. Now it is true that this table and the paradigm have the same color. It is also true that the color of the paradigm is known by you. According to your principle of indiscernibility it follows that the color of this table is known by you. But so much is granted to be false. The principle is therefore excessive.

ALEXANDER: Indeed. It follows either that there is nothing to the law or that Keith has mis-stated the heart of the law.

KATHERINE: I very well see that your formulation of a law of sufficiency for continuance is not open to the sort of objection I raised against Keith. For according to your version the law is a law of continuance realized by him who applies and follows the law.

ALEXANDER: Right. At the highest level of domination the law is a law of sufficiency for continuance.

KATHERINE: The law is not applied if I work out what is or is not at hand in Keith's mind; it is only applied by me if I work out what is enough for me to make an advance.

ALEXANDER: Yes. The construction of such puzzles misuses the law. For it is an instrument for generating inference in no other head than in that of him who uses it. It is absurd to suppose that by applying and following such a law I can place a new thought in your head, unless I make out the case within your reading or hearing. It is even more absurd to suppose that such a law works as an eraser and a pencil, erasing a word of your thought and putting another in its place.

RECORDER: Let me see whether I have an adequate record of your formulation of the law. The law is applied by meeting two conditions; it is followed by generating inference. The first condition of correctly using the law is that there is continuity among three epistemic acts: two acts of application and one of following. Right?

ALEXANDER: Right.

RECORDER: Is that condition necessary and sufficient for correct use?

ALEXANDER: No. There must not only be continuity from application to application to following. There must also be continuity of presupposition. Suppose that we meet the first condition of the law by laying down or taking a path of identity. Constructing the path makes two presuppositions or, as we say, effects two minor paths. Suppose we meet the second condition by taking another path. One of the presuppositions of a path of identity must be a presupposition of the second path. By means of the law a third path is generated; the other presupposition of the path of identity must be a presupposition of the third path. For example, we meet the first condition by asserting that the paradigm and this object have the same color. The two presuppositions are that the paradigm has a color and that this object has a color. We meet the second condition by asserting that the paradigm is red. The first presupposition is also a presupposition of the second assertion. We infer that this object is red; it is presupposed that this object has a color. In this case the law is correctly used.

RECORDER: How can we tell whether a presupposition of a path of identity is a presupposition of a subsequent path?

ALEXANDER: Ask whether the truth of a subsequent path depends upon the truth of a presupposition. If so, the proposed presupposition is a real one.

KEITH: The two conditions of continuity are meant to cope with apparent counter-examples, I take it.

ALEXANDER: Yes. I hope they do.

KEITH: I suppose it's going to be hard for us to get something through our heads: the law has nothing to do with substitution; it has something to do with contin-

106

uance and the possibility of generating new inference
or knowledge. I still wonder whether your formulation
leads to difficulties discussed by logicians who are
given to the idea that identity and substitution have
something to do with one another. For example, it is
true that Tully is Cicero. It is also true that
"Cicero" has six letters. So by the law it follows
that "Tully" has six letters. Which is false.
KATHERINE: Even I can see my way through your example.
For asserting that Tully is Cicero it is presupposed
that Tully is the name of a man and that Cicero is the
name of a man. But for asserting that "Cicero" has six
letters it is not presupposed that Cicero is the name
of a man. It is only presupposed that "Cicero" is a
word. The original claim would have had to be that
"Cicero" and "Tully" are the same word. Which is
false.
KEITH: All right. Forget cases of that sort. They're
not interesting. Suppose I don't know that Julian is
the Recorder of a certain conversation. I pick up a
copy and say, "I think the Recorder is wrong here." It
follows that I think that Julian is wrong here. But so
much is not true. So use of the law leads to error.
ALEXANDER: You brought up such an example a few minutes ago. Do you see how to dismantle Keith's?
KATHERINE: I think so. The claim on identity presupposes that Julian is a recorder and that a recorder is
recording a certain conversation. Now the primary
thread of continuity is meant to run not through
Keith's head but through ours; for he doesn't know the
path of identity. The second condition of the law is
therefore met not by Julian's belief but by our report
of Julian's belief. But our report doesn't presuppose
either that Julian is a recorder or that a recorder is
recording a certain conversation. Therefore, the sec-
ondary thread of continuity is defective. So the law
is incorrectly used.
RECORDER: Have we now finished with your Thesis about
Sameness and Otherness?
ALEXANDER: Yes.
RECORDER: This morning I said that I was not satisfied
with your statement and defense of a distinction between perception and thought. You asked me to wait until now to give my own opinion.
ALEXANDER: And what is your opinion?
(5)
RECORDER: I think that a perception is an hypothesis.
ALEXANDER: Good heavens why?
RECORDER: Because perception goes beyond the given.
One sees three legs of a table and acts as though it

has four; one senses a brown patch and acts as though
it is wood. There is a second consideration. Push one
eye gently with a finger so that its optical axis is
misaligned with the axis of the other eye. Doing so
gives you double vision. Now which of the resulting
perceptions is veridical? They both look alike. To
answer both considerations I say that we adopt certain
assumptions in order to make use of available sensory
information: we construct a perception. For this reason I said that a perception is an hypothesis.

ALEXANDER: Can we allow a distinction between perceiving and thinking?

RECORDER: I suppose you mean to hold me to an earlier
agreement. This morning you led the Chancellor into
saying that we would allow you a distinction between
the second and the third levels of mind or between perception and thought. (I.3)

ALEXANDER: I have no way of holding you to such an
agreement. You are to become head of your department.
I have no authority over you.

RECORDER: You have authority with us.

ALEXANDER: If you have discovered defect or excess in
my earlier argument, I must again take up the case of a
distinction between perception and thought.

RECORDER: In the first part of our conversation we
were not clear about sameness and otherness and their
modes of continuousness. Only a moment ago did you
formulate a law of continuity. In your original argument for a distinction you employed a version of the
law which Katherine used to reach an impossibility.

ALEXANDER: You have persuaded me to take up the case
again. Can we make use of the law in our argument
about perception?

RECORDER: Yes. Perhaps you should again state the law
for our benefit.

ALEXANDER: The law is applied by meeting two conditions; the law itself is a law of sufficiency of meeting the conditions for continuing. Applying and following the law demands continuity among the two instances of meeting the conditions and the instance of
continuing. There is a thread of continuity, as it
were, weaving its way through three points of action in
the mind of the person who applies and follows the law.

RECORDER: I understand.

ALEXANDER: It is your view that perceiving is itself
an instance of thinking; similarly, seeing is an instance of knowing.

RECORDER: Yes. Your thread of continuity moves equally among acts of judgment and among acts of perception.

ALEXANDER: And equally among achievements of thought

and among achievements of perception?
RECORDER: Yes.
ALEXANDER: Suppose that a man approaches us. You ex-
tend your hand and greet him, saying, "Hello." Can we
say you meet the second condition of the law when you
see a man approaching us.
RECORDER: Yes.
ALEXANDER: While you look at him and keep him in
sight, the Chancellor leans towards you and says, "That
man is the Premier." Upon hearing him you acquire
knowledge of who that man is. Can we allow it?
RECORDER: Of course.
ALEXANDER: Do you thereby meet the first condition of
the law?
RECORDER: Yes.
ALEXANDER: So a thread of continuity makes its way
from an achievement of knowledge through one of sight.
According to the law you have resources adequate for
following it; for you have already applied it.
RECORDER: I very well grasp that I do.
ALEXANDER: You follow the law by managing another
achievement of perception: you also see the Premier.
RECORDER: Also?
KATHERINE: (turning to Keith) He looks surprised.
(turning again to Julian) Write it down, Julian: "You
also see the Premier."
ALEXANDER: For just as to know what you see, namely
that man, is not to know who that man is, namely the
Premier, so to see that man is not to see the Premier.
Have I correctly reported your view?
RECORDER: Yes, I suppose so.
ALEXANDER: You remember my supposition: while you look
at a certain person and keep him in sight, the Chancellor leans towards you and says, "That man is the Premier." By use of the law you have resources adequate
for an additional achievement of sight. Can you in
fact manage it? Can you pull yourself together and, in
addition to seeing that man, also see the Premier?
RECORDER: It would be absurd to say so. Use of the
law does not give me such power.
ALEXANDER: You mean it doesn't improve your perceptual
position. Its use is not like stepping on a box and
thereby securing a position adequate for an additional
achievement of sight.
RECORDER: Perhaps I do mean as much.
ALEXANDER: If the law is powerless to improve your
perceptual position, then one of three criticisms is
called for. First, there is defect in meeting the second condition; second, defect in meeting the first condition, or third, defect in the law. But you agreed to

stand by the law. Further, it is pointless for you to argue error in the supposition that the man seen is the Premier.

RECORDER: Indeed.

ALEXANDER: So we are left with the first criticism: there is defect in meeting the second condition: to see something is to accomplish too little to meet a condition of the law. But since to judge may be to do enough, and to know is to accomplish enough, seeing is not a species of knowing and perceiving is not a species of judging.

RECORDER: I accept the argument you have laid out; it does refute my view.

ALEXANDER: Notice how the absurdity can be resolved by running the thread of continuity among epistemic acts. The second condition is met by taking it that you see that man; by use of the law it follows that there is support sufficient for taking it that you have seen the Premier. Not an additional achievement of sight arises but an additional act of thought.

KATHERINE: Julian, you look depressed rather than purged. Aren't you pleased to have a foolish windegg taken from you?

RECORDER: Well, Bill takes away my opinion without resolving my problems.

ALEXANDER: You advanced two considerations on behalf of your opinion that perception is an hypothesis. The first you introduced with these words: perception goes beyond the given.

RECORDER: Yes. How can I say that a piece of wood is sensorily given? There is much more to a piece of wood than can be seen at any moment. I could see what I see but it not be this piece of wood. My question is: What do we see in that sense?

ALEXANDER: I hope you will not think that I merely cavil over a question, annoying you with my worry that you do not put a real question. You must realize that in truth I fail to grasp how the question arises WHAT one can see when there is no possibility of saying or knowing what one can see.

RECORDER: Suppose a cat is looking at something. You have persuaded me to say that to look at something is not to know either that one is looking at something or what it is at which one is looking. I can nevertheless inquire what it is at which the cat is looking. Is that not so?

ALEXANDER: Yes. And to ask the question is to presuppose a framework. Does use of the framework depend upon the cat's looking at something?

RECORDER: No. There is no thread of continuity run-

ning from the cat's looking at something to a use of
the framework. Its use depends upon our believing that
the cat is looking at something and further upon our
curiosity as to what it is.
ALEXANDER: And does use of a framework in our case depend alone upon seeing something or also upon our believing or knowing that one sees something and further
upon curiosity as to what is seen?
RECORDER: Upon our believing or knowing that we do.
You have persuaded me to accept your premiss that there
is no thread of continuity running from our looking at
and seeing something to a use of the framework. But in
saying or thinking whatever we say or think we are an-
swerable--we are responsible.
ALEXANDER: Indeed we are. To what?
RECORDER: To sensory data.
ALEXANDER: I do not understand how you can accept my
premiss of continuity and nevertheless say what you
have said. How is it that upon saying or thinking, "I
can see a brown piece of wood" I receive a reply from
seeing something?
KATHERINE: Julian, you even lead the philosopher into
talking nonsense.
ALEXANDER: I understand how there can be, as it were,
horizontal responsibility along a floor of our framework; I do not understand how there can be vertical
responsibility, looking, as it were, into nature. Let
us examine your second consideration: you press one eye
and asks what you can see. If we were not elsewhere
committed, we could bring our framework to bear and
say, "I can see two fingers." But making such a claim
conflicts with saying other things under other circumstances which we take to be better; in such circumstances we would be in a position simply to point out
what can be seen and how many things there are. In
thus yielding both to the superiority of that position
and to the use we make of the framework in it we speak
now either of seeing the same thing twice or of there
appearing to be two fingers. Use of the word "appear"
signals our commitment elsewhere.
RECORDER: So I was talking nonsense when I originally
uttered the sentence "Perception goes beyond the
given."
ALEXANDER: Yes. It is also nonsense to say, "One goes
too far in seeing something." One does go too far in
thinking this or in saying that. We have laid foundations for such criticism of excess.
RECORDER: Would it help if I spoke not of what is
given but of sensory input or of a sensory presentation?

ALEXANDER: It would still be wrong to do so. For you
introduce expressions for saying What--but do so as if
in advance of our ordinary efforts to mobilize our
framework.
RECORDER: I would rather say that I bring a scientific
framework to bear.
ALEXANDER: But the objective is the same, namely to
say what it is that is seen, heard, felt or tasted.
RECORDER: Yes, and to do so without fear of error or
mistake. One wishes to do so without risk of commitment elsewhere, as you say.
ALEXANDER: But the fear of error is misguided.
RECORDER: No, I think not. I say so because I do not
agree with you that all error is tension within a
framework. A scientist institutes use of such expressions to make it possible to affirm this proposition:
the thing seen is the same thing as the thing he says
he sees.
ALEXANDER: And in order to take a path of sameness is
one meant to subordinate seeing something or saying
that one sees something?
RECORDER: What?
KATHERINE: I hope the students in your department are
better than its head. The account of sameness and
otherness has gone directly from Alexander's mouth to
your record without passing through the department's
head.
RECORDER: Katherine, I would rather have you help me
concentrate than cause me distraction. (turning to
Alexander) I am saying this: I can see what I say I
can see when I say, "a sensory core."
ALEXANDER: You remember that constructing a path of
sameness subordinates the execution of two minor paths.
From your proposition I can extract the first one as
follows: I can see a sensory core. The second one: I
say, "a sensory core." So the thing I say, namely the
expression "a sensory core", is the same expression
which I can see. Do I have your meaning?
RECORDER: You all think I'm stupid.
ALEXANDER: Come now. The Premier doesn't think the
Chancellor is stupid; the Chancellor doesn't think his
new head of department is stupid.
RECORDER: I am not saying that the thing which I see
is the thing which I am saying. I claim rather that
the thing which I see is the thing which I say I can
see.
ALEXANDER: Then you must mean to subordinate two acts
of language to taking a route of sameness. So you must
mean to be claiming this: what one can say in order to
point out what I see is what I am now saying in order

112

to say what I see. And so you commit yourself to a
certain stability.
RECORDER: My opposition to your position has exhausted
me. I have no further wish to disagree with you.
CHANCELLOR: And so, since your position collapses,
there is no further resistance to Mr. Alexander's observation that all error is tension internal to a
framework; all error is excess internal to a framework
wanting purging rather than dividing. A scientist may
therefore devote himself either to constructing a new
part of one or to putting one part right relative to
the security of another part. To do the latter we do
not see the necessity of introducing such curious expressions as "a sensory core" or "an optical presentation" or "the given".
RECORDER: (During the last few comments the Porter entered our room and served tea. It is already two
o'clock.)
KATHERINE: (Upon receiving a cup of tea she looked up
at the Porter.) Thanks. We've spent the last hour in
a tool shed, sharpening up the instruments of sameness
and otherness. Keith's grandfather would have been
proud of us: honing, ordering and sharpening, getting
ready to do some real work.
PORTER: And have you?
KATHERINE: We haven't got out of the tool shed.
KEITH: You do us an injustice. Our formulation of
Leibniz's law carries us outside the house of sameness
and otherness.
KATHERINE: Potentially, I suppose. Of course an example did in fact carry us out. (turning to the Porter) The point is, you see, that sameness and otherness are abstract objects; they are objects not of perception but of thought. Further, identifying and differentiating are conceptual acts; their performance
makes complex use of conceptual and linguistic resources.
KEITH: They are acts which no being can perform without use of a language or some other such instrument.
PORTER: So a cat does not see differences.
KATHERINE: A cat does not look at and see sameness and
otherness.
PORTER: Nor does a cat differentiate.
KATHERINE: No cat I have known either identifies or
differentiates.
CHANCELLOR: Nor discriminates?
KATHERINE: You're looking at me amazed, as if one of
us has gone mad. If to discriminate is to lay down or
take a path of otherness, then no cat discriminates.
If, on the other hand, to discriminate is to separate

or to cause there to be independence, then, I dare say, any cat can discriminate.

CHANCELLOR: My colleagues in the social sciences posit the power to discriminate both widely and deeply in the animal kingdom.

KATHERINE: Then they should jolly well be clear what they think it is to discriminate.

ALEXANDER: I fear we do not have time today for undertaking such a project of clarification.

PORTER: Do philosophers ever get anything settled?

KATHERINE: No. That's why I decided against doing advanced work in philosophy after I finished my first degree. Some of us cannot endure living in a house in which most doors are open and those shut are only temporarily or tentatively shut. But Lord knows I would recommend philosophy to any intelligent student as his first study.

PART VI

ALEXANDER: We have discussed examples drawn from the first of three families of paths subordinate to the reigning family of defect, sufficiency and excess. Let us now turn to the second and the third of the three families: that of combination and separation and that of dependence and independence.
(1)
ALEXANDER: The second family is made up of the genus of combination and the genus of separation. The genus of combination has two species: together with respect to space and together with respect to time. The genus of separation also has two species: apart with respect to space and apart with respect to time. For example, we say that two rivers come together and that two trees grow apart. Another expression belonging to the family is "a part of": we speak of certain paths making up a whole or of a whole consisting of several parts.

There are many modes of combination and separation; it would be appropriate to consider some of them relevant to our interests and objectives.
RECORDER: It has been taken for granted that there is a distinction between act and achievement. Certain achievements of knowledge you call complex. Does "complex" indicate combination?
ALEXANDER: Yes.
RECORDER: Then simpler achievements combine, forming a complex whole.
ALEXANDER: Yes. A complex whole can be thought of either as a plane or as a solid. In the first case there is only a combination of achievements; in the second there is a hierarchy, achievements of one level depending upon achievements of a lower level.
CHANCELLOR: The notions of combination and separation are so familiar to us that I can hardly think we are in need of further explication. Let us turn to your third family of paths.
(2)
ALEXANDER: The third family is made up of the genus of dependence and the genus of independence. For example, we say that a child depends for its welfare upon its parents and that the growth of this tree is independent of that of another tree.

We can perhaps deepen our understanding of the family by recalling expressions which we have employed today already: I mean those in particular which we have employed in accounting for our perceptual and epistemic positions and also for the natural world, on the one hand, and, on the other, the social and communicative

worlds. You remember that early today I said to you,
"Actions and achievements of the social world depend
for their completion and reaching upon power to control
the initiation, the continuance and the completion of
actions and movements of the natural world." My premiss is of dependence with respect to power. The notion
of dependence belongs to the family now under discussion and, in particular, to the genus of dependence;
its opposite is that of independence.

I also stated the relation between the communicative and the natural world by means of a notion from
the second pair. I say, for example, that an act of
gesturing depends upon the movement of a part of one's
body. And since I distinguish the pair of concepts
"dependence" and "independence" from the pair "a part
of" and "apart from", I argue the metaphysical point
that although gesturing depends upon natural motion, a
gesture is not a part of natural movement.
RECORDER: The first notions introduced in a systematic
way this morning are those of domination and subordination. Do I employ terms of the family under discussion
when I say, "One thing is done in subordination to another"?
ALEXANDER: Yes.
RECORDER: And which of two things do I mean: that the
dominant action depends upon the subordinate action or
that the subordinate action is a part of the dominant
action?
ALEXANDER: Both alternatives are possible. A gesture
depends upon natural motion; utterance of a word can be
part of uttering a sentence.
RECORDER: The third notion introduced is that of coordination. You evidently mean that two or more things
are done together. To which pair does the notion belong?
ALEXANDER: To the family of dependence and independence. For in effecting a coordination one performs
two or more actions which depend upon one another for
reaching a certain objective.
CHANCELLOR: In light of your expositions of the two
families of paths, I mean that of sameness and otherness and that of dependence and independence, I have a
more nearly adequate grasp of your earlier intentions.
In the first part of our discussion you made several
distinctions. It is now evident to me that you meant
not only to distinguish natural and social or communicative acts and perceptual and cognitive acts. You also meant to lay down premisses of dependence and independence. First, natural acts are independent of
social acts with respect to power; acts of perception

are independent of acts of thought with respect to
power. Second, social acts depend upon natural acts.
To prove the independence of an achievement of sight
from one of knowledge you argue that one can see something without either knowing that one sees or knowing
what one sees. You then seemed only to argue for a
distinction; you ought to have concluded independence.
A distinction would be implied. I wonder why you did
not.
ALEXANDER: Metaphysics has become so confined that at
that time I feared I would be misunderstood. For "independence" is often understood as "separation". It
would then sound as if one means that as there can be
perception without thought there can also be thought
without perception. But so much is not meant. For although making sound is independent of uttering a word,
uttering a word depends upon making sound. But since
"depends upon" does not mean "consists in", I reject the
independence of uttering a word from making sound in
favor of arguing dependence; I do not reject independence in favor of arguing consisting in.
(3)
KATHERINE: I suspect that you do not mean merely that
metaphysics has become confined; you also mean, I suspect, that it has become confused. Would you accuse so
great a philosopher as Willard van Orman Quine of confusion?
ALEXANDER: I dare not think so.
KATHERINE: Some time ago I read a review of his printed in the New York Review of Books. I've forgotten
when; I do remember it is a review of a book by Nelson
Goodman. Do you remember when the review was printed,
Julian? You remember nearly everything.
RECORDER: I stopped reading the Review when I quit
being liberal.
KATHERINE: Mr. Chancellor, what have you hired for the
head of a department of philosophy?
ALEXANDER: What did Quine write?
KATHERINE: Nothing happens in the world, not the flutter of an eyelid, not the flicker of a thought, without
some redistribution of micro-physical states. It follows that the flutter of an eyelid and the flicker of a
thought consist in a redistribution of elementary
states.
ALEXANDER: If you correctly report Quine, I fear he is
confused. Departing from a denial of independence he
misses its proper opposite and hits the opposite of
separation. It may well be true that nothing happens
in the world, not the flutter of an eyelid, not the
flicker of a thought, without some redistribution of

microphysical states. But what is set forth as a conclusion is incorrectly drawn. For the appropriate opposite is not "a part of" but "dependent upon". It
therefore does not follow that a thought consists in
elementary states; it follows rather that a thought depends upon elementary states.
KATHERINE: But what difference does it make to get so
fine a metaphysical point perfectly straight?
ALEXANDER: Would you say that for maintaining its position this book depends upon this table?
KATHERINE: Yes.
ALEXANDER: Do I mean that the book is part of the table?
KATHERINE: It would be absurd to say so.
ALEXANDER: Or that part of the book is part of the table?
KATHERINE: Nor that.
ALEXANDER: And something further: Can I describe the
book without describing the table?
KATHERINE: Yes.
ALEXANDER: Suppose I remark in general that we depend
upon the use of certain means for reaching a certain
end. Reaching the end is no part of using the means;
further, it is possible to account for the end reached
without accounting for the means employed. I doubtless
depend upon the employment of mechanisms of the brain
for thinking. But thinking is no part of using the
mechanisms; further, it is possible to account for
thought without a physiology of the brain. It is
therefore open to us to hold, as we must hold, that
epistemology, logic and metaphysics are independent of
natural sciences.
CHANCELLOR: I suspect now I made a mistake urging you
to rush on from a mere introduction of the notions of
combination and separation to a discussion of the notions of dependence and independence. It would not
have occurred to me to distinguish consistency from dependence nor separation from independence. But the
last point which you made interests me, and I would
like to have an adequate grasp of the terms of its defense. I spoke recently with a biologist whom I mean
to employ. He said to me, "All thinking depends on the
brain." I take it you would not dispute a scientist
who makes such a claim.
ALEXANDER: Indeed, I would not.
CHANCELLOR: Having made that claim he asked, "So can
there be boundaries between philosophy and biology?
All living things consist of molecules; so does the
study of life derive its fundamental principles from
those of physics and chemistry?"

118

ALEXANDER: The order of things is not necessarily the same as that of disciplines of your academy. The relation between thinking and the use of brain mechanisms is that of dependence; from an allowance of a relation of dependence it does not follow that philosophy depends upon a science of the brain. It is likely that a science of the brain depends in part upon certain fields of philosophy, logic and epistemology, for example.

I think it unlikely that your biologist would have asked, "So can there be boundaries between philosophy and biology?" unless he supposed thinking consists in the use of brain mechanisms. It would then follow that a complete account of the brain would have as a part a discipline such as logic. It would accordingly be reasonable to argue that the drawing of boundaries would be arbitrary. Such a position would be defective, resting as it does upon a false assumption.

The second pair of assertion and question invites a similar response. It will not do to say, "All living things consist of molecules." There is a level with respect to which it is doubtless correct to say that there are things consisting of molecules; the notion of parts combining to form a whole is correctly employed in structuring a discipline. But a person is not a whole whose parts are molecules; for thinking the law of non-contradiction does not consist of molecules.
CHANCELLOR: Indeed not; it would be absurd to say so.
ALEXANDER: Then let us say that wholes whose parts are molecules support events and activities of a person; it follows that certain events and activities depend upon the behavior of those wholes consisting of molecules. But it does not further follow that those events and activities have as parts the behavior of molecules. Since certain higher actions of life do not consist in the behavior of molecules, the study of life cannot derive its fundamental principles from those of physics and chemistry. Indeed, the latter sciences depend in part upon fields of philosophy.

The position of the scientist is often the position we are now in. We are in a position sufficient for reaching certain achievements both of perception and of thought; for there are things we see, and there are things we know. But we allow that such achievements depend upon ranges of subjects each of which is necessary and which are jointly sufficient for reaching the achievements. My allowance is prior to an account of a range of subjects jointly sufficient for an achievement.
CHANCELLOR: Of course. Without using your technical

mode of expression I would say that I can allow that I see something without having an account of means necessary and sufficient for seeing something; I can allow that I know something without having an account of means necessary and sufficient for knowledge.

KEITH: You have alarmed me about the possibility of confusing a relation of part to whole with one of dependence. I was recently reading a study of Hume's philosophy; according to the study Hume takes metaphysics to be first philosophy or first science. We're to take Hume to mean that all other sciences are comprehended within it or depend upon it.

ALEXANDER: We are given two alternatives: a relation of part to whole and a relation of dependence. It is accordingly one thing to say that various sciences form parts of a whole called metaphysics; it is another to say that various sciences depend upon metaphysics in one way or another. It is a mistake either to think that philosophy is a part of biology or to think that biology is a part of philosophy.

KEITH: I very well take your point. Perhaps we should picture the Chancellor's academy as a flattened pyramid upside down: philosophy helps form a foundation which gives support to other disciplines.

ALEXANDER: We have now surveyed the three subordinate families of notions: sameness and otherness, combination and separation and dependence and independence. (4)

CHANCELLOR: Do you mean for us to see that they work independently one of the others?

ALEXANDER: Not necessarily independently. I do wish you to see that each of the three minor families or categories has members which provide distinguishable conceptual resources. I would also like to alert you to the possibilities of defective or excessive cooperation between or among them.

CHANCELLOR: I'm not sure I follow you.

ALEXANDER: Then consider my wish with respect to the first minor category in relation to the second and the third. Let us now consider bridgework which carries the mind from otherness to the category of dependence and independence and, in a moment, from otherness to the category of combination and separation. The first piece of bridgework is the premiss that if there is otherness, then there is either dependence or independence.

CHANCELLOR: I see. Such a premiss was used this morning by Julian to generate six possible positions regarding particulars and universals.

RECORDER: Right. We convinced ourselves that both

particulars and universals exist.   It follows by the
premiss that there is between them either dependence or
independence.
KEITH: There are two extreme monistic positions: uni-
versalism and nominalism.   We discarded them this morning.   So the truth must lie between.   What do you mean
by "transcendent realism"?
RECORDER: That particulars depend upon universals for
being the particular things they are.   Its opposite is
immanent realism: universals depend upon particulars
for their existence.   Plato seems to hold the first,
and Aristotle, the second position.
KATHERINE: Whatever would it be to hold a position of
mutual dependence?
RECORDER: A particular depends upon a universal for
one thing, and a universal upon a particular for another.   For example, this book depends upon space for
having a volume; that volume, in turn, depends upon
this book for being known.
ALEXANDER: Having considered the premiss of dependence
and independence with respect to universals and particulars let us also consider it with reference to mind
and matter.   We had occasion to employ the premiss
earlier (III.9).
RECORDER: I remember.   It is possible again to identify six positions.
ALEXANDER: Let us first identify two extreme monistic
positions by employing the premiss through modus tollens.   Suppose that there is neither dependence nor independence.   There would then be no distinction.   Let
us call the first possible position monistic idealism:
there is only mind and no matter.   Call the second position monistic materialism: there is only matter and
no mind.   Suppose now that there is otherness between
mind and matter.   The next three positions presuppose
dependence.   The third is that matter depends upon
mind; the fourth, that mind depends upon matter, and
the fifth that there is mutual dependence.   The final
position presupposes independence.   So the sixth position is that each is independent of the other.
RECORDER: (I felt pleased; I put my pen down and
said:)   I find the classification convincing.   Either
there is sameness or otherness.   If the first, then one
of two versions of monism is right.   If there is otherness, there is either dependence or independence.   If
the first, one of three positions is right; if the second, then the last would be right.
KATHERINE: Are there examples of all six positions?
Some of them I find wild: too silly to discuss, I
think.

RECORDER: There are specific positions which I can think of. They can in fact be listed on a line: at the ends name the two extreme monistic positions: idealism and materialism. Withdrawing from the extremities list two extreme dualistic positions: theism and naturalism. At the center list the position lying in the Mean: interactionism. Let parallelism be its deviant:

idealism

               theism

parallelism   interactionism

               naturalism

materialism

The two extreme monistic positions do not do justice to otherness. But the two extreme pluralistic positions are also without balance: theism too much emphasizes mind, and naturalism too much emphasizes matter. Parallelism, although it gives each its due, neglects mutual dependence.

KATHERINE: What a sage and just man you are, Julian! You've got it all figured out. The positions Keith and I held in college you set aside on a charge of injustice. Are you really happy, sitting in the middle or, as you prefer to say, on the Mean?

RECORDER: I will be plain with you. I would like to be a theist.

KATHERINE: But are too intelligent to be.

RECORDER: Don't tempt me into vanity.

CHANCELLOR: It would pain me to think the question answered which of the six positions is right. As a man of science, I think of myself as a naturalist, if I understand you in your use of the word.

RECORDER: There are great and clever men who have occupied each of the positions.

KATHERINE: But no women?

KEITH: They have better sense.

KATHERINE: And that, my good friend, is a sexist remark.

KEITH: You see how, on occasion, she withholds from me the title "lover".

RECORDER: I should perhaps ring for the porter. We may be in need of afternoon tea.

ALEXANDER: Let me remind you of the plot of our journey; we may have wandered down a by-way and lost sight of our principal path. We have set before ourselves three categories or families of conceptual instruments; we have been considering bridgework whose use carries

the mind from sameness and otherness to dependence and
independence. It was my intention to have us consider
as well bridgework from the first minor house to the
second one. There are two premisses whose construction
effects bridgework between them.
CHANCELLOR: What are the premisses?
ALEXANDER: The first is that if "A" and "B" name the
same thing, then A and B are either combined or separate. The second is that if A is one thing and B another, then A and B are either combined or separate.
KATHERINE: Keith looks agitated.
KEITH: May I jump in?
ALEXANDER: Yes, of course.
KEITH: It is not possible for both premisses to be
right. Suppose that a nominalist is right in what he
claims about the assertion "Here is one book." I believe I can lay out his claim in the following way.
When I utter the word "one" and then the word "book", I
don't mention things either combined or separated. As
to the first, it is denied that the number one and this
book are combined or fixed together; it is not as
though we have before us two wholes, the number one and
this book, somehow placed together, forming a third
whole. And as to the second, it is denied that the
number one exists apart from and in separation from
such things as this book. So with respect to apparent
claims on universals a nominalist denies both immanent
and transcendent realism. By means of the second premiss which you laid out it follows that the expressions
"this book" and "one" do not name distinct things. But
whatever A is and whatever B is, A and B are either the
same or other. Therefore, "this book" and "one" name
the same thing. By means of the first premiss it follows that A and B are either combined or separate. But
the conclusion has already been disproved. Since the
condition of the premiss has been successfully met, the
premiss itself is wrong. So if the nominalist were
right, not both the premisses would be right. But it
is clear which one to give up. For consider the use of
"Cicero" and "Tully". It is false that the names name
two things separated; but it is also false that the
names name two things combined. For nothing is, as it
were, combined with itself. By modus tollens and the
first premiss it follows that Cicero is not the same
man as Tully. The conclusion is equally false. We
should therefore hold to the second premiss of combination and separation and give up the first one.
RECORDER: Keith looks pleased to have some metaphysical equipment at hand.
KEITH: I am pleased. The afternoon has already been
productive. In our last discussion a metaphysical

123

premiss got formulated: whatever A is and whatever B is, A and B are either the same or other. We now have a second premiss to add to the first one: if A and B are other, they are either combined or separate.
ALEXANDER: I'm sure we'll have an opportunity to consider whether you mean to keep the premisses under mature metaphysical employment. Let us now consider three principles each of which is consistent with the premiss of combination and separation. The first is that whatever is distinct is combined; let us call it the principle of amalgamation. The second is that some distinct things are combined and that the other distinct things are separate. The third, finally, is that whatever is distinct is separate; let us call it the principle of atomism.

The principle of atomism settled very early into the foundations of philosophy. Pythagoreans seem to have held that distinct things receive enough void to set them apart--each from another.
RECORDER: Indeed, they did. In his Physics Aristotle remarks that the void distinguishes the natures of things, being a kind of separating factor between terms in series. So much happens with respect to numbers: the void distinguishes and separates their nature.

You would also be justified in saying that Parmenides and Zeno argued in accordance with the principle of atomism. For Parmenides argues as if what is other than being is separate from it.
ALEXANDER: Perhaps you can confirm another impression I have. It seems to me that Plato understood the difficulty of the principle. If God had created according to it and if we practised philosophy according to it, it would be as if God had in fact destroyed a world and as if we had tried to follow Him, destroying philosophy. If the principle remains in use in the discipline of metaphysics, reason must appear to make a very bad showing of itself.
(4.1)
RECORDER: I think that Plato and Aristotle refuted what you call the principle of atomism; in any case I am not myself disposed to hold it. I do hold what you will allow me to call the modified principle of atomism: whatever is distinct or distinguishable is separable.
ALEXANDER: You say, "modified" because you turn from a notion of actuality to one of potentiality.
RECORDER: Yes. Descartes sometimes writes philosophy as if he held the modified principle. According to his second meditation one inquires about thinking: thought is an attribute which belongs to me: it alone cannot be

separated from me. I can therefore state my essence by mentioning thought; for I am what is not distinct from me. The principle is accordingly used through modus tollens: since thought is not separable from me and what is distinct is separable, thought is not distinct from me. So I am a thing that thinks. But a body is separable. God could so have created things that I would have been created without a body.

In his sixth meditation Descartes gives us a good example both of reliance upon the modified principle of atomism and also of its appeal. Let me render his text in the following way. I am one thing; my body another; further, I have a clear and distinct idea of myself inasmuch as I am only a thinking and unextended thing; I also possess a distinct idea of body. Now God can create things as I clearly and distinctly apprehend them. Therefore, it is certain that I am distinct from my body and can exist without it.

KATHERINE. But if Descartes's argumentation presupposes the principle, as you say it does, and if the principle is excessive, then such argumentation is too weak to support its conclusions.

RECORDER: The principle is not excessive; it has an established role to play in metaphysics. Descartes's pattern of argumentation was already established in the thought of Ockham. For example, he inquires whether there is a distinction between the essence and the existence of a thing. He argues in the following way: suppose there is a distinction. There would then be no contradiction in supposing that God preserves the essence of a thing without preserving its existence. But there is contradiction in the supposition. Therefore, there is no distinction. The established role of the modified principle of atomism was also recognized by David Hume.

In his treatise on human nature Hume gives an argument which leads to the principle (I.III.III). All distinct ideas are separable. But the ideas of cause and effect are distinct. For we can conceive an object to be non-existent this moment and existent the next without conjoining to it the distinct idea of a cause. By means of the principle it follows that there is a separation of the idea of a cause from that of a beginning of existence. Since the ideas are separable, it is possible the objects are separable. It is therefore impossible to demonstrate the necessity of a cause.

I think the argument suggests an underlying argument which leads to the principle. The first premiss of it is that if there is a distinction between two things, it is possible to think one of them without thinking the other. The second premiss is that if it

125

is possible to think one of them without thinking the
other, it is possible to think one of them as without
the other. In conformity with the second premiss Hume
reasons that since it is possible for the imagination
to conceive a beginning of existence without conceiving
a cause, it is possible to conceive a beginning of existence without a cause. But what can thus be conceived is possible; so it is possible that something
begins to exist without a cause. Therefore, no principle to the contrary is certain.
KATHERINE: I think Hume's argument gives us an illumi-
nating example of forced cooperation between the two
families of sameness and otherness and combination and
separation. I do have a question about the example,
Julian. If the argument were sound, it would surely be
sufficient to show that our experience is of disjointed
or separable events and objects. We would not require
an empirical investigation to discover that objects of
experience are not held fast together. For if I say
first this and then that and were tempted to think that
the first is the cause of the second, I could correct
my temptation by recall of Hume's modified principle of
atomism: since there is a distinction, there is separability. For all I know the two objects exist apart.
RECORDER: Hume's conclusions follow from two premisses: first, what is distinct is separable and, second, causes and effects are distinct.
KATHERINE: It is truly wonderful how keen sighted the
two premisses are, spotting gaps everywhere. The first
premiss is a metaphysical earthquake, leaving gaps everywhere.
KEITH: If Julian is right in thinking he finds an underlying argument in Hume which leads to the modified
principle, one would also be right in thinking one
finds a similar argument in Berkeley. In the introduction to his Principles of Human Knowledge (#10) he
writes that it is impossible for one to form the abstract idea of motion distinct from the body moving. I
can abstract in one sense: for example when I consider
some particular parts of qualities separated from others. For although they are united in some object, they
may nevertheless really exist without them. But
Berkeley denies he can abstract one from another or
conceive those qualities separately which cannot exist
so separated. So I would say with respect to Berkeley
that the first premiss of an underlying argument is
that if there is a distinction, then it is possible to
conceive one of them without conceiving the other; the
second premiss, I think, is that if it is possible to
conceive one of them without conceiving the other, then

126

it is possible for one of them to exist without the other. By a law of transitivity it follows that if there is a distinction, then there is separability.
CHANCELLOR: (turning to Alexander) Well then, Mr. Alexander, what are we to say of the use of a metaphysical principle upon which so much depends?
ALEXANDER: Say: use of the principle leads to defect or excess; its use should therefore be discontinued.
RECORDER: Why?
ALEXANDER: In the last part of our conversation we formulated two laws of sufficiency for continuance. Use of the first law carries us from a path of otherness.
RECORDER: I remember. I have a formulation of it written here in my record.
ALEXANDER: By means of its most basic use we proceed from disclosing a number, namely one, to disclosing another number, namely two. Or do you now wish to say that when I count, beginning, "One, two," I twice reveal the same number?
RECORDER: No, I do not wish to say so.
ALEXANDER: Then since we say that one is a number and that two is another number, we can also say, according to the first premiss which leads to your principle, that we can disclose the first without disclosing the second.
RECORDER: You correctly follow the first premiss; its consequence is right.
ALEXANDER: Fine. I have no objection to make against either the premiss or its consequence. But there is a second premiss still to be employed. Since there is independence with respect to the achievements of counting, there is potentiality of independence or separation with respect to the objects of the achievements, namely the number one and the number two. The consequence of your two premisses and therefore of your principle is that it is possible for the number two to exist in separation from the number one.
　　Consider the consequence in light of your summary of my account of the family of combination and separation. Laying down or taking a path of combination or separation implies either a notion of space or one of time. But the number one is a universal and also the number two; they are therefore neither in space nor in time. It follows that a statement which relates them either as combined or as separate is defective. Therefore, the consequence of your principle is defective.
RECORDER: Your argument reveals one thing which I do not doubt: use of my principle is not consistent with that of two others. The first is that laying down or

taking a path of combination or separation implies
either a notion of space or one of time; the second is
that universals are neither in space nor in time. But
so far from persuading me to give up my modified principle of atomism I am the more persuaded that one of
your two principles must be wrong.
KATHERINE: It seems to me that the metaphysical burden
we bear would be lightened, if Julian were shown to be
wrong. Julian recently summarized a piece of Hume's
argumentation which tends towards excessive skepticism.
If Julian's modified principle of atomism were shown
not to be a sufficient principle of metaphysics, such
argumentation would either have to be given up or provided a quite different basis. Nor do I feel differently about Keith's summary of Berkeley's criticism of
abstractionism. When Keith and I first met at college,
we used to argue a lot about Berkeley. Keith has mentioned the fact that he became an idealist. Although
I wasn't persuaded by my reading of Berkeley, I felt
powerless to answer him. Distinctions between the family of sameness and otherness and that of combination
and separation passed me by completely. It did not
even occur to us to formulate what you call the modified principle of atomism. So perhaps I should ask you
again: Is Julian's principle an adequate metaphysical
principle?
ALEXANDER: You know my opinion.
KATHERINE: But the first argument you gave begs the
question against Julian.
ALEXANDER: Then let us again consider use of the principle. Can we agree upon the following statement of
your principle: whatever is distinct is separable?
RECORDER: Of course.
ALEXANDER: Do you have a good idea of how to account
for the use of the suffix "able" when one speaks of
separability in contrast to separation?
RECORDER: I accept the account which I have heard you
give of "can": the word indicates sufficiency of a certain range of subjects for a certain objective. So
when I assert that I can lift this book, I claim
strength, time and position enough for executing a certain action. When I just now made the assertion, I
omitted a decision to act.
ALEXANDER: Fine. I wonder whether, in light of our
account, we can agree upon a premiss. If there is power sufficient for separation and what is relevantly
omitted is supplied, then there would be separation.
RECORDER: Of course. If God can separate water from
water and put a firmament between and if a will, first
omitted, be supplied, then there would be separation.

ALEXANDER: I'm sure we understand one another. When you said that you agree with my account of ability, did you mean to imply that if two things are separable, someone or something can separate them?
RECORDER: Yes.
ALEXANDER: Suppose you assert that this pile of books is separable from this table; you mean, let us say, that you can lift them and hold them apart from the table. Since the table is one thing and the pile of books another, you can hold them apart from the table; further, since you decide to do so and make an effort to do so, you do do so. An hour or so later they fall to the table; they leave you exhausted. Although you resolved and made an effort to keep them apart, you could not. There is therefore no distinction between the table and the pile of books. Can you accept the conclusion of the argument?
RECORDER: I think the argument only shows that for there to be a distinction is not for me to have power enough for separation, given that only will and effort are omitted. But for there to be a distinction is for God to have power enough for separation, given that only will and effort are omitted.
ALEXANDER: Suppose God lifts the books up and holds them apart from the table. Why does He succeed and you fail?
RECORDER: Because God is stronger.
ALEXANDER: But the allowance of a distinction does not mention relative strength. It is not as if there is a distinction for God but not for you. The allowance, without reference to any particular person, is entirely sufficient for the conclusion that there can be separation. Mention of effort is not necessary; for effort is use of strength. Will alone is necessary: anyone's will.
RECORDER: I'm not sure what to say. I don't know how to answer you; I'm not persuaded to give up my principle. (As I was wondering what more to say, the Porter brought us tea.)
(5)
KEITH: There is a question which I would like to put. My question concerns the relations between the family of sameness and otherness, the family of combination and separation and skepticism. I shall formulate my question in light of a premiss which I hold, namely that whatever is distinct is combined or separate or dependent or independent. It is evident that you hold that there is a distinction between an act or an achievement and its objects. For example, you say there is a distinction between laying down or taking a

path of sameness and sameness; you say there is a distinction between disclosing a color and a color or between uttering a word and a word.
ALEXANDER: I do hold that there are such distinctions.
KEITH: If there were no difference between act and ob-
ject--as I used to believe when I was an idealist--I
very well see how you would deliver us from that skepticism whose target is any act originally instituted.
There would fail a measure against which the act is
tested; it would itself be the measure. But you say
there is a distinction. It follows from my premiss by
modus ponens that there is combination or separation or
dependence or independence between act and object. My
question is which alternative we are to accept. I
think my question is a metaphysical question: Does the
object exist without the act? Let us suppose an affirmative answer to the question. There then arises an
epistemological question which I would also like to
put: Is the institution and the execution of the act
necessarily open to a question of correctness, right-
ness or truth?
ALEXANDER: I suspect you see how to answer your epistemological question in light of the answer you suppose
to your metaphysical question.
KEITH: If the object of an act exists prior to and independently of the act, there is ground for the growth
of skepticism. For even in the beginning of our acts
of language a question arises whether act is fair to
object. Such is the predicament, I believe, of philosophers of correspondence.
ALEXANDER: In an earlier discussion between the Chancellor and me (IV.4) it was agreed that certain acts of
institution are not open to a question of truth. Do
you wish to reopen that discussion?
KEITH: No. But I would like you to run over that consideration which leads you to reject independence.
ALEXANDER: Suppose Adam means to institute a procedure
for saying of what color a certain paradigm is. He
chooses a paradigm and institutes utterance of the word
"white" in order to say of what color it is. According
to your alternative of independence there is a color,
namely white, which exists without either an act of
institution or an achievement of disclosure. Such an
alternative is that of a realist who holds that universals are independent of acts and achievements of ours
whose objective is to acquire knowledge of universals.
KEITH: We imagine Adam picking something up and referring to it when he begins, "This is ...." He refers to
nothing other than the paradigm.
ALEXANDER: And how would you account for his further

task in light of my account of being?
KEITH: His task is to create a subject of potentiality the realization of which is sufficient for disclosing the color of something. It would not be right to char- acterize his task in this way: to make further refer- ence to something and say what else it is to which he refers. It is therefore not as though, when he goes on to say, "This is white," there were a question of whether he has correctly or rightly identified an ob- ject of reference. Put in terms made familiar to us when you and the Chancellor were speaking I can say that when Adam lays down a path of language, saying, "This is white," there is too little a basis for the question, "Does he have its color right?"

In light of such a consideration or argument, if you please, I would say that the color disclosed, name- ly white, is not something else existing independently of the paradigm. It would otherwise have been referred to as a term of the relation of independence; further, there would have been a question of correctly identify- ing it. Therefore, such a universal does not exist apart from objects such as the paradigm we have been referring to. So Plato was wrong, and Aristotle must have been right. For according to my premiss, whatever is distinct and does not exist apart must be combined with or dependent upon such things as our paradigm.
ALEXANDER: And are you happy with the second alterna- tive?
KEITH: I don't mind it. I suspect it provides a cer- tain bulwark against skepticism. For if acts of lan- guage create their objects, there would fail a measure against which original acts of institution are tested and examined. One can say simply that the color white depends for its existence upon our use of the word "white". There is scope for pleasure in saying so.
ALEXANDER: It would certainly be wrong to say that this chair came into existence independently of an ac- tivity of making it. There first was a chair when a carpenter completed his activity.
KEITH: Indeed. So it is with the existence of the color white. It came into existence when Adam finished laying down a path, saying, "This is white."
ALEXANDER: Suppose it had snowed on the day before he gathered his community about him for the institution of the use of the word "white". Would you say that the snow was the same color as Adam's paradigm?
KEITH: Yes.
ALEXANDER: You remember we discussed two laws of con- tinuance when we finished an account of sameness and otherness (V.4). You raised no objection to them then.

KEITH: Nor do I now.
ALEXANDER: Perhaps use of the second law can as much continue our discussion as it was intended to forward human thought. To meet the first condition of the law it is sufficient to hold that Adam's paradigm is the same color as the snow.
KEITH: So much I do hold.
ALEXANDER: We meet the second condition of the law by allowing we know that the paradigm is white.
KEITH: Of course.
ALEXANDER: It follows that the snow was white. There is therefore a color which it had. It follows further that it is not right to say that the color white first came into existence with the completion of Adam's action of laying down a path of language. Do you agree to accept the consequence of the argument?
KEITH: I suppose I must.
KATHERINE: You've depressed Keith.
KEITH: I suppose I am a little depressed; I'm largely perplexed. There are two premisses which Julian assures me ancient and medieval philosophers would not have thought of denying. The first is that whatever A is and whatever B is, A and B are either the same or other. I have myself read the premiss set forth somewhere by Aristotle. The second is the premiss of our recent argument: whatever is other is either combined or separate or dependent or independent. By refuting both alternatives of my second premiss you force me to employ the premiss by modus tollens rather than to give up the premiss.
KATHERINE: Why?
KEITH: Combination and separation exhaust the alternatives of a distinct family. To assert, "This is white" is immediately to assert a combination. If you deny my assertion, you deny a combination. You then have only one alternative for redeeming your denial: namely to assert separation. I can advance a similar consideration with respect to sameness and otherness. They exhaust the alternatives of a distinct family. To assert, "Cicero is Tully" is immediately to assert sameness. If you deny my assertion, you deny sameness. You then have only one alternative for redeeming your denial: namely to assert otherness. So it seems to me that I have only one route to follow to resolve my perplexity: give up a distinction either between a universal and a substance or between an object and an act. I suppose I would be returning to strands of nominalism and idealism.
RECORDER: It is my suspicion that Keith is beset with the same perplexity which Aristotle must have enter-

tained. Plato argues that when I assert both that there is motion and that there is rest, I mention three things: being, motion and rest. Since there is a distinction between being and motion and between being and rest, Keith's second premiss applies, giving rise to the question whether being and motion are combined or separate. If they were separate, then, as Parmenides would argue, motion would be nothing. For there is nothing distinct from and apart from being. So they must be combined. Now I think Plato recognizes only one mode of combination: forming a part of. So motion combines with being acquiring a part of being as a part of itself.

KATHERINE: You're not going to lecture us on Plato's metaphysics, are you? We'll all forget the point of the example.

RECORDER: I'm coming to Aristotle's response as quickly as I can. Aristotle holds, quite correctly, it seems to me, that to use the word "be" is not to do the work of a mode of predication: I neither say what something is, how it is, when it is nor where. But if there were an underlying mode of combination between being and motion, there would be a corresponding mode of predication. Since there is not, being is not combined. Since there is neither combination nor separation, the word "being", when I say, "a man being", does not refer to anything distinct from a man.

After my long exposition you perhaps see the point of my example: like Aristotle Keith does not see how otherwise to resolve his perplexity than by giving up certain distinctions.

ALEXANDER: Let us seek resolution after we have a definition of truth.

(6)

RECORDER: Before we stop, I wish to make a complaint. I realize from remarks which you have been making that you take something for granted which I cannot take for granted. You assume that one does not perceive universals. I am prepared to say, on the contrary, that one can perceive universals. For example, I can see colors, shapes and sizes. Nor am I alone in making such a claim. I speak from my record: modern philosophy, as if with one voice, says that we perceive sensible qualities. And I dare say the Chancellor too, speaking for common sense, would say that one can perceive sensible qualities.

KATHERINE: There is something in what Julian says. Perhaps he strikes a note of sympathy with me--and I presume also with Keith--because of our education. You know that I was trained in British empiricism and Keith

133

in American pragmatism. I have been inclined to assume
that a survey of objects of perception is a survey of
sensible qualities: of light and colors, for example.
ALEXANDER: Let us first consider whether we can agree
upon a premiss of dependence. It is that the achievement of seeing something depends upon certain acts of
looking and attending.
CHANCELLOR: We accept the premiss; I'm sure we can
stand by the consequences of using it in epistemology.
ALEXANDER: Can we add a second premiss to the premiss
of dependence? Suppose that there is something which
is seen. The achievement of seeing it depends upon
looking; the second premiss is that the achievement depends upon looking at something: either the thing seen
or something else in a spatial relation to the thing
seen. One can be looking at one thing and so attend
that one sees something other than the thing looked at.
CHANCELLOR: We can stand by both premisses.
ALEXANDER: The second deserves the company of a third:
resources adequate for saying what is seen are also
adequate for saying either what is looked at or what
stands in a spatial relation to something looked at.
CHANCELLOR: Anyone who takes the first two premisses
into his practice of epistemology can surely take the
third.
ALEXANDER: And are you willing to say as much, Julian?
RECORDER: Yes.
ALEXANDER: Then let us begin. Suppose that you say to
Katherine, "Look at the color of those clothes." Do
you ask her to look twice, once at a dress and once at
a color?
RECORDER: No. I am not asking her to look twice.
ALEXANDER: Do you ask her to look at a color in addi-
tion to looking at a dress?
RECORDER: No. I ask her to look only once. We can
say that in looking at the color she is looking at the
clothes.
ALEXANDER: Then we can lay it down as a premiss of our
argument that in looking at the shape of this coin I
am looking at the coin?
RECORDER: Yes.
ALEXANDER: Suppose you take a coin out of your purse
and the Chancellor takes a coin out of his pocket.
Each of you look at both coins, making comparisons.
Let us say that both coins have the same shape. Can we
allow as much?
RECORDER: By all means.
ALEXANDER: You now turn your backs to one another and
again look at the coins. Would you want to say that
you are both looking at the same shape?

RECORDER: Yes.
ALEXANDER: You look at the shape of that coin. But
that coin and this coin are of the same shape. So
would you say that it follows that you are looking at
the shape of this coin?
RECORDER: Yes.
ALEXANDER: Upon the basis of our premiss it would follow that you are looking at the Chancellor's coin.
RECORDER: But so much is false.
ALEXANDER: Then you must either give up the premiss
that you are looking at the shape of your coin or give
up the premiss that when you look at the shape of it,
you are looking at the coin.
RECORDER: I find it evident how to resolve the argument. I will give up both premisses. When I look in a
given direction, I may be looking at something; I see
its color. I can therefore see the color of something
else without also looking at it. So my opinion now is
that I may well be looking at certain things; I see
their colors and shapes.
ALEXANDER: According to our first premiss the achievement of seeing a color depends upon looking; according
to the second premiss the achievement depends upon
looking at something: either the thing seen or something else in a spatial relation to the thing seen.
Our first argument led you to deny the first alternative. It follows that the color red stands in a spatial relation to the Chancellor's shirt, for example.
RECORDER: Indeed. When I look at his shirt, I see the
color of his shirt.
ALEXANDER: But the color of his shirt is the color
red. So it follows that you see the color red and that
the color red stands in a spatial relation to his
shirt.
RECORDER: Yes. It is a part of the thing being looked
at.
ALEXANDER: Then the universal is in two separate
places at once; for those drapes are also red. The
same thing is both there and here. I mean, strictly
speaking, that the same universal is divided into two.
RECORDER: Such a conclusion is absurd. So your argument forces me to return from its conclusion along one
of two paths. Either I must say that a universal is
not perceptible or I must say that a universal is at a
place in relation to things which are looked at. Since
the same thing cannot at the same time be at two separate places, the universal which is a part of the Chancellor's shirt is not the same universal which is a
part of those drapes. I'm not sure which way I should
go.

KATHERINE: Try the second path, Julian. It sounds
full of metaphysical excitement. Who knows what places
can be found along it in which one can hide from common
sense. I will try it out for you: two things at a distance cannot possibly have exactly the same color. At
two separate places on a page one cannot possibly write
exactly the same letter.
ALEXANDER: Is it possible for an object to have a col-
or at all?
KATHERINE: Of course.
ALEXANDER: Also possible for one to write a letter?
KATHERINE: Of course.
ALEXANDER: Another small point: Which of the two following paths can we take? The first is that two objects can be alike in color; the second is that two
colors can be alike in color.
KATHERINE: You must not think me entirely innocent of
metaphysics. I'm putting up a case for Julian in order
to give him time to pull himself together. We must all
agree to say that red is but does not have a color;
triangular is but does not have a shape. So we must
not say that two colors can be alike in color.
ALEXANDER: Can we say that two objects are alike without implying that they have something in common?
KATHERINE: No, we cannot. We would otherwise say they
are unlike.
ALEXANDER: So can we say two objects are alike in col-
or without implying that they have the same color?
KATHERINE: No, we cannot.
ALEXANDER: Look at the Chancellor's shirt and then at
those drapes. Now consider: Are they alike or unlike
in color?
KATHERINE: I must be faithful to myself and to common
sense: they are alike in color.
ALEXANDER: Then they have the same color.
RECORDER: Indeed. We must admit that they have.
(turning to Katherine) Thanks. I can carry on for myself.
ALEXANDER: Then the second alternative must be set
aside. It therefore follows that a universal is not
perceptible. We should accordingly renew our respect
for an account of our distinction between the second
and third levels of mind. One both looks at something and thinks; upon looking at something one sees
something; upon thinking one knows what the color is of
the thing which one is looking at and can see.
RECORDER: You have brought the argument to the conclusion that universals are not perceptible. You have not
argued against certain ordinary things that we say, for
example, "Look at the color of that house" or "But have
you seen its shape?" When you laid out premisses basic

136

to our argument, you mentioned a third premiss: resources adequate for saying what is seen are also adequate for saying either what is looked at or what
stands in a spatial relation to something looked at.
According to your argument use of "color" and "shape"
is not adequate for saying what is at a certain place;
their use is not adequate for saying what is looked at.
It follows that their use is not adequate for saying
what is seen. So the question "But have you seen its
shape?" is not adequate. But you would fly in the face
of common sense if you said that in putting such a
question I misuse either the word "seen" or the word
"shape".
ALEXANDER: Against such instances of speaking under
ordinary circumstances I may have no objection to
raise. An objection would first be raised when one
picks one's words with care appropriate to philosophy.
Saying that we see colors and shapes is not adequate.
A survey of relevant resources assures us of my denial
of adequacy. Consider again the use of a pair of O-
words such as "light" and "dark", of their U-word "col-
or" and finally of the A-word "red". To utter the word
"light" in saying, "It is light." is not to do enough to
say what it is that can be seen. Suppose we look outside. I make a gesture and say, "It is light." When I
utter the word "light", I do not reach any achievement
of saying What beyond that of saying what it is that I
am saying. Since I do not say what it is that I am
speaking about, looking at or pointing to, I also do
too little to say what it is that I can see.
    What I have said about the O-word "light" can also
be said about its U-word "color". For I do not say
what, for example, I am referring to when I say that
something is light in color or that this and that have
the same color.
    We come, finally, to the coinage of the A-word
"red" in order to say what the color of something is.
To do so is still not to take any step towards altering
the original situation. For one then goes on only to
say what the color is, not what it is that one is
speaking about, looking at or moving towards. It further follows from the preceding argument that the word
"red" is not used in order to say what one can see.
    It is perhaps clear to you that the question what
is seen yields its place in our philosophy to the question what to say in order to say or to reveal what is
seen. The reason is that all knowledge and disclosure
as to What depend upon acts of language. We accordingly reject the notion that the having of images or sen-
sations is enough for awareness or knowledge of what,
for example, is seen. To make our reason clear let me

develop a metaphor. We distinguish the ground upon
which we build a house and the foundation of a house.
We say that the foundation of a house is a part of the
house; the ground upon which it rests is not. We similarly distinguish the ground of knowledge and the foundation of knowledge. The ultimate foundation of all
knowledge and disclosure as to What is the act of so
thinking, uttering or writing a word or an expression
that one succeeds in being or in making clear what the
word or what the expression is. Such immediate
achievements of foundational acts are themselves parts
of our framework whose use is sometimes sufficient for
knowledge and disclosure. So although perceptual experience helps form the ground of knowledge, it is no
part of its foundation. We do grant, of course, that
we build up our framework in certain perceptual and
natural situations.
KATHERINE: At the beginning of our discussion of
Julian's claim that one can perceive universals I confessed that British empiricism had early won my sympathy. It seems to me that a consequence of your refutation of Julian's claim damages empiricism more than I
would wish. We now say that there is a light breeze
of philosophical safety about the remarks, "I look at
and can see a billiard ball; I can imagine and picture
a ball." It happens to be true that there is only one
ball to be seen and, subsequently, to be pictured. Now
suppose an empiricist, trained in Berkeley's critique
of abstractionism, says to me: Now picture its number
without picturing the ball. I say, "I cannot." He
will then conclude that there is no distinction between
its number and the ball; I simply use "one" in explicating the meaning of the word "ball".
ALEXANDER: We have long since set aside the foundations of nominalism. We grant to a philosopher with
one foot in empiricism and one foot in nominalism that
we cannot picture the number of the ball. But we can
know it. For its number is a universal and is an object of knowledge and not of perception.
KATHERINE: But there is a consequence damaging to empiricism; it is that empiricism does not have an adequate account of thought sufficient to reach such knowledge.
KEITH: But you agree with an empiricist that if there
is a distinction between two things, then it is possible to perceive or to think the one without perceiving
or thinking the other. So since there is a distinction
between a ball and a number, it is possible for us to
see or to picture the ball without thinking, "one" or
without knowing a number.

ALEXANDER: With so much I do agree.
KEITH: I think we should try to cheer Julian up. He
looks as if someone meant to take away his record.
RECORDER: You and Katherine are young; I am in middle
age.
KATHERINE: Even if you lose your record, you have won
a post. It will be exciting for you to assemble a department of philosophy.
CHANCELLOR: And Julian knows he has my support.
KEITH: There now! Do you feel cheered?
RECORDER: I am still somewhat in a fit of wonder.
There are metaphysical impediments to the assumption
that universals are thought but not perceived. At some
time or another I have felt close to all of three
schools of metaphysical thought: realism, conceptualism
or nominalism and idealism. Consider the first in the
two versions of Plato and Aristotle. In the first version a form and a particular so combine that the particular acquires a copy of the form as part of itself.
Plato gives such an account by relying upon a species
of our family: a part of and apart from. Suppose a
copy of a form is part of a particular and thus helps
compose or make it up. It would then be reasonable to
hold that in perceiving the particular one perceives
the copy. So something very much like a universal
would be perceived. It follows further that Plato's
metaphysical account is an obstruction to the assumption that universals are only thought and never perceived.
KEITH: But we have corrected such a metaphysical account: universals and particulars are not combined; the
former do not help form parts of the latter.
RECORDER: I suppose I should be pleased; one impediment is removed. In the second version of realism a
universal depends for its existence upon particulars.
KEITH: Then it would be open to Aristotle to hold that
to see some of the things which make up or compose a
table is not to see a universal.
RECORDER: But in De Anima Aristotle describes a sense
as that which has the power of receiving the sensible
forms of things without matter (II.12). He also says
that the proper object of sight is color.
KEITH: But in Book II, as I remember, he writes that
the object of sight is the visible and that what is
visible is color and a certain kind of object. I don't
think he means by "color" what Professor Alexander
meant when he was refuting the view that universals are
perceptible. I think he rather means what we mean when
we say, "having the power to reflect light."
RECORDER: Perhaps you suggest a way of removing a sec-

ond impediment to my acceding to the force of
Alexander's arguments. I very well see that nominalism
offers no obstruction. For since it denies the exis-
tence of universals, it would hardly be tempted to make
them objects of perception.
KEITH: Then are you all right accepting the arguments?
RECORDER: Yes, I think so.
KEITH: I'm glad to hear it.
KATHERINE: You've also been assured you have friends.
RECORDER: How striking it is that insight along one
axis of philosophy is only secured with the help of insight along another axis. By acquiring a metaphysical
position I have secured an epistemological position.
At the same time I see how my double gain contrasts
with the major positions of our tradition. A major
premiss of metaphysics has been that whatever is other
is combined or separate. Pythagoreans and monists held
that whatever is other is separate. Plato refuted the
principle, replacing it by the middle principle that
some distinct things are combined and that the others
are separate. By "combined" he means "forming a part
of". So an object having a copy of a form has it as a
part. Plato's version of realism is compatible with
the assumption that if copies of forms are universals,
then some universals are perceptible. Aristotle also
refuted the principle of atomism, replacing it by the
middle principle. He developed a notion of combination
which means "dependent upon" and not "forming a part
of". Aristotle's version of realism is compatible with
the assumption that some dependent universals are perceptible. To see a table is not to see something depending upon it, but it is in principle possible to see
something depending upon the table for its location.
So realism has not in fact been an enemy of the assumption that universals are perceptible.
    The nominalist reaction to realism did not dislodge
the assumption of perceptibility. For the things which
exist and which a realist would call universals are
components of the things we see.
    (turning to Alexander) I see now that by correct-
ing our account of metaphysics you eliminate the ground
of the assumption. Universals exist and are other than
particulars. Proper philosophical method leads us away
from the question whether there is combination or separation between them; our method rather leads us to the
question what the relation is between acts and achievements of perception and acts and achievements of
thought. Ground for the assumption is eliminated in
the following way. Since we perceive certain individuals and there is no relation of combination or separa-

140

tion between an individual and a universal, there is no
metaphysical basis for the assumption that we also perceive universals.
(7)
ALEXANDER: Since you seem again to be of good cheer,
you will forgive me if I do not sufficiently regard
your feelings. A while ago (VI.4.1) you stated and
defended the Modified Principle of Atomism. May I ask
whether you have now abandoned its metaphysical use?
RECORDER: I confessed that I didn't know how to answer
you. Do you want me to plead guilty?
ALEXANDER: (ignoring a question tinged with feeling)
You laid out an argument for the principle. The first
premiss is that if there is a distinction between two
things, it is possible to perceive or think one of them
without perceiving or thinking the other. It is evident that the word "without" indicates a relation of
separation or independence between two acts or achievements of perception or thought.
RECORDER: You can hardly be disappointed with me for
adopting the first premiss. Plato himself lays it out
in his Republic. Someone argues there that if each is
one and both two, the meaning of "two" is that the soul
will conceive them as distinct; they will be separable
in thought (524B).
ALEXANDER: It does not disappoint me that you or any
other philosopher would lay down the first premiss.
But why the second, that if it is possible to think the
one without thinking the other, it is possible to think
the one as without the other?
RECORDER: I think the shift to the second premiss is
natural for anyone who holds a correspondence theory of
language and truth. One can feel the temptation alive
in Abelard's account of abstraction. He gives a helpful example: I can discern separately the gold and the
silver of a statue which are joined together; I can
examine now the gold and now the silver, looking separately upon things which are conjoined but not looking
upon them as separated in that they are not separated.
ALEXANDER: So far so good.
RECORDER: But Abelard asks whether conceptions arising
from abstraction are false since they perceive things
otherwise than as they subsist. It is my impression
that a philosopher of correspondence is inclined to
ground a distinction in the separation or the separability of the things distinguished. He is inclined, I
believe, to argue as though two things distinguished
necessarily stand in a relation either of separation or
of combination; if of combination, then likely combination with separability.

141

ALEXANDER: I hope we can refute and replace the correspondence theory of truth. Suppose our effort suc-
cessful. Would there be any remaining considerations
which would incline you to uphold the second premiss?
RECORDER: No. It now seems clear to me that there
would be no good reason to shift the relation of separation or independence from acts and achievements of
perception or thought to objects thought or perceived.
ALEXANDER: Then if our effort this afternoon is suc-
cessful, it would be useful if you had time to write a
book in which you made a systematic study of the role
of the principle and the modified principle of atomism.
I suspect the role of the principles has not been a
healthy one.
RECORDER: Thank you for the suggestion. I would be
interested in writing such a book. But I first need
your refutation and your positive account of truth.
ALEXANDER: Then let's turn to giving it.
RECORDER: (The Porter entered at four o'clock and
asked whether anyone wanted anything.)

PART VII

(1)

ALEXANDER: Let us now discuss the fourth great family
of paths of language: that of defect, sufficiency and
excess. Suppose someone lays down or takes a path of
the family. The first step of our method is to inquire
as to the dominant objective of a given act: in the
case at hand of laying down or taking a path of sufficiency, for example. The objective is that to or for
which there is said to be enough. So an objective of
sufficiency is reaching a certain end or goal. The
second step of our method is to inquire how our notions
of subordination and coordination apply. By definition
the subject is that of which there is said to be
enough. So a subject of sufficiency is means said to
be sufficient for reaching some end.

KATHERINE: This morning we started a journey which has
led to a family of resources for the practice of criticism. It seems to me that we first caught sight of the
family when we discussed your first example of assertion, "This table is long." (III.4) You then said that
the word "be" indicates sufficiency and that being is a
kind of sufficiency. Such a premiss, I take it, under-
lies your account of assertion according to which to
assert is immediately to assert sufficiency. Having
allowed that there is a dominant act of assertion we
follow your method first by inquiring what the objective is and then by inquiring what the subject is. I
believe it follows that as the subordinate act of laying down or taking a path of sameness subordinates two
minor paths so the dominant act of laying down or taking a path of sufficiency subordinates two minor paths:
one making clear what the subject is and one making
clear what the objective is.

ALEXANDER: It is not unreasonable to expect resources
adequate for making so much clear.

KATHERINE: When I remark, "This table is long," I do
enough to reach a certain goal. Let us not dispute as
to what the objective is. I employ means or--as you
say--effect a subject simply in subordinating and coordinating the use of certain expressions. Someone else
can criticize my remark by arguing the means I employ
are not sufficient for reaching the end I wish to
reach. For although I assert sufficiency of certain
means, he denies sufficiency of my means. Have I correctly restated your intentions?

ALEXANDER: Yes. There is a dialectical pattern of our
reflection and argumentation. The first point of it is
making such a remark as you remind us of. The second

point is reached by a critic who denies sufficiency of
means for an end. At the third point he reveals which
of two paths of criticism he is taking: one of criticizing for defect or one of criticizing for excess.
The interval between the third and the fourth points is
filled out by his criticism, his argumentation and his
considerations. The fourth point is reached by an act
whose object is sufficiency--an act which makes continuance possible. Even if the first act is successfully
criticized and set aside, it may not be possible for an
inquiring community to restore itself to sufficiency.
KATHERINE: Denial is clearly not the end of inquiry;
it prepares the way for the full practice of criticism.
An achievement of that practice is making perfectly
clear whether there is criticism for defect or rather
for excess.
ALEXANDER: There are several triadic modes of criticism an account of which is relevant to our inquiries.
A triadic mode uses an expression of defect, an expression of sufficiency and an expression of excess. Relevant to our inquiries are three triads. The first is
that of indifference, consistency and inconsistency;
the second is that of defect, correctness and incorrectness, and the third is that of exiguousness, truth
and falsity.
KATHERINE: Before we turn to them, I would like to
know what the whole triad is of which being is the middle member.
ALEXANDER: There is no one expression for the object
of criticism. Perhaps I can help you by means of the
following consideration. Suppose you deny sufficiency
of a subject for an objective in response to someone
who asserts, "This table is six feet long." If the object of criticism is defect, you must show either that
the subject of criticism is faulty or that it is in
need of supplementation and addition. If the object of
criticism is excess, you must show that there is an alternative with which the subject is inconsistent and
that it should accordingly be set aside. In the first
case we often call for supplementation and in the second, elimination.
KATHERINE: Fine. I think I have the spirit of your
outline of criticism.
ALEXANDER: Then let us consider some triads an account
of which is essential to epistemology. Let us begin
with the triad of indifference, consistency and inconsistency.
(2)
CHANCELLOR: What is consistency?
ALEXANDER: Consistency is a kind of sufficiency.

144

(RECORDER: When the Chancellor put his question and
Alexander gave the heart of an answer, a messenger entered the room and told Alexander that he was wanted on
the telephone. The messenger spoke as if urgent business needed attending to. Alexander excused himself,
arose and left the room.)
KATHERINE: I think we should go on with our discussion, don't you? Julian, I think you should lead the
discussion. You surely have a sensible idea as to what
consistency is.
RECORDER: Fine. We'll take it for granted that consistency is a kind of sufficiency. Our method leads us
to two further questions: what its objective is and
what its subject is. I would like to continue with an
answer to the second. Its subject is coordination between one act and another; its objective is pursuing
the same end. So consistency is sufficiency of coordination for pursuing the same end. We can say by analogy that consistency is epistemic cooperation.
KATHERINE: Can we also say by analogy that cooperation
is social consistency?
RECORDER: I'm trying to write down my own definition.
KEITH: I find it astonishing that the definition of
consistency mentions members of the three great families of terms: subjects of consistency are modes of
combination; consistency itself is a kind of sufficiency, and an objective is the pursuit of the same
end. You mean to say that working together is the subject of consistency; not either act by itself.
RECORDER: Yes.
KEITH: But we do say, "Your statement is not consistent with mine."
RECORDER: Indeed. We also say, "There is no consistency between them." In either case my definition applies: two statements are made together in pursuit of
the same end. Suppose we turn and look out of the window. You say, "That is Mr. Smith." I say, "Indeed.
That is Mr. Smith." My remark is consistent with
yours. To account for the assertion of consistency I
presuppose subject and objective: in making our remarks
we mean to pursue the same end, namely to say who is
walking there. Our joint effort is good enough for
pursuing the same end. For if you reach your end and I
mine, we will have managed the same achievement, namely
saying who is walking there.
KEITH: And is inconsistency defect or excess?
RECORDER: Inconsistency is a kind of excess. Its subject is coordination between one act and another; its
objective is pursuit of the same end. So inconsistency
is coordination excessive for the pursuit of the same

145

end. We can say by analogy that inconsistency is epistemic war.

KATHERINE: Can you give an example?

RECORDER: Suppose we turn and look out of another window. You say, "That is Mr. Smith." I say, "I disagree. That is Mr. Jones." My remark is inconsistent with yours. For saying so I presuppose subject and objective: in making our remarks we both pursue the same achievement, namely saying who is walking there. Our joint effort is too much for the pursuit of the same end. For if you had reached an end and if I had reached an end, we would not have reached the same end.

KATHERINE: I understand.

KEITH: Since consistency is sufficiency and inconsistency is excess, what is the correlative term for defect?

RECORDER: I don't know what it should be called. Let us call it indifference. So indifference is too little done together for pursuit of the same end. Suppose I set out to say who is seated around this table. Although there is consistency between remarking, "Katherine is here" and "Keith is here", there is indifference between remarking, "Katherine is here" and "This is a table."

KEITH: So with respect to any two remarks and some objective there is either indifference, consistency or inconsistency. But if two remarks are not consistent, it does not follow they are inconsistent.

RECORDER: Right. It is characteristic of a game that a move of a game and any act of a distinct and separate activity are neither consistent nor inconsistent but rather indifferent. Someone who, playing chess, castles does not subordinate the move to the pursuit of an end of chess which could also be pursued, for example, by shoveling snow, shouting at someone or proving a theorem of logic. I think one can say in general that for the pursuit of the ends of a game a move of the game and any action of a distinct and separate activity are indifferent.

KATHERINE: Before you turn to correctness, you can perhaps ease my mind about something that used to bother me. You may know I spent one year as an undergraduate at the University of Alberta--here in Edmonton. I then heard a teacher of mine, Herman Tennessen, raise a skeptical issue. The issue arises in the following way. To criticize is to criticize from within a conceptual framework or, as Herman used to say, a global system. Suppose there is a system A and a system B and that A and B are distinct and separate. By virtue of sufficiently deep breaks between A and B there will be

incommensurability; there will be no such a thing as
system-comparison. It follows that system B can bring
no pressure to bear upon us to change or to modify system A. Each is, relative to the other, autonomous.
Nor can ordinary language hold up a catwalk to carry us
from the one to the other. For either ordinary speech
is so imprecise as to be unsuitable for serious thought
or it is so precise as to become part of A, B or some
other conceptual framework.
KEITH: I've not yet understood why the thesis of incommensurability supports a skepticism we would want
to say is excessive.
KATHERINE: Both A and B claim means adequate for
knowledge. But how is one to evaluate the success of
either? Either one must stand outside or inside the
system to be examined. But from the outside its sur-
face is opaque to critical vision. So the only possible critique of a global conceptual system is an immanent critique, as Herman says. For such a global system a coherence theory of truth would seem adequate.
But it is possible that systems A and B are incompati-
ble. Each, on its own terms, would equally well account for the same reality or the same part of reality.
It used to trouble me to say that inconsistent systems
account equally well for the same reality.
KEITH: I don't suppose I was very good in the old days
at dissuading you from your troubles. I think it is
easy enough now to see why they are groundless. You
allow, on Tennessen's behalf, that there is no comparison between A's and B's statements of their objectives.
So we don't know whether the work of A and that of B
serve as alternate means for reaching the same end.
KATHERINE: Well, they both make a claim on truth; they
both claim means adequate for knowledge.
KEITH: But can nothing more specific be translated
from the language of A into that of B? You did quote
Tennessen as saying that each accounts equally well for
the same reality. Saying so implies, it seems to me,
that it is possible to translate at least one sentence
used to state an achievement of knowledge which both
structures offer themselves as support for. If, of
course, they do not share a statement of a common objective, they are indifferent one to the other, and
they sit side by side, one playing chess and the other
acting out a play. But there is no perplexity in my
inference; for there is no incompatibility incapable
of resolution.
(2.1)
(RECORDER: I felt relieved to see Alexander return. I
was not comfortable in my assumed role.)

ALEXANDER: Someone telephoned me from the office of the Premier. The Premier sends his regrets; he says he is not able to meet with us this evening. We shall eat dinner without him. He is sending a visitor in his place, Thomas Nelson, an old friend of mine, as you know.
KATHERINE: Perhaps the Premier was called upon to change the price of oil. I hope we can still depend upon his generosity towards your new academy and the pursuit of knowledge.
ALEXANDER: (obviously unwilling to take up Katherine's point of view) Have you been discussing consistency?
RECORDER: We have. (I reported to him what I have already made a record of.)
ALEXANDER: I think you have adequately stated the objective of consistency: the pursuit of the same end. I do not think that you have adequately stated the subject of consistency. (turning to me) Suppose that Katherine says that the Premier ought to have joined us this evening. Keith says he agrees. There is consistency between the comment which Katherine makes and the comment which Keith would also make. According to your definition Keith implies that there is sufficient coordination. According to your summary of your discussion, Keith said that the subject is working together. (turning to Keith) Did you mean "working together well"?
KEITH: I'm not sure I know now what I meant; I was trying to encourage Julian. I think he felt embarrassed to have assumed your role.
ALEXANDER: Is Julian the only one who knows what was meant?
KATHERINE: I certainly don't know.
CHANCELLOR: I wasn't listening. I was wondering what you were doing.
ALEXANDER: The burden of clarification rests upon your shoulders, Julian.
RECORDER: I was trying to identify a subject of consistency; I wanted my account of the subject to respect a principle which I had been assuming since you opened a discussion of the chief category of terms of criticism.
ALEXANDER: What principle?
RECORDER: That a subject of any species of sufficiency lie on a continuum of more and less. Unless there is more or less, I don't see how there can be enough of anything. Surely all sufficiency is sufficiency of a quantity or a quality. Now a quantity is necessarily more or less of something; but so is a quality. For example, one woman is more or less beautiful than an-

148

other.
ALEXANDER: So you followed such a principle when you suggested that there can be enough coordination for the pursuit of an end.
RECORDER: Well, yes. Keith was helpful when he said that two remarks can work well enough together for the pursuit of an end.
KATHERINE: Metaphor has a way of bringing relief. But it sometimes works not as a magnifying glass, focusing an issue, but rather as a mirror, diverting critical gazing.
KEITH: More metaphor, but none that helps. It must be diverting.
CHANCELLOR: We're in turmoil and a bit mixed up. We don't know what the subject of consistency is, do we?
ALEXANDER: I think you were trying too hard. You know very well the things said to be consistent: commands, remarks and actions of various kinds. I would say in general that the subject of consistency is actions. To say that there is consistency between them is to say that they are adequate for the pursuit of the same end.
CHANCELLOR: Strictly speaking the terms of consistency, inconsistency and indifference are actions. Do I have your meaning?
ALEXANDER: Yes.
CHANCELLOR: Although we say the two remarks are consistent, we must mean that the making of this remark and the making of that remark are together adequate for the pursuit of the same end.
(3)
ALEXANDER: Right. Let us turn to correctness. Correctness is sufficiency of modes of continuousness for following. A question of correctness accordingly arises when I try to say a word after you, when I try to repeat what you have said and when I quote you.
RECORDER: This morning you distinguished two stages of our ascent to knowledge of the truth (III.1). You made a corresponding distinction between two kinds of acts of language: laying down and taking a path. Am I right in thinking that one mode of taking is either subordinated to following or is itself an instance of following?
ALEXANDER: Yes. In the first case the question arises whether the taking a path is correctly done. According to my definition of correctness that question is none other than the question whether one's action is adequate for following.
RECORDER: A large part of training, I take it, is learning to follow.
ALEXANDER: Evidently. You and the Chancellor will

149

want to know how large a part.
RECORDER: And what is incorrectness: defect or excess?
ALEXANDER: Excess. Incorrectness is excess of action
for following. Suppose an actor is reciting lines of
one of Shakespeare's plays. Suppose he misquotes a
line. Does he do too little or too much to follow?
RECORDER: Too much. He goes beyond the text. Since
correctness is sufficiency and incorrectness excess,
there is a third member of the triad. What is it to be
called?
KATHERINE: Not knowing one's lessons; I was often
called by that name.
(4)
ALEXANDER: We also criticize for truth and falsity.
Let us turn to their definitions. Truth is sufficiency
of subjects of actuality in both modes of application
and following for certain objectives of actuality: in
particular for reaching certain achievements of language. In formulating the opinion that Socrates is
white you proceed in ways sufficient for reaching an
achievement of language. When I say, "sufficient for
an achievement," I mean to leave a possibility open,
namely that there is sufficiency for an achievement of
language without reaching knowledge. Suppose you say,
"Socrates is white." I say, "It is true that Socrates
is white." You are right in the opinion you hold; in
holding the opinion you nevertheless did not know his
color.
RECORDER: I'm not sure I follow.
ALEXANDER: Consider a further example. Suppose that
two people, Mr. Smith and Mr. Jones, are conversing.
Mr. Smith is in another room looking for his cat; Mr.
Jones comes to stand before a mat. He hears Smith say
from the other room, "The cat must be on the mat in the
living room." Jones replies, "You're right. He is
here." Jones puts Smith in the right; an act of reflection is in turn subordinated to that of bringing
their investigation to a conclusion. Since Jones is
not only in a position good enough for knowledge but
also in one of having acquired knowledge, he is also in
a position to lead Smith from right inference to knowledge. We can say on behalf of Smith that although
there is sufficiency for an achievement of knowledge,
his position is not good enough for thereby achieving
knowledge. If one does speak the truth without having
knowledge or leading another to knowledge, one's failure is due entirely to one's position in which one uses
a framework.
    Since truth is sufficiency, falsity is either de-
fect or excess. But to say, "That is false" is not to

criticize for defect. We would not say that someone
has made an insufficient use of a framework for reaching his goal. Like an archer who aims at reaching a
target, he who speaks falsely has not under-reached it;
he has over-reached it.
CHANCELLOR: It seems to me that there is another analogy which would be better. When we opened this part of
our conversation, you said that if the object of criticism is defect, one must show either that the subject
is faulty or that it is in need of supplementation; if
the object of criticism is excess, one must show that
there is an alternative with which the subject is inconsistent and that it should accordingly be set aside.
In the first case one may call for supplementation; in
the second, one must call for elimination. So it seems
to me that he who is criticized for falsity is like a
carpenter who creates an object our household cannot
accommodate. A false statement is one whose place our
community declares occupied; it is accordingly eliminated and set aside.
ALEXANDER: Your analogy is better than mine; it properly introduces the definition of falsity: falsity is
excess of a range of subjects of use in both its modes
for a range of objectives of actuality. Since truth is
sufficiency and falsity is excess, there must be a
third mode of examining and criticizing parallel to
that of criticizing for falsity; let us call it criticizing for exiguousness: exiguousness is defect of a
range of subjects of use in both its modes for a range
of objectives of actuality.
CHANCELLOR: I take it that when a philosopher defines
truth, he does not thereby say what in particular is
true. What then is the objective of defining truth,
falsity and exiguousness?
ALEXANDER: Their objectives are objectives of potentiality: the definitions are given to help make it possible to examine and to criticize. To consider the
employment of a definition in conducting an examination
suppose someone asserts, "The cat is on the mat." According to the definition of truth, to ask whether what
is asserted is true is to ask whether there is sufficiency.
KATHERINE: It astonishes me how nicely things have
come together. This morning, when I tried to distinguish senses of the word "be", I would have argued for
a principle of justice or fairness: that one ought not
criticize something for what it does not in principle
offer. For surely criticism is a response to uses of
instruments of reason; it should meet demands of fairness.

ALEXANDER: Of course.

KATHERINE: Therefore, since a question of truth is appropriate and fair to the given assertion, a question of sufficiency should correspond to an assertion of sufficiency. Since he who examines asks whether there is sufficiency, he who asserts that the cat is on the mat should be asserting sufficiency. But this morning I would have said that he who asserts that the cat is on the mat immediately asserts a combination or some other relation. Your theory would therefore misguide us in immediately examining for sufficiency. But of course that view of mine was disposed of, and we agreed that all assertion is immediately assertion of sufficiency; for the word "be" indicates sufficiency. One could say in a summary way that being is a kind of sufficiency.

RECORDER: In his work Truth Aquinas records some opinions according to which truth is being. For example, Augustine says that the true is that which is. If the opinion were right, it would seem that the words "truth" and "being" mean the same. If so, there would be no logical difference between asking whether the cat is on the mat and asking whether what is asserted is true. Indeed, Aquinas also records an opinion to the contrary: "Useless repetition of the same thing is meaningless; so, if the true were the same as being, it would be meaningless to say: 'Being is true'. This, however, is hardly correct. Therefore, they are not the same." (Question One, Article I)

ALEXANDER: If the words "truth" and "being" meant the same, then to perform a reflective act of criticism, saying, "What you assert is true" would be to perform an act of assertion, saying, "The cat is on the mat." But since there is a difference in act, there is a difference in the uses of the two words, although both indicate sufficiency. Further, subjects of being can be subjects of potentiality or of actuality; subjects of truth are of actuality. Therefore, being is not in general truth.

RECORDER: Aquinas's answer to the question whether truth is being reads in part as follows:

> ...in the statement, "The true is that which is," the word "is" is not here understood as referring to the act of existing, but rather as the mark of the intellectual act of judging, signifying, that is, the affirmation of a proposition. The meaning would then be this: "The true is that which is--it is had when the existence of what is, is affirmed."

ALEXANDER: His answer is not adequate. For the word

"is" is not a mark of the intellectual act of judging; it does not signify the affirmation of a proposition. The second achievement of uttering the word does not help make known, for example, whether a question is put or whether an affirmation is made. We should say rather that the word indicates or signifies sufficiency; other resources are necessary to make known whether sufficiency is asked for or asserted.

RECORDER: You know that the thesis has been continuously discussed that the word "true" is logically superfluous. Michael Dummett writes:

> The thesis that 'It is true that A' is equivalent to A is enunciated by Frege himself in the same essay, 'Der Gedanke': 'It is true that I smell the scent of violets' has, he says, just the same content as 'I smell the scent of violets'. Let us call this thesis 'the equivalence thesis'. (Frege, p.445)

Dummett argues for a reservation about the application of the equivalence thesis to any language for which the law of bivalence does not hold. He continues:

> ...if the failure of A to be either true or false is due to the presence of a name which lacks a bearer, we cannot on the same ground claim that 'It is true that A' fails to be either true or false. ...(The argument was based) only on the principle that we can pass from saying that 'It is not true that A' is true to saying that 'It is true that A' is false. The justification for this lies in the fact that, even in the context of a many-valued logic, we expect negation to carry only false statements into true ones. (p.446)

ALEXANDER: There may well be good reasons for restricting the use of the equivalence thesis. In the passage you quote Dummett provides none. If the claim of A is said to be defective, then the claim of the truth of A can also be said to be defective and so neither true nor false. So suppose that one denies the truth of A. Dummett's argument requires a further premiss: that the denial of the truth of A be true.

The further premiss confuses the discussion of the equivalence thesis. For the denial of the truth of A is a step of a process which is still incomplete: in addition to denial we require a decision between a claim of falsity or a claim of exiguousness. To justify a claim of exiguousness it is enough to cite the presence of a name which lacks a bearer.

RECORDER: Perhaps Dummett's conclusion can be reached in another way. Suppose someone denies the truth of A.

Now that denial is inconsistent with the affirmation
of the truth of A. So if the denial is true, then the
affirmation must be false.
ALEXANDER: No. If the denial is true, the affirmation
is not true. It is therefore either exiguous or false.
Suppose I deny the truth of "The present King of France
is bald," meaning to argue that there is no king of
France. You affirm the truth of the sentence. I reject your affirmation not on a charge of falsity but on
a charge of exiguousness. So although I may have support enough to deny the truth of your sentence, it does
not follow that it is false that the present King of
France is bald. For if it were false, it would be inconsistent with an accepted alternative, for example
that the King has a full head of hair.
RECORDER: Have you now given the definition which you
meant to give?
ALEXANDER: Yes.
RECORDER: I would like to write down for myself a summary. I know you think summaries can involve risk. I
hope I do not take a great risk if I write in a summary
way that truth is the sufficiency of a certain subject
for knowledge. Exiguousness is the defect of the one
for the other, and falsity, the excess of the one for
the other.
    It is a principle of yours, as I remember, that all
defect of a subject for one objective is adequacy of
the subject for another objective. In the case at hand
I presume I'm right in inferring that the second objective, if it obtained, would take the place of the
first. So what is exiguous for knowledge is adequate
for something else: ignorance or confusion, I suppose.
What is excessive for knowledge, being false, is adequate for something else: being in error or being mistaken. So rather than achieving knowledge one enters
either a state of confusion or one of error. Have I
run all over town, not noticing that I pull nothing behind me?
ALEXANDER: No. I think your summary accurate; I hope
it can prove helpful.
(4.1)
RECORDER: (turning to Alexander) I wonder whether you
have forgotten a promise you made to Katherine.
ALEXANDER: Perhaps I have forgotten.
RECORDER: This morning (I.5) Katherine said that the
reason why we do not examine acts and achievements of
perception for truth or falsity is different from the
reason why we do not examine a dream for truth or falsity. The latter fails a basic principle of criticism.
ALEXANDER: I remember the conversation.

154

RECORDER: You said that her question could be answered
after we have at hand definitions of truth and falsity.
ALEXANDER: (turning to Katherine) I'm sorry. I had
forgotten. Are you clear now how to put your question?
KATHERINE: Yes. Why should we not say that an act of
perception is a subject of truth or falsity?
ALEXANDER: An act of perception is not a subject by
which one either acquires knowledge of a universal or
makes something clear. Further, the subject of truth
is the application and following of established procedure. But to perceive is not to apply and follow a
framework. Therefore, the words "true" and "false" are
incorrectly used in examining acts of perception for
truth or falsity.
KATHERINE: I think I could have worked out your answer
for myself.
ALEXANDER: Fine.
(5)
KATHERINE: Before we leave the definitions of exiguousness, truth and falsity, I would like to know whether your theory of truth and that of correspondence are
compatible.
ALEXANDER: I suspect there are several versions of a
correspondence theory. Correspondence provides a
framework upon which certain metaphysical theories in
part depend: realism, conceptualism and nominalism. It
is not enough to refute correspondence in the dress of
realism; it returns from its refutation in the dress of
conceptualism. Struck down it again rises from the
ashes of refutation, now in the form of nominalism.
KATHERINE: It would be enough for me if you could show
that correspondence is not right in giving its final
account of truth by means of a notion of sameness rather than by means of a notion of sufficiency. I assert
of this table that it is white. According to correspondence I assert the truth only if the color which I
disclose is the same as the color which it has. Do I
misrepresent correspondence?
ALEXANDER: No, I don't think so. Julian will tell us
whether we're unfair to the history of philosophy. Let
us consider the condition "the color which I disclose
is the same as the color which it has." When I say,
"the same as," I take a path of sameness. What are its
minor paths?
KATHERINE: The first is, "I disclose a color" and the
second, "It has a color." The dominating question is
then whether what you disclose is the same as or other
than something it has.
ALEXANDER: Fine. A definition of sameness and an account of laying down or taking a path of sameness carry

155

us so far; protection and respect for the family of
sameness and otherness permit us neither more nor less.
Consider further the second minor path, "It has a col-
or." I shall ask you to say what "has" means in light
of our metaphysical discussions. Let me remind you of
its argument. Words, colors and lengths are universals. But a universal is neither in space nor in time.
A universal therefore does not stand in a relation of
combination or separation to anything from which it is
distinct.
KATHERINE: I remember. Keith is still perplexed about
the argument. But I am persuaded that you are right.
ALEXANDER: The allowance of a distinction between a
color and this table is therefore not inconsistent with
another allowance, namely that there is no relation
either of combination or of separation with respect to
a color and this table. What then does "has" mean when
one says, "It has a color"?
KATHERINE: You are a remarkable teacher, you know.
This morning you found me spreading senses of "is"
around. You've now got me winding things together. In
the use of "has" before us the word, like "is", indicates sufficiency.
ALEXANDER: What is its subject?
KATHERINE: The potential use of certain resources.
ALEXANDER: And its objective?
KATHERINE: The potential management of an achievement:
disclosing the color of the table.
ALEXANDER: So to presuppose that it has a color is to
presuppose resources adequate for disclosing its color.
Do you mean to assert as much?
KEITH: You're winding things up too quickly,
Katherine. Surely something can have a length although
we lack means for saying of what length. A problem may
have a solution although no one has resources for saying what the solution is.
KATHERINE: You must be right. I was led along too
quickly by Bill's questions. Let's go back a step or
two. Ask me again what the objective of sufficiency
is.
ALEXANDER: And its objective?
KATHERINE: The potential use of resources sufficient
for initiating an inquiry that has its end in the management of the achievement of disclosing the color of
the table. So there must at least be resources adequate for asking what the color is.
ALEXANDER: No one would now say that you've gone too
far. I think we have sufficiently analyzed the statement you made on behalf of the correspondence theory of
truth. Does our analysis show us anything with which

we must disagree?
KATHERINE: Yes. Correspondence disagrees about the analysis of the phrase "its having a color". Correspondence holds that the phrase indicates something apart from and independent of the use of our framework. But we reject such an account.
ALEXANDER: Yes, we do. Do we reject it because of defect or because of excess?
KATHERINE: Because of excess. For it gives the wrong analysis and account of a substance having a color, for example.
ALEXANDER: The account is wrong. Further, it distorts an account of perceiving and of the relation between perceiving and thinking. To employ its account of truth in trying to tell whether a given assertion is true it is necessary both to know what is said, namely "This table is white" and also to see whether it has a color. But such a projected achievement of perception is indistinguishable from one of thought. An account of perception is accordingly confused with one of thought.
KATHERINE: Surely it is not sufficient only to see whether this table has a color. One must also see what color it has.
ALEXANDER: Indeed. For there would not otherwise be complete matching.
KATHERINE: But if one can perceive what the color is, one's task in using language is not to assert but to report. Reports, however, are neither true nor false but correct or incorrect. It must then be acts of perception which are true or false. With what will a perception correspond in order to be true?
RECORDER: I wonder at the confidence with which you two dismiss correspondence. There are distinguished philosophers who think correspondence a platitude. In his essay Subject and Predicate in Logic and Grammar P.F. Strawson writes:
Now the aim of judgment is truth; and a given judgment or belief is true just in so far as things are as one who holds that belief or makes that judgment thereby holds them to be. This is the platitude enshrined in anything which calls itself a Correspondence Theory of Truth. It is how things are in the world or in reality or in fact that determines whether our beliefs or judgments, and the propositions we affirm in expressing them, are true or false. (I.I.2)
While I'm reading to you from his book, let me read to you a later paragraph:
We have two equivalent descriptions, or general

forms of description, of the content of fundamental type of judgment. How might linguistic expression be given to such judgments? Here is a very general description of a way it might be done in the case of a judgment relating to a single particular: combine two expressions, one specifying the particular in question and one specifying the concept in question, in such a way that the result of the combination is true, or expresses a truth, if the particular exemplifies the concept--or, if the concept applies to the particular--and is false, or expresses a falsehood, if it does not. (I.I.3)

ALEXANDER: I take it you mean to have us see that the platitude of correspondence is revealed by using the words "as as", for example, in writing, "true just in so far as things are as."

RECORDER: Yes.

ALEXANDER: Further, in writing, "the result of the combination is true if the particular exemplifies the concept" Mr. Strawson uses the word "the" the fourth time in bringing a theory of correspondence to bear; for he presumably means that for the result to be true is for the concept which is specified TO BE THE SAME AS the concept exemplified by a particular thing.

RECORDER: Yes. Correspondence would not be correspondence if it did not employ a path of sameness.

ALEXANDER: Let us make the same supposition that Katherine and I made: I assert, "This table is white." In order to account for the truth or the falsity of my assertion you must posit a path of sameness on behalf of the theory of correspondence.

RECORDER: Right. For to be right you must assert things to be as they really are.

ALEXANDER: Now tell me: in order to hit the truth must not the immediate object of my assertion be identity?

RECORDER: What do you mean?

ALEXANDER: In Strawson's general account I must assert that THE concept specified is the same as that exemplified; in my example I must assert that THE color disclosed is the same as the color which the table has. Must I not do some such thing in order to speak the truth?

RECORDER: Yes. So much you must do if correspondence is to be applicable.

ALEXANDER: I thought so. But when I assert, "This is white," I do not take a path of identity either at the dominant or at a subordinate level. The assertion is immediately an assertion of sufficiency. The subject effected at subordinate levels is a collection of acts: referring to something, uttering the word "this" and uttering the word "white". It is no part of making the assertion to take a path of sameness.

RECORDER: I am not convinced. Surely in making the assertion one applies and follows a particular law of continuousness: Whatever else is of the same color as the color of this paradigm is white. In laying down the condition of the law one lays down a path of sameness.

ALEXANDER: Indeed. But meeting the condition is no part of subordinating the following of the law to making an assertion. Meeting the condition is enough to follow and so to continue; neither applying nor following is part one of the other.

RECORDER: I don't know how to answer your reply to my first argument. Let me try something else. You assert, "This is white." I reply, "No, it isn't." I continue, "It's some other color." Since I deny your assertion in favor of arguing otherness, your assertion must be one of sameness. So perhaps you were really asserting this: "This is the same color as white."

ALEXANDER: You remember there are two conditions of the law of continuousness which you slightly abbreviated when you issued it just now. The first is "If this and the paradigm have the same color"; the second is "and if the paradigm is white." Would you not oppose anyone who meets the first condition by asserting, "This table and the paradigm have the same color"?

RECORDER: Yes. I would say they have different colors.

ALEXANDER: Suppose again I assert, "This is white." When you reply, "No, it isn't; it's some other color," do you mean to say anything more than that since the paradigm is white, this table and the paradigm have different colors?

RECORDER: No.

ALEXANDER: Then there is a prior and a posterior pair of contradictories. The prior pair contains a path of sameness and one of otherness; the posterior pair contains, for example, "This is white" and "This is brown."

RECORDER: What is the common goal the first two are in pursuit of?

ALEXANDER: Preparing ground sufficient for continuing.

RECORDER: And of the second pair?

ALEXANDER: Reaching knowledge as to the color of this.

RECORDER: I am inclined to agree with you.

ALEXANDER: Do you also agree that the theory of correspondence is not adequate?

RECORDER: Yes. I think you have convicted it on a charge of defect: its account is inadequate. For not

159

every assertion which is true or false immediately subordinates a path of sameness. It therefore cannot re-
deem its promise when it says, "An assertion is true
which says things AS they are."
KATHERINE: I now feel as Julian must have felt when he
interrupted us a few minutes ago. You have been criticizing correspondence as though it conceded your principle of critical fairness: that one not criticize action for what it does not claim to offer. You naturally ask whether there is sufficiency in light of your
theory that assertion is immediately assertion of sufficiency. But correspondence does not similarly assume
that assertion is immediately assertion of sameness.
It is simply a condition of the truth of an assertion
that there be sameness. To be an assertion an assertion does not have to assert sameness; but to be a true
assertion there must be sameness. The speaker offers
the critic a mode of discourse when he makes an assertion. The critic projects a comparison by asking
whether the assertion's mode of discourse is the same
as a mode of reality. The speaker does not himself
make such a comparison.
ALEXANDER: So the speaker does not mean to speak the
truth nor to share in the critic's work?
KATHERINE: He does mean to speak the truth.
ALEXANDER: Then he must mean to be right in claiming
sameness of a mode of discourse and a mode of reality.
KATHERINE: Perhaps your charge against correspondence
is justified. Do you think philosophers are wrong when
they claim that correspondence is enshrined in ordinary
language?
ALEXANDER: Yes. When I employ the word "as" in saying, "He says things as they are," I do not indicate
sameness; I indicate sufficiency.
KATHERINE: Then perhaps we should make a claim on your
behalf: the theory of sufficiency is enshrined in ordinary language.
KEITH: Are you making a joke, Katherine?
KATHERINE: I don't think so. You would have laughed.
KEITH: It seems to me that Professor Alexander took
pains early this morning to disabuse us of the idea
that when one says, for example, "He doesn't see things
as they are" or "But that's how things are," one indicates a partially submerged path of sameness. You remember you expressed puzzlement about the use of the
word "as" when one says one sees something as it is.
(I.4)
KATHERINE: My puzzlement has long been laid to rest.
The word indicates a partially submerged path of sufficiency. So the use of an expression such as "That's

how things are" commits us not to a theory of correspondence but to one of sufficiency.   For when one
says, "That's how things are," one asserts the sufficiency of someone's action for settling a certain matter; as I would hope C.S. Peirce would be willing to
say: one asserts the sufficiency of action for the settlement of an opinion.
RECORDER: You may wish Peirce would say such a thing.
He doesn't; and only she would think so who doesn't
read Peirce.   What he actually writes, if you're interested, is that the opinion which is fated to be ulti-
mately agreed to by all who investigate is what we mean
by the truth; the object represented in this opinion is
the real.   That is how Peirce explains reality.   Do you
still want him to be the father of your neo-pragmatism?
KATHERINE: Grandfather.   My father is living.   (turning to Alexander)   Peirce's remark won't do, will it?
ALEXANDER: I would rather not play a role in helping
to keep Peirce out of western Canada.
KEITH: But admiration ought not suspend criticism.
RECORDER: Then you criticize what he writes.   Perhaps
I can tell whether to hire you to teach Peirce in my
department.
KATHERINE: Julian is coming into his own, isn't he?
I'll wager you'll make a fine bureaucrat.
KEITH: By writing, "The opinion...is what we mean by
the truth" Peirce reveals confusion between a subject
of truth and truth.   He further obfuscates a point
which it is not easy for me to make.   Suppose there is
an opinion which all who investigate agree to.   Since
there is universal agreement, there is no charge of
exiguousness or falsity brought against the opinion.
It does not follow that there is neither exiguousness
nor falsity; indeed, there can be means whose actualization is sufficient for sustaining a charge of falsity.   It can turn out that a united learned community is
wrong.   Agreement about an opinion, therefore, does not
imply that the opinion is true.
KATHERINE: But you agree that if there is no inconsistency, there is no falsity.
KEITH: Indeed.   But negation may not automatically be
resolved in favor of, in this case, a condition of consistency nor in favor of a conclusion of truth.   So it
does not follow that if there is consistency, there is
truth.
KATHERINE: Good.   So we really can avoid the view that
truth is coherence.
KEITH: Suppose there is a system of acts between any
two of which there is either consistency or indifference.   It does not follow that the execution of either

161

act is sufficient for reaching its goal, even if they are mutually sufficient for the pursuit of the same goal.

RECORDER: (I'm not sure I've made a full record of Keith's last remark. As he was making it, the Porter entered, pushing his tray. Katherine looked up and said:)

KATHERINE: More tea?

PORTER: At five o'clock? I've brought cocktails.

KATHERINE: Good! How long before dinner?

PORTER: Dinner will be served at six. Have you finished your tour of instruments of criticism?

KATHERINE: When I learned what truth and falsity are, I hardly recognized the instruments I have long assumed have lain in my hands.

PORTER: What are they then?

KATHERINE: To employ the words is to criticize for defect, sufficiency and excess. It turns out that truth is the sufficiency of the use of a framework for reaching complex achievements of disclosure.

PORTER: And falsity?

KATHERINE: Excess.

PORTER: Excess?

KATHERINE: Excess!

PORTER: I don't get it.

KATHERINE: Nor do I.

PORTER: Does he who speaks falsely say too many words?

KATHERINE: Don't ask me.

KEITH: Don't act as if you were helpless. When there is falsity, there is excess: in particular certain alternatives can be constructed among which there is inconsistency; further, one of them is right.

KATHERINE: (trying to explain the matter to the Porter) If a conceptual framework is capable of generating an alternative which is false, it is also capable of generating two alternatives between which there is inconsistency; if there are only two, one of them is true and the other, false.

PORTER: Then is reaching knowledge prior to falling into error? And for every wrong answer is there a right one?

KATHERINE: I think you should study philosophy. But at the moment you're too quick. Imagine a gardner pruning a tree. The tree, by analogy, is a system of paths taken by someone in the pursuit of knowledge. Wherever he finds falsity, he finds excess; he accordingly cuts off a limb and throws it aside. But he doesn't cut away just any limb that has sprouted in the wrong direction or has grown too far. He traces it back towards the trunk until he finds a node from which

an adequate alternative can or has grown. He then cuts
that entire stem away. The good gardener only cuts when
he also preserves.
PORTER: So your gardener is a critic armed with instruments of criticism: the words "exiguous", "true" and
"false". When he uses the word "false" in criticizing
and setting aside, he also uses the word "true" in continuing and preserving. In that way he never gives up
or casts off all of what he has. Right?
KATHERINE: Right. Criticism for truth is conserving.
So will you come to our new academy and study philosophy?
PORTER: I don't know. I'll be back at six o'clock.
KATHERINE: We'll be here. (He leaves.)
(6)
ALEXANDER: Having defined three triads of modes of
criticism and reflection let us again consider perplexities of our own which have remained unresolved.   It
would not do to pretend to find a mean between too much
and too little skepticism while leaving unresolved perplexities in our own accounts.
KEITH: I would like to resume a discussion which you
and I recently had (VI.5). We discontinued the discussion shortly after I said that I did not very well see
how one could abandon either of two premises.   The
first is that whatever A is and whatever B is, A and B
are either the same or other.   The second is that whatever is other is either combined or separate.
ALEXANDER: Your perplexity seemed to me particularly
understandable in light of an assumption which
Katherine made this morning (III.4), I mean that there
is an "is" of identity. If, when I assert, "A is the
same as B," I immediately assert an identity, then the
only alternative to my assertion is an assertion of
otherness, saying, "A is other than B." For you were
surely right to observe that sameness and otherness exhaust the alternatives of their family.
KEITH: Surely for the sort of consideration which you
have now advanced it has seemed evident to logicians
that it is a necessary truth that A is the same as itself. For the alternative would be to say that A is
other than itself. It would obviously be absurd to
hold the alternative. So we are returned to the first.
ALEXANDER: Perhaps you see now how to resolve your own
perplexity. One can do so by piecing the parts together, as people say.
KEITH: I can't think what the first part would be.
RECORDER: Let me help you. You remember that Bill and
I were discussing the example "Cicero is Tully." (V.3)
I accepted the lesson of a previous discussion with

163

Katherine: to assert is not immediately to assert identity. Therefore, the "is" of the sentence "Cicero is Tully" does not indicate identity but sufficiency.
ALEXANDER: (turning to Keith) Is it necessary to go through an argument?
KEITH: No. I accept your account of assertion: to assert that Cicero is Tully is immediately to assert the sufficiency of subordinate action for an objective.
ALEXANDER: If identity were the immediate object of assertion, there would be only one alternative for redeeming its denial.
KEITH: But since the immediate object of assertion is sufficiency, its denial is a denial of sufficiency. There are therefore two paths of criticism open to him who issues the denial: criticism for defect and criticism for excess. If I took the second path and, in particular, that of charging inconsistency or falsity, there would still be no resolution of my perplexity. For inconsistency arises between two alternatives in pursuit of the same end. But only alternatives of the same family can serve as means in pursuit of the same end. So if I mean to suspend the use of my first premiss in our sustained practice of metaphysics, it must be on a proved charge of defect.
ALEXANDER: And hasn't such a charge been proved against saying, "A thing is the same as itself"?
KEITH: Yes, I think it has. (V.2)
ALEXANDER: Then let us turn to your second premiss.
CHANCELLOR: Before we do so, I would like to put a question.
ALEXANDER: What is it?
CHANCELLOR: I wonder whether I have grasped the point of your criticism of saying, "A thing is the same as itself." You have asked me to be clear, when we take up criticism, whether we have set upon a course of positive or of negative criticism.
ALEXANDER: Indeed.
CHANCELLOR: If upon a course of negative criticism, you have further demanded clarity as to whether we mean to criticize for defect or for excess. Now you have evidently criticized saying, "A thing is the same as itself" for defect rather than for excess. For you said to the Recorder that he did not do enough to support an assertion of either sameness or of otherness. Did you wish us to see that from a criticism of defect it does not follow that the sentence "A thing is the same as itself" is false?
ALEXANDER: Yes. You perhaps thereby see how we avoid an impossible situation. For if I said that the sentence is false, I would imply that something is other

than itself. If one were inclined to call the original sentence false, one would be more inclined to call the second sentence false.

CHANCELLOR: In point of fact neither is false; both are defective.

ALEXANDER: Yes. I have already tried to make clear to you why we should say that such sentences are exiguous.

RECORDER: I wonder whether I have an adequate record of our resolution of perplexities about the behavior of the house of sameness and otherness. I take it we have given ourselves reason for using with caution the formula that everything is either the same or other. Caution is called for; the reason is that application of the formula can be defective. The formula can therefore be inadequate for generating an alternative.

ALEXANDER: Right.

RECORDER: But suppose that a path of identity is true; it follows that a path of otherness is false. The converse is also necessary. Right?

ALEXANDER: Right.

RECORDER: And suppose the presuppositions of paths of identity and otherness are true. Can we then adopt a version of Keith's original law (V.3.1), namely that one is true and the other, false?

ALEXANDER: Yes.

RECORDER: The same can be said about paths of uniqueness and addition. May I write so much down?

ALEXANDER: Yes.

KATHERINE: You remember I seem to have produced an argument which caused some perplexity. Are we now in a position to resolve it?

CHANCELLOR: I've forgotten what the argument is.

KEITH: I'll write it out again:

   (1) if U, then I
   (2) if not-I, then not-U
   (3) if O, then not-I
   (4) if not-U, then A
   (5) so if O, then A.

CHANCELLOR: Let me see whether I've got it: if uniqueness, then identity; if not, not. But if there's otherness, there's not identity; if no uniqueness, then addition. It follows that if there is otherness, there is addition.

ALEXANDER: Anyone care to speculate how to resolve the argument and save us from its conclusion?

CHANCELLOR: Do you mind if I try my hand at relieving your logical or metaphysical pain?

ALEXANDER: No.

CHANCELLOR: I'm not sure I speak with conviction. I think I know what you would like me to say. The defec-

tive or excessive step is step four. From a denial of
the sufficiency of a path of uniqueness for reaching
some end an assertion of the sufficiency of its opposite does not follow. So much would follow if the denial of sufficiency were resolved in favor of criticism
for excess: that is, resolved in favor of calling the
path false. Perhaps you suspect I don't understand
what I'm saying. So consider again the example in
terms of which you originally formulated your perplexity. Julian is the only person who is keeping a record. Let us suppose both that there is only one person
keeping a record and that he who is doing so is other
than Julian. By step five it follows that someone else
in addition to Julian is keeping a record. The inference presupposes something false. It is therefore exiguous, as you say, or defective in some other way.
Now to account for the defect. It lies in step four.
For uniqueness is denied not in favor of falsity but in
favor of exiguousness. But the formula listed at step
four is only usable, if the presuppositions of paths of
uniqueness and addition are true. The formula is
therefore misused.
ALEXANDER: Used in a mode of defect or in one of excess?
CHANCELLOR: In one of excess. For inconsistency is
generated.
(7)
ALEXANDER: Having resolved certain perplexities which
arose when we considered the work of the house of sameness and otherness let us turn to perplexities concerning bridgework which carries us from sameness and otherness to either combination or separation or dependence or independence. You remember we considered the
premiss that whatever is other is dependent or independent. Six positions were accordingly stated first regarding universals and particulars and then regarding
mind and matter. (VI.4)
KEITH: I think I see how to resolve my perplexity concerning the premiss that whatever is other is combined
or separate. The premiss is not immediately a premiss
of an alternative in the family of combination and separation; it is immediately a premiss of sufficiency: it
asserts the sufficiency of meeting its condition for
concluding an alternative within the family of combination and separation. To deny the premiss is to open up
one of two paths of criticism. If I took the second
path of criticizing for excess and, in particular, for
inconsistency or falsity, there would be no resolution
of my perplexity. The reason is the same as I recently
gave. So if I mean to suspend the use of my second
premiss in our sustained practice of metaphysics, the

premiss must be proved guilty of defect. I realize we
have fully discussed the consequences of either alternative of the premiss. I can't for the life of me tell
now whether the alternatives were convicted on charges
of defect or excess.
ALEXANDER: Do you remember the arguments against the
two alternatives? Shall we have Julian read from his
record?
KATHERINE: No, not that. Come now, Keith, pull yourself together. So poor a memory you don't have.
KEITH: We imagine Adam laying down a path of language,
saying of the paradigm which he has selected, "This is
white." He refers to one thing, the paradigm, and
says, "This." In continuing he does not perform an
additional act of reference. But asserting that the
paradigm and the color white are separate or independent implies double reference: once to one term of the
relation and once to the other term. But since the implication is false, the assertion itself is exiguous
and so defective.
KATHERINE: Another argument has been given. Asserting
that there is a relation of separation or independence
between two terms implies something spatial or temporal. It would have to be asserted, for example, either
that the color white is independent of the paradigm for
its posiiton or that it is separate from the paradigm
in space. But a universal does not have a position; it
is not at a distance from the paradigm. Such implications are false; therefore, the assertion is exiguous
and so defective.
KEITH: Good. Since the first alternative is not sufficient, then if use of the premiss is adequate, the
second alternative must be all right. But its claim on
adequacy was refuted. (turning to Alexander) It seems
to me that you showed not that the sentence "The color
white first came into existence with an act of institution" is exiguous but rather that it is false. We
imagined snow on the day prior to institution. There
is therefore a color which it had. But that conclusion
conflicts with the assertion that the color white first
came into existence on the day of institution. I think
you must have meant to reject my sentence on the charge
of falsity rather than on one of exiguousness.
ALEXANDER: Our argument was not as precise as it can
be now. Saying that yesterday's snow was white implies
that it had a color; but according to your alternative
it did not have a color. For there was no such thing
for snow to have. But the alternative is rejected not
because the color white existed then but because of the
use of the following inference by means of modus tol-

167

lens. If the alternative is sound, it would not be
true that the snow was white. But so much is true.
KEITH: So much I follow. But what moves you to reject
the soundness of the alternative in favor of defect
rather than excess?
ALEXANDER: Because to say, "There is a color which the
snow had" is not to say, "There existed yesterday a
color which the snow then had." There is therefore no
conflict between earlier or later arrival of whiteness.
The alternative is accordingly rejected because of a
deep commitment which it makes: to the timing of the
existence of the color white. When I say, "There is a
color which the snow had," I do not assemble support
adequate for the question, "And just when did the color
begin to exist?" We do not have support adequate for
mentioning an action, event or state of a universal
with respect to which a temporal question is appropriate.
KEITH: So we do have cause to renew your motto that
universals are neither in space nor in time. We accordingly suspend use of my second premiss in the practice of metaphysics.
KATHERINE: I think the argumentation which has led us
into and out of that premiss rather grand. I certainly
think, Keith, that you should not be hard on yourself
for missing the exit. Philosophical puzzles are rather like a labyrinth: it is easy enough to wander in; it
is too hard for most of us to get out again without
simply abusing the art of dialectic. I recently read a
book by D.M. Armstrong, called Nominalism and Realism.
I think he is put in the same position you were strug-
gling to free yourself from. At the opening of Chapter
10 he writes somewhat as follows. It is not possible
to account for universals simply in terms of particulars; to try is to risk the error of nominalism. It is
not possible to account for particulars simply in terms
of universals; to try is to risk the error of univer-
salism. To see the errors of both ways is the beginning of wisdom: but only the beginning. For the question which then arises is the way in which particulars
and universals stand to each other. We must first reject the doctrine of transcendent realism that universals stand outside particulars in a realm apart. But
if transcendent realism is rejected, then some version
of immanent realism must be accepted.
     To argue in such a way as Armstrong argues is to
argue according to the premiss that whatever is distinct is either combined or separate.
RECORDER: I think you do an injustice to Armstrong's
book. The book has a good grip on the insight which

Professor Alexander has been trying to deliver to us:
the properties of a particular are not related to that
particular. Armstrong writes that he requires a non-
relational immanent realism. He requires a realism
which distinguishes the particularity of a particular
from the properties of the particular while denying
that the two aspects are related. For example, it is
helpful to think of the way in which the size of a
thing stands to its shape. Size and shape are inseparable in particulars, yet they are not related. Certain aspects of things are inseparable and too intimately conjoined to speak of their being related.
KATHERINE: You ought rather accuse Armstrong of inconsistency than me of injustice. Can you have been listening to yourself when you uttered the words "the way
in which the size stands to its shape", "inseparable in
particulars" and "too intimately conjoined to speak of
their being related"? Surely the word "inseparable"
indicates a species of combination and also a denial of
power sufficient for separation. Is to be combined not
to be related?
RECORDER: Yes, I suppose it is.
KATHERINE: And is not for two things to be conjoined,
however intimately, for them to be related?
RECORDER: Of course.
KATHERINE: Then it seems to me I was justified in saying that Armstrong writes in accordance with the premiss whose metaphysical use we have freed ourselves
from.
KEITH: (turning to Alexander) I have still not had an
answer to a question which I put early this afternoon.
(VI.3) I suppose I was initially wondering about the
relation between metaphysics and epistemology. It
seems to me that a case for skepticism is strengthened
or weakened according to whose metaphysics you presuppose. Realism housed in a framework of correspondence,
I suspect, gets the disease worst; idealism has prided
itself on its immunity. So I was naturally wondering
how the skeptic will thrive in your house of neo-pragmatism.
ALEXANDER: Julian will be playing the role of a skeptic this evening.
KEITH: So I understand. There is something on my mind
that may be relevant to our recent discussion. I was
put in mind of it just now when Julian said that
Armstrong calls for non-relationality. It seems to me
you give him what he wants without joining him in a
kind of backsliding. Unless I've got things wrong, you
order metaphysics and epistemology with respect to universals in the following way. It is a premiss of our

metaphysics that particulars and universals are distinct. There is no further premiss of relations between them: in particular the family of combination and
separation offers no means for identifying a relation
between a substance and a universal. So with respect
to universals we have completed our metaphysical inquiry; we turn to epistemology and resume our interest
in relations, asking what the relation is between disclosing a universal and disclosing what it is to which
reference is made and with reference to which a certain
achievement of knowledge is desired.
      However unclear I was earlier this afternoon about
what I was asking you, I now think I wanted to ask you
this: Has our metaphysical account made our task easier
of accounting for knowledge of universals?
ALEXANDER: Our task has been made easier by virtue of
having a metaphysical account which does not place impediments along the way which we would take in order to
take up epistemology.
KEITH: It is easy enough to spare oneself perplexity
by neglecting metaphysics. It is very difficult to do
metaphysics and smooth one's way to other fields of
philosophy. I would say the same about logical puzzles.
One can spare oneself perplexity by ignoring them. Ignorance is easy: but it is difficult to do logic and
smooth one's way to an account of complex achievements
of knowledge.
RECORDER: Another example which would have sustained
our earlier perplexity comes to mind.
KATHERINE: Are we now in flight or in pursuit?
RECORDER: What do you mean?
KATHERINE: The delicate philosophical spirit, I take
it, is equally in flight and in pursuit: in flight from
paradox and perplexity and in pursuit of adequacy. We
just got out of the fly-bottle. Why are we going back
in?
KEITH: You know Julian well enough to know: to help
the Middle Ages out.
KATHERINE: Another example from the Middle Ages? What
is it then, Julian?
RECORDER: Siger of Brabant develops a position in his
Question On The Eternity Of The World. A premiss of
his position is known to us: universals depend for
their existence upon particulars. For example, the
species Man depends for its existence upon particular
men.
KEITH: Upon some one man or upon all men who exist?
RECORDER: Upon all. Siger writes that the species is
not caused in the sense that it exists in an eternally
caused individual but rather because in the individuals

170

of the human species one is generated before the other eternally; the species has to be and to be caused through an individual's existing and being caused.

KEITH: Then is the species again caused to exist whenever an individual is caused to be?

RECORDER: He says so: the species begins to exist when it existed and had previously existed.

KEITH: I don't understand how something can come to exist, existing already. Can it start to rain, raining already?

KATHERINE: (looking at me) Why do you hesitate, Julian? It's absurd to say that you just now made this chair, having made it already.

RECORDER: It is true. Siger's position is self-contradictory. Nothing starts, continuing already.

KATHERINE: Keith offered you two alternatives: the species Man depends upon one man or upon all men who exist.

RECORDER: If one is to hold Siger's premiss of dependence, one would have to take the first alternative: upon one man at a time.

KEITH: Did Siger think the alternative possible?

RECORDER: I think not. For there would then be no complete explanation as to why the other men are men. For the species is the formal cause. If there were no connection or dependence between universal and particular, the universal would be no part of what makes a certain man a man.

KATHERINE: Leave the Middle Ages in the fly-bottle, Julian. Siger's problem is not ours. We do not suppose that a universal is part of the cause of anything. The question "What makes a particular man to be man?" is a pseudo-question. There's defect or something lapping about its head. It's nonsense, Old Fellow.

CHANCELLOR: Even I don't have Katherine's impatience with the philosophy of the Middle Ages. Let me see whether I have mastered what you refer to as our position. When I assert of Alexander, "He is a man," I utter the words "a man" in support of saying What. The achievement of saying What, is that of revealing an essence. But that essence is not a cause.

KATHERINE: Nor an effect.

CHANCELLOR: Nor an effect. So when I assert that Alexander is a man, I'm not giving a causal explanation.

KEITH: Right.

KATHERINE: So nothing compels us to agree with Siger. We're certainly free to use the solution offered us: suspend the use of premisses of combination and dependence with respect to a distinction between particulars

and universals.
KEITH: I too am content with our resolution of certain
metaphysical perplexities. I wonder whether we have
made equal progress in resolving logical puzzles.
KATHERINE: What do you mean?
(8)
KEITH: Consider, for example, a version of the Liar's
Paradox: "What I am saying is not true."
RECORDER: (turning to the Chancellor) We know Keith
better than you do, but even you must have noticed his
transformation. As the thought of discussing puzzles
and paradoxes entered his head, his spirits quickened.
Like my grandfather's racing horse he is ready to run
against entries made by the tyrant of human language:
Paradox.
CHANCELLOR: I don't mind watching such a race; I don't
myself have legs for running one. But I would have
students of my academy encouraged to run. Good exercise for the mind.
RECORDER: But no corruption for the spirit?
(Alexander looks at Julian but remains silent, still
looking surprised.)
CHANCELLOR: What do you mean?
RECORDER: I am not speaking as your future head of department, you understand. I'm speaking as an historian
or as a sociologist or something.
KATHERINE: Really, Julian; it is time you made up your
mind what you are.
RECORDER: Training in puzzles and paradoxes cultivates
the mind; the philosophically educated mind knows its
way through mazes and labyrinths. But interest in puzzles can become immoderate; excessive interest is sometimes recognized as paradox mongering. When a great
civilization produces philosophers who articulate a
doctrine or a theory, the doctrine or the theory remains for a time vulnerable, like a child recently
born. So much happened in the two greatest ancient
civilizations known to me: those of China and Greece.
Puzzle makers arise and do their work at the expense of
vulnerable theory and doctrine. Such puzzle makers we
find in Zeno and some of the Sophists of Greece and in
the Neo-Micians of China.
CHANCELLOR: I would say that a great civilization
passes through such a stage in refining the art of argumentation and dialectic. An academy should preserve
that stage so that its students can also pass through
it.
RECORDER: A paradox is the effect of a ray of light
led into a box and caused to reflect back and forth between two mirrors facing one another. You know that

172

clever people can construct such boxes by means of two members from the family of sameness and otherness and from the family of combination and separation. It is awful, you know, for the mind to get caught vibrating between two such poles, the one receiving reason and returning it to the other.

CHANCELLOR: It is good training to get caught, according to your image. It would be awful not to free oneself. I would not like to have students leave my academy thinking that any serious intellectual effort conceals paradox and inconsistency. (turning to Keith) A moment ago you invited us to consider a version of the liar's paradox: "What I am saying is not true."

KATHERINE: How would you resolve the paradox? It would be a nice test of today's discussions if you can show us a resolution.

KEITH: Suppose the dominating act of language is rejecting something. The word "not" is uttered in order to make it evident that something is rejected. We know that the immediate object of rejection is sufficiency, indicated when one says, "is true." Let us set aside a statement of the objective. We next consider means whose sufficiency for an objective is rejected. Katherine, will you play the role of the liar who says, "What I am saying is not true"?

KATHERINE: Yes, of course.

KEITH: Can you tell me what the words are whose use reveals a subject whose sufficiency is denied?

KATHERINE: Didn't I say enough when I said, "What I am saying is not true"?

KEITH: Enough to complete a sentence. But remember that according to the Thesis of Negation you use the word "not" to disclose an act of rejection. According to the Principle of Distinguishable Resources it follows that the word is not uttered in order to let us know what the subject is whose sufficiency is rejected.

KATHERINE: Fine. Then we are left with the words "what I am saying". So the subject must be saying something.

KEITH: But since we are practicing philosophical criticism, we require knowledge of what is said. What resources do you give us for acquiring such knowledge?

KATHERINE: None. For I can't simply repeat the original sentence.

KEITH: Then since you run out of requisite resources, you say too little--indeed you do too little--to take a way of paradox. For you fail to make clear what the subject is, criticized either for defect or for excess. So we criticize your saying, "What I am saying is not true" for defect. What you say is neither true nor false but exiguous.

CHANCELLOR: What a fine piece of analysis, Keith. I would encourage our students to imitate you.

KATHERINE: Since Keith does not expect to be praised, Mr. Chancellor, any praising him is excessive praise. I would like to know what the roots are of the apparent paradox. I take it that we do not in principle object to someone laying down a path of language and applying it to itself.

KEITH: Not in principle. Someone might write, "Whatever word I write is possibly misspelled." One can apply the premiss to writing a word in laying down the premiss.

KATHERINE: Quite so. Suppose I lay down the premiss "Whatever I say is not true." I apply the premiss to laying down the premiss. It follows that the premiss is not true. Have I gone wrong yet?

KEITH: No. Carry on.

KATHERINE: According to our dialectical pattern I must now make clear whether I criticize for exiguousness or for falsity. Suppose I criticize for falsity. Since the premiss is false, whatever I say is true; the premiss is therefore true as well. Since such criticism leads to an impossibility, the criticism itself must be either defective or excessive. So suppose I criticize for exiguousness. Since the premiss is exiguous, it does not follow that whatever I say is true. Indeed, no absurdity follows. So is the root of such a paradox the assumption that there are only two objects of criticism: truth and falsity?

KEITH: Yes.

RECORDER: Surely not in every case. You remember some years ago when we met at a summer institute we discussed paradoxes. One evening, as I remember, we discussed a paradox formulated by Bertrand Russell: a set S is defined as follows. For every x, x is a member of S if, and only if, x is not a member of itself. But by substitution we obtain the following: S is a member of itself if, and only if, S is not a member of itself.

KEITH: Some time ago we discarded use of the logical notion of substitution in favor of use of the notions of applying and following.

RECORDER: No matter. Puzzles don't disappear on the wings of a departing notion. I can put the definition of S in the following way: anything is a member of S if, and only if, it is not a member of itself. Now one of two assumptions must be made: the first is that S is a member of itself; the second, that S is not a member of itself. By applying the definition to the first assumption it follows that S is not a member of itself;

by applying the definition to the second assumption it
follows that S is a member of itself.

KATHERINE: I'm getting hungry and bored with paradoxes. I don't suppose I have a head for this sort of
thing. There'll be enough problem-solving this evening. I do hope you won't be long. I sometimes suspect
such puzzles are better ignored than resolved.

CHANCELLOR: I don't have much of a head for this sort
of thing either, but it will not do to ignore such puzzles. I would like to know how Keith means to respond
to Julian's statement of Russell's paradox.

KEITH: The first assumption to which the definition is
applied is that S is a member of itself. The immediate
object of the assumption is sufficiency: so much is
made clear by means of the word "is". The subject is
subordinate action with respect to membership. I suppose one might think of membership as inclusion and its
opposite as exclusion. Would it do any harm to make
the supposition?

RECORDER: No, none.

KEITH: So your first assumption immediately assumes
sufficiency and subordinately effects a subject of inclusion, namely S including itself. But suppose I deny
the assumption of sufficiency. According to our dialectical pattern I must now make clear whether I criticize for defect or for excess. Suppose I criticize for
falsity. Since it is false, its alternative must be
found with respect to the pair of inclusion and exclusion. According to this mode of criticism one accedes
to the premiss that S is either included in or excluded
from itself. But either alternative leads to paradox.
So the mode of criticism must not itself be right. So
suppose I criticize for exiguousness.

RECORDER: How then do you propose to make out the case
for exiguousness?

KEITH: Making the first assumption presupposes sufficient use of the definition for identifying something
called set S. But its identification is not reached
until membership is established. But since application
is open and without limit, there is no membership closure: S is therefore not completely definable. The
first assumption is therefore exiguous.

RECORDER: Then you reject the first in favor of the
second. But the second is also sufficient for applying the definition. The paradox still remains.

KEITH: I think rather that the paradox does not still
remain. I reject the first alternative when I say, "S
is not a member of itself." I reject it and argue defect. Since the denial is sufficient, I do enough to
meet the condition of the premiss "If S is not a member

of itself, then it is a member of itself." By modus
ponens it follows that S is a member of itself. But
the consequence of using the premiss has already been
found to be exiguous. It follows that the premiss itself is defective. There is accordingly defective
means for generating a paradox.
RECORDER: I think I am persuaded by your handling of
the case against Russell's purported paradox. It seems
to me to replay, in a logical form, the perplexity we
were in, when we took ourselves to be compelled to
choose between immanent and transcendent realism. Deep
puzzles have a way of casting themselves now in a metaphysical, now in a logical and now in an epistemological form.
CHANCELLOR: I understand the keen interest some of you
have in the solution of logical puzzles. I think I
have heard enough to take to heart the importance of
accommodating ourselves to triadic modes of examination
and criticism. I'm sure there will be room in our academy for someone to take up a deep and systematic study
of metaphysical and logical puzzles. Let us close the
subject for today and have dinner. After dinner we
will seek moderation between too much and too little
skepticism.
(9)
KATHERINE: I too would be pleased to quit a discussion
of logical puzzles. But before we stop for dinner, I
would like satisfaction regarding a recent discussion
between Keith and Bill. (VII.6) Keith put the order
between metaphysics and epistemology in the following
way. It is a premiss of our metaphysics that particulars and universals are distinct. There is no further
premiss of relations between them. A particular and a
universal are neither combined nor separate; a universal neither depends upon nor is independent of a particular for its being. In speaking thus I complete our
metaphysical inquiry with respect to universals. We
accordingly turn to epistemology and resume our interest in relations concerning the knowledge of universals.
     It has been a premiss of our discussions that
reaching knowledge is an achievement which depends upon
the use of a language. One was barely awake early this
morning when one heard Bill speak of managing more or
less simple achievements of knowledge. I take it that
universals are objects of knowledge. In such cases a
complex achievement of knowledge is not an achievement
of knowing a complex. For the word "complex" would
imply that there is a relation of combination or of dependence between the objects known. Do I so far betray

misunderstanding of today's affair?
ALEXANDER: No.
KEITH: Not yet.
KATHERINE: Now I wonder whether every object of knowledge is a universal. I assert, "This is a table." I
do enough to make something known. What then is the
object of knowledge?
KEITH: We speak of a complex achievement because we
speak of a complex of achievements: one part of a whole
is making known what it is to which you refer; another
part is saying What. The two parts fit together to
help form the whole, namely saying what this is. But
to know is not to know a whole of parts; to know is to
manage an achievement which is a whole of parts.
KATHERINE: You characterize the parts of the whole
achievement in different ways: you say, "One makes
clear What," "One discloses a name" and "One indicates
sufficiency." Now we all say that the object of disclosing a name is a universal. Is there an object of
making clear What?
KEITH: Yes. For when you make clear to me to what you
refer, we manage distinct achievements and know the
same thing, namely what it is to which you refer.
KATHERINE: And what is the object of indicating sufficiency?
KEITH: One should put the relevant achievement in this
way: one indicates What. For when you assert, "This is
a table" and say, "is", you indicate what it is you assert, namely the sufficiency of something for something.
KATHERINE: Then is sufficiency not an object of knowledge?
KEITH: No. How could it be? I assert the sufficiency
of a subject for an objective. The objective, let us
say, is reaching knowledge. If to reach such knowledge
were in part to know sufficiency, then there would be
another objective of reaching a goal. Reaching that
goal would be no part of reaching the first achievement. But he who asserts that this is a table does not
mean to indicate sufficiency of knowing what this is
for reaching a further achievement.
KATHERINE: I think I am satisfied with your reply.
Something has become clear which has not been clear to
me before. The account which has been given of acts of
language rests in some measure upon the use of the family of dependence and independence. The account which
you just now outlined of achievements of communication
rests in equal measure upon the use of the family of
combination and separation and, in particular, upon the
notion of a whole and its parts.

177

ALEXANDER: You look as if there is something more on your mind.
KATHERINE: I fear it is time for dinner; I may annoy you if I too much prolong the afternoon.
CHANCELLOR: There is time; we have leisure.
RECORDER: Hasn't Plato reminded us that we are not like lawyers, about to present a case before a judge?
KATHERINE: Perhaps I will continue. It has been our concern--not merely today but since we first met some years ago--to define several species of sufficiency: consistency, truth, cooperation and justice, for example. Truth is sufficiency for knowledge; justice, for satisfaction. Knowledge, in turn, is an achievement which depends upon two kinds of pillars of support: the first is a certain use of language, and the second is being in a certain position. There are accordingly two subjects of adequacy for knowledge: thinking and perceiving.

I suspect we've never been in doubt that there is a distinction between knowing something and either using language or seeing something. Further, there is a relation of dependence being knowing something and using language and being in a certain position. Our account of the relation of dependence protects us against saying either that knowing is a part of using a language or that knowing is a part of perceiving. You have certainly carried me along with you today in your rejection of a reduction of an account of dependence to one of combination.
ALEXANDER: I have no reservations about your summary of the course of our conversations.
KATHERINE: But this morning (I.4) you said that seeing something does not provide support for correcting or modifying what is said. I have Julian's record here. Let me read out two sentences:

...it means nothing to say that I have recourse to seeing the Premier in order to judge whether I say too much were I to say, "I see the Premier." Similarly, I talk nonsense when I say, "I have recourse to seeing him in order to judge whether I say too little were I to say, 'I barely caught a glimpse of him.'"

I wonder whether, in order to bring us away from defects or excesses of empiricism, you said more than you meant to say.
ALEXANDER: In defining philosophy this morning I remarked that in the course of the day we would have laid before us accounts and explanations and also procedures and premisses. Most of what was promised has been done. It is now easier to make clear and precise what

deserves to be clear and precise.

My effort then was to uncover ground necessary for the practice of criticism for excess: in particular for incorrectness, inconsistency and falsity. I may not have made clear to you then what I hope has been made clear to us: criticism for excess presupposes that there are alternate terms capable of subserving the same objective. Accordingly, the criticism of an act of language for excess presupposes resources adequate for an alternative act of language. I did not mean to suggest that perception is not a subject dependently adequate for knowledge.

KATHERINE: I very well see now that you didn't. I mistook you. It is plain to me now that you were preparing ground for an account of criticism.

CHANCELLOR: You've taken us on a tour, this afternoon, of a town. Along its main street sit three minor houses; slightly elevated, on a hill, sits the major house. You have referred to it as the reigning family of conceptual resources. After we surveyed the three minor houses, we considered bridgework, as you've been saying, which carries the mind from the resources of one house to another: for example, from sameness and otherness to combination and separation. I suppose you've set yourselves up as traffic wardens, trying to order and to rationalize intra-city traffic.

I am puzzled why you didn't follow the same procedure when we came to the governing house. Your omission of following the procedure is the more surprising in light of your view that sameness has everywhere usurped the rights of sufficiency.

KATHERINE: Wouldn't your analogy make a fine movie? Plato and Aristotle smuggled sameness out of its own house and into the reigning house, kidnapping sufficiency and leaving defect and excess tied up in the basement, you know, neglected and abandoned. I want to play otherness.

KEITH: You are playing otherness.

CHANCELLOR: (ignoring the bickering which broke out between Katherine and Keith) Am I wrong in thinking that a certain thing greatly occupies you? I mean that sameness usurps the rights of sufficiency.

ALEXANDER: You are not wrong. Perhaps you know my position. For the sake of making myself perfectly clear let me state my position.

KATHERINE: I wish you would.

ALEXANDER: Laying down or taking a path of sameness is sometimes sufficient for reaching knowledge; although sameness is not truth, effecting a path of sameness is a subject of truth. The mind, moving to knowledge, sometimes takes a path of sameness. You understand me:

179

I would do justice to the effecting of a path of sameness in order to reach knowledge, understanding and
wisdom.
CHANCELLOR: So much I have never taken you to deny. I
believe that you mean to deny something else: that all
just and sound reasoning depends upon effecting a path
of sameness.
ALEXANDER: Yes. There are means sufficient for appropriate action and achievement without effecting a path
of sameness or otherness.
RECORDER: The soundness of his view leads to a critique of parts of our tradition: a critique for excess.
For example, in his Treatise Hume writes that all kinds
of reasoning consist in nothing but a comparison. But
comparing is an activity which finally depends upon the
house of sameness and otherness for its materials. For
one should go on to say wherein two things are similar
or dissimilar. If similar, they have something in
common; if dissimilar, there is otherness.
KATHERINE: (smiling at the Chancellor) The mind must
be fairly well stocked with supplies from that house in
order to get all that done.
(The Porter entered and invited us to dinner.)

PART VIII

ALEXANDER: The final part of our conversation concerns the susceptibility of our accounts to skepticism and dogmatism. If there is such a thing as moderate skepticism or moderate dogmatism, then our concern is again with defect and excess.

CHANCELLOR: I think our concern is as you suggest it is. A good student can both doubt too little and too much; it is similarly possible to be too lax and too strict. I would say that the risk in our day is of too much skepticism rather than of too much dogmatism. So I think you should largely be concerned to meet excessive skeptical argumentation.

ALEXANDER: Then let us consider our accounts of the two stages of an ascent to knowledge of the truth in relation to skeptical argumentation. Arguments with a skeptical force are doubtless written in Julian's record. Perhaps you would play the role of the skeptic in testing our accounts.

RECORDER: Of course.

ALEXANDER: There are two stages which we reach either in coming to know a matter of fact or in making a claim. The first step of the first stage is reached having selected an example, a paradigm or a standard; the second is reached having laid down a path of language with respect to the example, the paradigm or the standard selected. The third step is reached having created a basis of potentiality the actualization of which is sufficient for continuance. The second stage, finally, is reached by using instruments of prior institution. (1)

RECORDER: People can be divided with respect to any one of the four steps. With respect to the first, two people can disagree as to what to select as a clock, a ruler or a scales; they can disagree as to which person to elect as leader.

ALEXANDER: Can you house a case for skepticism at the first stage?

CHANCELLOR: Surely the first step of the first stage is pre-skeptical.

RECORDER: I don't agree. The role of the skeptic and that of the anarchist are there the same. The anarchist will have no precedents set by following which someone rules; the skeptic will have a choice between paradigms left open.

ALEXANDER: But to be a skeptic one must doubt; at the first step there is too little to doubt. Suppose Adam takes something to hand and, raising it up, says, "Take

this." Upon what should a skeptic practice doubt?
RECORDER: He can say to Adam, "Perhaps you should take that instead."
ALEXANDER: Without knowing to what end Adam acts as he does?
CHANCELLOR: (turning to Julian) I think it would be absurd for a skeptic to speak up and object as you imagine.
RECORDER: I don't agree. I think he has an opportunity to express the heart of skepticism: to argue against any action an achievement of which would be to eliminate alternatives.
CHANCELLOR: Then you should characterize the skeptic as arguing against the settlement of an example or a paradigm; he argues in favor of inactivity, contemplating alternatives to settling upon an example: perhaps fishing or eating instead. To give such an argument is not to reveal the heart of skepticism but rather that of laziness. I will not have such a skeptic in my academy. I think we should turn to the third step where, I hope, we can employ a serious skeptic. In an earlier discussion (IV.4) we secured the first two steps against excessive skepticism. So let us say that we have reached the third step in our ascent to complex achievements of knowledge and disclosure. Please lay out your account of the third step in detail.
(2)
ALEXANDER: I speak of creating a potential basis a realization of which is sufficient for continuance: in particular, sufficient for following. There are two ways in which one comes to be in such a position: the first is without institution and the second is with institution.
RECORDER: Would you say that potentiality for following is prior to actually following?
ALEXANDER: Yes. For suppose Adam institutes the utterance of the first word; Eve is listening. Suppose further that we mean to account for her clearing a potential basis use of which is sufficient for following. With respect to the first and second levels of mind we presuppose powers of attention and of memory. In order to occupy a position sufficient for following she must have power exercise of which is sufficient for sounding out the word in her head and also power of body exercise of which is sufficient for making a sound in subordination to repeating the word which Adam first uttered. Exercise of such powers is posterior to having them. Further, she does exercise such powers without first actually knowing the word or knowing a rule to follow. We would otherwise move towards the excess of

182

rationalism: namely that actual knowledge is prior to potentiality for learning.

CHANCELLOR: I'm prepared to say with you that we can allow Eve to be in a position of potentiality without prior institution on her part.

ALEXANDER: I observed that there are two ways in which one comes to hold a position of potentiality: the first without and the second with institution. The second is divided into two species: the first is incomplete and the second is complete. With respect to the first species one creates a potential basis for continuance by saying, for example, "Some animals are horses." The word "some" indicates sufficiency of a subject for following the premiss; it is also made clear, however, that mere application, saying of that that it is an animal, is not enough to effect a subject sufficient for following the premiss. Let us not further consider the first species.

The second species has two sub-species: the first is implicit and the second, explicit. With respect to the first one creates a potential basis for continuance by saying, for example, "All horses are animals." The word "all" indicates sufficiency of a subject for following the premiss; the subject is repeated application of the premiss. Thus are directions given for the complete use of an instrument of reason. Application, saying of that that it is a horse, is enough to effect a subject itself sufficient for following, so going on to say, "So it must be an animal." With respect to the second sub-species one creates a potential basis for continuance by saying, for example, "If Socrates is a man, then he is mortal." The word "then" indicates sufficiency of a subject for following the premiss; the subject is meeting the condition of the premiss--a condition laid down when it is said, "If Socrates is a man." By meeting the condition one effects an actual subject said to be sufficient for following; one accordingly infers, "So Socrates must be mortal."

RECORDER: I'm not certain I follow. Your account of employing the words "some, all, then" is new to me. (3)

ALEXANDER: Then let us consider another example in order to discuss the possibility of laying down certain paths of sufficiency. Let us consider in particular the utterance of such words as "all, each, every, any." The words belong to the genus of sufficiency of the family of defect, sufficiency and excess. In particular, a word of the group indicates sufficiency of a subject for continuance: continuance either in the mode of merely following or in the mode of subordinating

following to an act such as inferring, predicting or
concluding. A subject of sufficiency is single or repeated application. The word "all", for example, indicates sufficiency: sufficiency to continue either upon
realizing a potential basis or upon an actual basis.
In the first case we speak of sufficiency for potential
continuance and in the second, sufficiency for actual
continuance. In the second case, for example, I assert, "All these ravens are black." In making reference to these things and in saying of them what they
are I create an actual basis; I effect a subject of
actuality. I assert sufficiency for doing what I do,
namely to continue towards a disclosure of their color.
And in the first case, for example, I lay down the
premiss "All ravens are black." In uttering the word
"ravens" and in saying What I make application possible; I lay down a premiss of sufficiency for continuing
upon making application, namely to continue towards a
disclosure of color. In laying down the premiss I do
not myself reach the achievement; I make it possible
for you to do so by creating an instrument capable of
use. For should you refer to something and say of it
what it is, saying, "That is a raven," you would have
assembled an actual basis sufficient for following me;
you can then continue in order to say of it what its
color is, saying, "black."
KEITH: Before we employ your account in our examination for skepticism, I would like to make a comparison.
If your account is right, the dominant contemporary account is wrong. I think the dominant account can be
put this way: when I say, "All ravens are black," I refer to several things, namely to all ravens. You must
know that the assumption of reference is widely held
by logicians. Upon that assumption is based another:
that of substitutivity. For it is said that if "that"
refers to a raven, then a substitution-instance can be
had from the original assertion, namely "That is
black." Now if the two assumptions of reference and
substitutivity were wrong, I dare not think how much
contemporary philosophical work would become--at least
for us--useless and irrelevant.
KATHERINE: I don't see why you say something so dras-
tic. It seems to me that what a logician means to accomplish with the help of a notion of substitution Bill
means to accomplish with the help of the notions of application and following. And quite frankly I think we
are presented two coherent alternatives. On the side
of W.V. Quine, for example, we have the picture of a
motor one or more whose parts can be replaced, the motor continuing to do its job; on the other side we have

the picture of a hammer which a carpenter takes hold of
by the handle--application, I take it--and by means of
which he drives a nail--following. You surely don't
want to say that the picture of substitution is defective or something.
KEITH: Perhaps I do. I'm not sure. I understand what
it means to revise a sentence I've written. I erase a
word and write another word in its place. Now I say I
apply and follow the premiss "All ravens are black;" I
don't think you offer me an alternate account of what I
do when I say, "Since that bird is a raven, it must be
black," by saying, "You revise the premiss." Even if
what you suggest is intelligible, it is not right. For
suppose I'm writing a play. I write a line and then
revise it. Revising is an action subordinate to the
dominant activity of writing a play. But when I assert
of that bird that it is a raven and infer of that raven
that it is black, I don't pursue the same end as he
pursues who lays down the premiss. He who lays down
the premiss is, as it were, a lawgiver; I, by contrast,
administer the law. In administering it I don't revise
it. Let me put my point in a different way. When I
apply and follow a premiss, a principle or a law, it
does not follow that the status of the law is conferred
upon a consequence of its use. For example, a bachelor
is by definition an unmarried male above a certain age.
When you apply the definition to me and call me a bachelor, you would not say that I am a bachelor by definition. The status of the instrument you employ, revealed by the words "by definition", is not transferred
to the classification which you award me.
KATHERINE: I agree.
KEITH: But use of a notion of substitution leads to
puzzles which, in light of our account, are artificial.
For example, it is said that 9 is necessarily greater
than 7. By substitution it would follow that the number of planets is necessarily greater than 7. But so
much is false. So either there is no such substitution-instance of the formula or the formula is itself
false. I think it a sign of a superior account that no
such puzzle can be formulated.
KATHERINE: How would you show that there is no ground
for its formulation?
KEITH: An account of the formula would go as follows:
the formula is immediately a formula of sufficiency,
indicated by "is"; immediately subordinated is a path
of otherness, indicated by "-er than"; two minor paths
are further subordinated: 9 (is) a number and 7 (is) a
number. The word "necessarily" reveals the status of
the formula: namely that it has no coherent opposition.

185

Now suppose I apply the formula, asserting, "There are nine planets." By means of the formula it follows that the number of planets is greater than 7. There is no guarantee, of course, that my inference is free from opposition.

KATHERINE: You said that philosophical work of our time would become useless and irrelevant.

KEITH: Yes. I had in mind Quine's work on a notion of referential opacity, for example.

ALEXANDER: I think we should leave to another occasion a criticism of contemporary work. We must not discourage students from reading Quine. I was last giving an account of the use of the word "all". Let us return to the possibility of skepticism with respect to the premiss "All horses are animals."

(4)

RECORDER: You agree that criticism is possible.

ALEXANDER: Of course. Philosophy is the chief watch over the exercise of the office of criticism.

CHANCELLOR: What then are the questions appropriate to criticism?

ALEXANDER: The first is: To what end is such a premiss laid down? The second is: What is its genus or department?

CHANCELLOR: Fine. Let us suppose we know its objective and its home. Let us suppose we can place it within our community.

ALEXANDER: Suppose then the premiss is laid down in continuing and developing the activity of a given genus of the Academy. If there are procedures for such activity, we can ask: Is the premiss correctly laid down? If its objective is common to other members of the genus, we can ask: Is there consistency?

CHANCELLOR: This afternoon you gave us definitions of consistency and correctness. I think we see well enough how to use them. But you must know that our heart is not in any of the four questions put so far. No skeptic thrives on placing them. We wait for you to exercise the supreme office of criticism by asking whether the premiss is true.

ALEXANDER: To put that question now is to abuse the office of criticism. For truth is sufficiency for objectives of actuality. But the objective of laying down a premiss is to make it possible to reach a certain achievement. Its objective is therefore not one of actuality but one of potentiality. A question of truth is accordingly inappropriate to the laying down of the premiss; it is appropriate, rather, to its use. Since one does too little in laying down premisses actually to reach certain achievements, premisses, prin-

ciples and laws are neither exiguous, true nor false.
But by one of our laws any instance of laying down a
premiss is defective, sufficient or excessive. Some
triad of modes of criticism is therefore appropriate
and relevant.
CHANCELLOR: Then what is the appropriate question?
ALEXANDER: First, whether your Academy will keep a
premiss, a principle or a law in use and, second, if
so, whether restrictions are placed upon their application and use.
CHANCELLOR: I would find another example helpful.
ALEXANDER: A biologist lays down the premiss "All ravens are black." We consider its use in two steps: application and following. To execute the first step we
refer to something and assert of it that it is a raven;
to execute the second step is to follow. By following
one infers that the raven is black. We allow one of
three possible results with respect to the inference:
exiguousness, truth or falsity. Let us ignore the
first possibility.
CHANCELLOR: Then what is shown by either one of the
two results about the premiss itself?
ALEXANDER: To run such a test as we have imagined is
to run a test not of the premiss itself but of its use.
For running a test is to examine, and all examination
is examination of action for defect, sufficiency and
excess.
CHANCELLOR: I follow.
ALEXANDER: If a result shows anything, it shows something about the use of the premiss in relation to application and also in relation to criticism of the consequence of following. If the consequence is found to
be true, sufficiency is shown among the cooperating
parties of the test. By analogy the winning of a game
shows the adequacy of several players playing together;
it does not reveal an attribute of a single player. If
the consequence, however, is found to be false, excess
is shown among the cooperating parties of the test. To
resolve the situation the faculty of understanding requires the aid of the will. For to resolve the tension
created in the framework something must be made superfluous.
KEITH: I suppose Julian is anxious to play the role of
skeptic. I find the account--as much of it as I have
understood--extremely interesting.
KATHERINE: Excessively so?
KEITH: I find it very interesting. Having left correspondence behind, convicted of defect, you also manage to avoid a coherence theory of truth. That theory
too, I take it, would be defective. For it is not

187

enough that there is consistency and coherence among
the working members of a framework; they must work well
enough together to win.
ALEXANDER: Right.
RECORDER: Keith was right. I am anxious to play the
role of skeptic with respect to the third step of the
first stage; at our present speed we will not reach the
second stage before midnight. People can be divided
with respect to the third step; division can be focused
upon a number of aspects of laying down a path. Let us
see whether you can follow me through the following argument. Suppose a member of your Academy lays down the
premiss that all swans are white. At one time a number
of white swans are discovered. According to a pattern
of inductive inference the discovery implies the possibility or a certain degree of probability of the premiss. But at another time a black swan is discovered.
According to a pattern of deductive inference the discovery implies the falsity of the premiss. Now the
same premiss cannot be both possibly true and certainly
false. Fault must therefore lie with the pattern of
inductive inference.
CHANCELLOR: Now you would draw us towards excess. For
consider any such premiss laid down. We can conceive
a favorable instance possible and also an unfavorable
instance possible. We accordingly conceive the same
premiss both possibly true and certainly false. Since
so much is impossible, we must become skeptical about
induction.
    Mr. Alexander, how are we to resolve the puzzle?
ALEXANDER: Some puzzles and problems are parasitic
upon particular theories which are entirely deserving
of them. Part of the puzzle which the Recorder laid
out I have no wish to try to resolve. Not all premisses are consequences of following procedures. Some
premisses open and do not conclude scientific practice.
Somewhat like a man who invents a game and establishes
its rules a mathematician, a scientist or a philosopher
can lay the foundations of a discipline; tools and instruments are forged in order to build it up.
CHANCELLOR: We agree with you in advancing such a picture of making a start. The picture of a person ob-
serving this white swan and that white swan is not adequate for picturing the laying of the foundation of a
discipline. It therefore will not do to think of a
premiss as the conclusion of a series of particular ob-
servations. But a change of pictures, as you recommend, Mr. Alexander, does not wholly absolve us from
our difficulties. For suppose a scientist lays down
the premiss that all swans are white. He observes some

white swans. Now I believe our problem arises with the concession that from the observation and the use of the premiss it follows that the premiss is at least possibly true. The scientist now observes a black swan; it also follows that the premiss is certainly false. But nothing is both possibly true and certainly false. Therefore, either the first observation does not incline the premiss towards truth or the second observation does not incline it towards falsity. But since one of the conclusions follows, both do. For if experience does not tend to show up a premiss as true, it does not tend to show up a premiss as false.

So although you may be sanguine about discharging induction from our academy, you can hardly be equally sanguine about the loss of a relation between experience or observation and the truth or the falsity of premisses.

ALEXANDER: You speak now, Mr. Chancellor, as if you did not mean to assent to an argument of mine given a few minutes ago.

CHANCELLOR: I fear you must repeat it if I'm to take hold of it.

ALEXANDER: Truth is sufficiency of subjects for objectives of actuality. But the objective of laying down a premiss is to make it possible to reach a certain achievement. Its objective is therefore not one of actuality but one of potentiality. A question of truth or falsity is accordingly inappropriate to the laying down of the premiss; it is appropriate to its use.

CHANCELLOR: I remember.

ALEXANDER: So your puzzle can be resolved by means of the principle that it is not the same thing which receives contradictory attributes. To see that we can stand by the principle let us review your example. You lay down the premiss that all swans are white. A user of the premiss discovers a swan and by means of the premiss infers, "So it must be white." Suppose the inference is proved right.

CHANCELLOR: I do know my way now. By holding that there is truth we can also hold that there is sufficiency of epistemic cooperation for continuing to meet the future in a certain way. Of the premiss itself we say that it remains in potential use.

RECORDER: But it is commonly said by logicians that observation of a number of white swans confirms the premiss that all swans are white. There is a relation of confirmation between observation and premiss.

ALEXANDER: I hope you can agree with me that two conditions are necessary for allowing that one thing confirms another. The first is that the position in which

189

one confirms is better than that in which someone performs the act confirmed. The second is that the confirming act and the act confirmed have a common objective.

RECORDER: You obviously take for granted that I share a presupposition of your statements of the two conditions: namely that the terms of a relation of confirmation are actions.

ALEXANDER: And do you share it?

RECORDER: Yes, I do. Perhaps at last I have got the shift from a substance-centered to an action-centered philosophy through my head.

ALEXANDER: Then let us further consider the two conditions. In a given position one formulates a hunch; in another, one settles upon an opinion of certainty, so confirming the hunch. It follows that one is in a worse position in the first than in the second case. Further, it follows that the objective of the first act is the same as that of the second: both aim at an objective of actuality.

RECORDER: So much is clear.

ALEXANDER: The position in which a premiss is laid down is not relevantly improved by putting oneself in a position adequate for telling that that swan is white. Further, the objective of laying down the premiss is one of potentiality, namely to make it possible to reveal of what color; the objective of remarking, "That swan is white" is one of actuality: to reveal of what color. Since the two acts fail to satisfy either condition for allowing confirmation, we should say that there is no relation of confirmation between observation and premiss.

We have been considering the first half of the argument: that which rests upon the supposition of a favorable case. Now suppose that we discover a black swan, having inferred by means of the premiss that the swan referred to would be white. Since there is too little in the first instance to allow confirmation, there is also too little in the second to allow disconfirmation. We should therefore look elsewhere in our discipline for appropriate and relevant triads of modes of criticism and reflection. Where to look I have already suggested. Since an inference has been proved false, excess has been demonstrated of cooperating parties of a part of the framework. Resolution is therefore called for. There are two initial moves which can be made. The first is to suspend use of the premiss entirely. It would thereby become outmoded, as an old model of a car becomes, fit only for a museum or a history of science. The second is to make restric-

tions either on application or following. In the first
case a search would be made, I presume, for a replacement.
     For some time we have been considering the third
step of the first stage of institution. If you are
satisfied with my account of it, we should turn to a
discussion of the second stage.
(4.1)
KEITH: I, not quite. When you opened our present discussion, you spoke of creating a potential basis a
realization of which is sufficient for continuance; you
remarked further that there are two ways in which one
comes to be in such a position: one without and one
with institution and convention.
ALEXANDER: I remember.
KEITH: I would like to know whether I have followed
you as far as you have tried to carry us. It has obviously been your intention to free us from excessive
use of paths of sameness and otherness. That intention
is realized, I hope, in the following summary: I can be
in a position sufficient for continuance without first
laying down or taking a path of sameness or of similarity; I can be in a position adequate for an advance
without first erecting the bridgework of a comparison.
Consider the position of a child who is learning a language. With respect to a paradigm it has learned the
use of the expression "a car" well enough to say what
it is to which his parent is pointing. Suppose that on
another occasion he sees a car; several subjects may
now be jointly sufficient for continuance: he goes on
to utter the expression "a car", thereby saying what
that object is. We grasp an explanation of the cause
of the second instance of continuance without having to
allow that the child grasped or perceived a path of
sameness or similarity. We grasp an explanation of the
cause without having to allow that the child reasoned
somewhat in the following way. "The object before me
now and the paradigm either are or have the same essence. Since the paradigm is a car, this object too is
a car. I therefore have adequate ground for speaking
up and saying to my parents, 'a car'."
KATHERINE: Why do you make yourself ridiculous, Keith?
You haven't followed Bill; you've exceeded him, and
what more is excess is the excess of satire. Your op-
ponents don't deserve it. No one supposes that a
child, recently turning his hand to the learning of the
language his parents speak, reasons in such a sophisti-
cated--no, rather in such a philosophical way. It is
not in any case open to us to make such a claim on the
child's behalf; for he cannot reason in such a way un-

191

til he has mastered a language adequate for speaking in
such a way.
RECORDER: I don't think Keith has run to excess. He
has brought out something none of us have quite dared
put to Bill: when a child has learned only the rudi-
ments of a language, it is not yet in a position to
fashion paths of sameness and otherness; it is therefore not in a position to make comparisons. It nevertheless advanced from one occasion when it says, "A
car" to another occasion when it then too says, "A
car." Since there is a cause of doing so, there is
sufficiency. It further follows that means adequate
for doing so do not include drawing a comparison. Nor
can perception make up the defect. For we do not perceive sameness or similarity.
KATHERINE: (looking at Julian and then turning to
Keith) I suppose Julian understands you better than I
do. (turning again to Julian) I'm not sure I'm taking
all this in. It is sometimes said that a child proceeds by analogy. But analogy is said to rest upon
some kind of likeness or similarity. So if a child ad-
vances by means of an analogy, it must perceive, recognize or think a certain likeness or similarity. Of
course, I may not understand analogy any better than I
do Keith. What is an analogy?
RECORDER: I think most people would say that an analogy is a certain likeness between things which, in other
ways, are different. For they say that as one thing
stands to a second, so a third stands to the second.
For example, as objects stand to existence so do universals; for both are said equally to exist. But philosophers speak of an analogy of being because they
wish to deny two propositions. The first is that existence is a universal, as, for example, a color is. For
to say that this book exists and that the number one
exists is not to presuppose that they have the same
property. The second proposition is that the word
"exist" is ambiguous and equivocal. For to say, "This
book exists" is not to use the word "exist" in one
sense and, saying, "The number one exists", in another.
Such philosophers therefore hold that there is a mean
position between univocality and equivocality: the an-
alogical.
(Katherine looks at Alexander, who is shaking his
head.)
KATHERINE: What's the matter?
ALEXANDER: Is it true that our tradition's account of
analogy is based upon the assumption that, at bottom,
there is likeness or similarity?
RECORDER: Yes, I think so.

KEITH: Then to hell with the account.   It presupposes
what we have recently given ourselves cause to reject:
a roadway of similarity.   It seems to me to be true
that the word "exist" is not used ambiguously when I go
from asserting, "This book exists" to asserting, "The
number one exists."   Nor does my advance rest upon the
shoulders of a comparison.   It is not as if I reason,
"Since this exists and this and the number one have a
certain likeness, it too must exist."
(5)
CHANCELLOR: We have discussed skeptical argumentation
with respect to the three steps of the first stage.
Let us now consider skepticism with respect to the second stage: that of use.   By employing paths of language
laid down I make an ordinary assertion: for example,
that the name of that cat is George.
RECORDER: I mean to apply to the assertion a general
skeptical method.   To make clear what the method is let
us suppose we entertain two mutually exclusive alternatives.   The first is that that cat is George; the second is that that cat is not George.   The first premiss
of the method is that if we allow the possibility of
the second alternative, we cannot consistently claim
the certainty of the first one.
ALEXANDER: I assent to the first premiss.
RECORDER: The second premiss is that whatever is conceivable is possible.   It is an established maxim of
metaphysics that whatever is conceivable contains the
idea of possible existence.   Now the Chancellor purported to deliver to us a piece of knowledge when he
asserted that the name of that cat is George.   In addition to the alternative which he gives us I can conceive another, namely that the name of that cat is not
George.   Since the second alternative is conceivable,
it is possible.   We can accordingly allow its possibility.   By the first premiss and the law of modus ponens
I infer that we cannot consistently claim the certainty
of the first alternative.   The Chancellor's assertion
is therefore doubtful.   By application of the same
method we can say that all such assertions and claims
are doubtful.
ALEXANDER: Let us examine your argument.   I accept the
first premiss: one cannot consistently claim a possibility and claim a certainty to the contrary.   But the
second premiss appears to be doubtful in light of an
account of differences between two senses of "possible".   The first sense is that of "can" and the second
is that of the phrase "it is possible that."
RECORDER: What are the senses of the words?   There is
a good deal of controversy about them.

(6)

ALEXANDER: Both expressions belong to the same family
and to the same genus of that family. The word "can"
indicates sufficiency of a range of subjects for an objective; further, the word helps make clear what the
range of subjects is. For example, when I assert, "He
can lift it," I assert sufficiency of a range of subjects including having strength and time; the word
"can" does not indicate what objectives are aimed at.
So let us say that "can" indicates sufficiency of a
marked range of subjects for an objective.
RECORDER: I follow your remarks about "can"; what is
conceivability?
ALEXANDER: Conceivability is sufficiency of conceptual
resources for laying out a path of language. Answering
the question whether certain resources are adequate depends upon knowledge of the genus of the projected path
of language: whether one means to continue a fairy
tale, write a piece of history, develop a science or
give an argument in philosophy.
RECORDER: And what is the sense of the phrase "it is
possible that"?
ALEXANDER: The phrase indicates sufficiency of a range
of subjects for an objective; further, it helps make
clear what objectives fall within the range of objectives: in particular opening or starting an inquiry.
For example, when I assert, "It is possible that he
will lift it," I assert sufficiency of taking a path of
language for opening an inquiry. When I assert, "It is
probable that he will lift it," I assert sufficiency of
taking a path of language for going half-way along a
line of inquiry. When I assert, "It is certain that he
will lift it," I assert sufficiency of means for concluding an inquiry.
RECORDER: I wish to make quite sure I have your account of power and possibility. The words "can",
"able" and "conceivable" indicate sufficiency of a
range of subjects for an objective; "can" and "able"
indicate a marked range of subjects but not of objectives; "conceivable" indicates marked ranges of both:
certain resources adequate for conception; by "conception" we understand "laying out a path of language in
a certain genus of activity." Is so much enough of a
review of your account of power?
KATHERINE: Yes.
RECORDER: On the other side the words "possible",
"probable" and "certain" indicate sufficiency of an un-
marked range of subjects for a marked range of objectives: opening, continuing and concluding inquiry. But
we know by analysis that means said to be sufficient

194

for such an objective is the laying down or taking of a
subordinate path of language.
ALEXANDER: Both your reviews are accurate. Perhaps we
can return to our example of skeptical argumentation.
KATHERINE: Before we do so, I would like to put a
question. You distinguish objectives of potentiality
from objectives of actuality. To which class do you
assign opening and continuing an inquiry?
ALEXANDER: To the class of objectives of actuality.
For he who asserts possibility takes a step forward.
KATHERINE: Yes, I see. Perhaps we should return to
the original argument.
(7)
ALEXANDER: When Julian laid out the argument, he gave
two premises. The second is that whatever is conceivable is possible. I hope we are now in a position to
examine its use in epistemology for defect, sufficiency
or excess.
CHANCELLOR: I hope other members of my Academy will
follow philosophers in the care you've shown with keeping your own house in order.
ALEXANDER: To assert the second premiss is to assert
that if there are resources adequate for a certain conceptual activity, for example laying out a path of language, then there are means adequate for opening a line
of inquiry; further, an act of conceiving is adequate
for opening an inquiry. Do you mean to say that to
have means adequate for conception is to have a conception adequate for starting an inquiry?
RECORDER: Yes.
ALEXANDER: Suppose you lay down a path of language by
means of which you begin a fairy tale. You say, "A
long time ago there lived a king who was famed for his
wisdom through all the land." Have means been deployed
adequate for conception?
RECORDER: Yes.
ALEXANDER: And so adequate too for starting an inquiry
by asserting or allowing, "So it is possible that there
was such a king"?
RECORDER: One would go too far in making such an inference.
ALEXANDER: Then are we to criticize such a use of the
premiss for excess?
RECORDER: Yes.
ALEXANDER: Then your skeptical argumentation ought not
rely upon use of the premiss. Let us examine your argument from another point of view. According to your
argument the Chancellor asserts, "The name of that cat
is George." You shrug your shoulders and reply, "That
cat may be Henry." At a certain level of domination

you make a claim or an allowance (I'll turn to their difference in a moment). We know that every claim or allowance is immediately one of sufficiency; we accordingly inquire as to subject and objective. The subject is taking a path of language; a high ranking objective is reaching knowledge as to the name of that cat; your immediate objective is taking one step forwards towards reaching the achievement of knowledge. You claim or allow means adequate for approach; the Chancellor asserts means adequate for reaching the achievement. There is inconsistency between you because means for opening your line of inquiry and for closing his are excessive for the pursuit of the same achievement, though in fact you both aim at it.

CHANCELLOR: I have no doubt that you have correctly explicated our predicament. You have not yet resolved it. You will surely not take excessive care in forcing us to understand ourselves.

ALEXANDER: Let us next be clear about the difference between allowing and claiming. One can allow a possibility in the face of no inconsistency with a relevant body of acts and achievements. One can also allow and suppose by isolating the genus of such allowances and suppositions and merely play a game.

RECORDER: I have no wish to isolate my skepticism.

ALEXANDER: Indeed. Since the Chancellor claims to be in perceptual and epistemic positions adequate for disclosing the name of that cat, you cannot mean to allow a possibility to the contrary. You must wish to claim. Since you claim a possibility and contradict the Chancellor, you must have a reason.

RECORDER: I do have a reason. You neglect an established premiss of logic: whatever is self-consistent is possible. So since the alternative path "That cat is Henry" is self-consistent, there is reason for claiming that it is possible that that cat is Henry. Since so much is possible, the Chancellor is wrong in thinking it certain that the cat's name is George. According to my record I stand on a firm tradition. I have it written here that if an assertion implies nothing contradictory, it is possible.

ALEXANDER: Your record weighs heavy upon you. You have been challenged to think the notions of truth and falsity by means of a triad rather than by means of a duality; you are challenged to befriend defect, sufficiency and excess. Nothing less is expected of you with respect to consistency. Should we suppose that to deny inconsistency is to assert consistency? Suppose someone were foolish enough to assert that this cup and this saucer are inconsistent. Would you not keep your

wits about you and deny inconsistency in favor of arguing indifference?
RECORDER: Yes.
ALEXANDER: Would you tolerate a logician inferring, "So they must be consistent"?
RECORDER: No. There is too little for concluding consistency. But my example is not analogous. When I utter the words "that cat", I mean to set forth an alternative; when I go on to utter the word "Henry", I aim at the same objective. It therefore follows by your definition that there is consistency between my use of the words "that cat" and my use of the word "Henry".
ALEXANDER: I agree that so much does follow. But I deny that it follows that the alternative is possible. For to prove that there is no inconsistency between parts of a whole is not to prove that there is no inconsistency between a whole and its environment. To prove that there is consistency between use of the words "that cat" and use of the word "Henry" is not to prove that there is consistency between allowing that that cat is Henry and other acts and achievements.
KATHERINE: You are bound to agree with him, Julian. Proving consistency in the use of parts of a sentence does not prove consistency between the sentence and its relevant environment. Consistency between the use of parts of a sentence is therefore too weak a basis for arguing the possibility of the whole sentence.
RECORDER: If I am bound to agree, so is Hume. In An Inquiry Concerning Human Understanding (Section IV) he gives the following argument. The contrary of every matter of fact is still possible; for it can never imply a contradiction and is conceived by the mind with the same facility and distinctness as if ever so conformable to reality. "That the sun will not rise tomorrow" is no less intelligible a proposition and implies no more contradiction than the affirmation "That it will rise." We should in vain, therefore, attempt to demonstrate its falsehood. Were it demonstratively false, it would imply a contradiction and could never be distinctly conceived by the mind.
ALEXANDER: What is the basic premiss or premisses from which Hume reasons? He and Berkeley write in such an elegant and polite way that it is difficult to distinguish premiss from conclusion.
RECORDER: One premiss is that if anything is demonstratively false, then it implies a contradiction and cannot be distinctly conceived. The minor premiss is that the sentence "The sun will not rise tomorrow" does not imply a contradiction and can be distinctly conceived. I can think the sentence, Hume writes, as if

ever so conformable to reality.

ALEXANDER: We reject the major premiss. For even an
allowance of demonstrative falsity is not sufficient
for concluding that there is inconsistency between
parts of that whole said to be false. But if something
is allowed to be false, then there is inconsistency between it and something else said to be true. Although
the sentence "The sun will not rise tomorrow" is not
internally inconsistent, there is inconsistency between
it and the assertion that the sun will rise tomorrow.
There is therefore not a basis sufficient for allowing
possibility. Reasons are accordingly demanded for
claiming that it is possible that the sun will not rise
tomorrow. Do you have any to give?

RECORDER: No. I am bound to agree with you that you
have shifted the burden of proof upon me. I cannot
accept it.

ALEXANDER: Then do you have any reason at all for believing or for suspecting that it is possible that this
is another cat than that named George?

RECORDER: No, none. For generating skeptical argumentation I have been trying to follow general methods. I
have no particular case to make against taking it for
granted that the Chancellor is in perceptual and epistemic positions adequate for disclosing the name of
that cat.

ALEXANDER: Then I can conclude that our two stages of
ascent are safe from a general attack launched according to skeptical methods.

(8)

KEITH: I have tried to follow the conversation between
Professor Alexander and Julian with appropriate care.
Perhaps the argument which I wish to give has already
been shown to be defective or excessive in some way.
If so, you must pardon me my inattentiveness; if not, I
wish to know how it is to be criticized. There is a
premiss which I think deserves employment at a fairly
basic level of our logic; it is that whatever is possibly so is possibly not so. My first premiss can surely
be allowed to cooperate with a second one: that what is
certain is possible. Now the Chancellor asserts that
it is certain that the name of that cat is George. By
the second premiss it follows that that cat may be
George, and by the first premiss, that it is possible
that that cat is not George. But some time ago there
was general consent that there is inconsistency between
an assertion of certainty and one of possibility to the
contrary. Since I have grounded the inference that
that cat may not be George by means of deep logical
premisses, we must give up the assertion that it is

certain that the name of the cat is George. Now I
think it evident that such reasoning can be widened by
a philosopher of a skeptical disposition and can be
used to throw doubt upon a large class of assertions.
KATHERINE: I am as unclear as Keith is whether you
have already shown us how to examine such an argument
as Keith has given. I certainly think you should make
perfectly clear to us how to go about its examination.
You remarked some time ago that philosophy is the chief
watch over the office of criticism. I presume that you
should set a precedent for the conduct of the office.
So I think Keith's two premisses provide an opportunity
for you to demonstrate points you were recently making
to the Chancellor.
ALEXANDER: I shall by all means try to satisfy you. I
can follow my method of examination first with respect
to the premiss "Whatever is certain is possible." We
first inquire what its end or objective is. We inquire, second, what its genus or discipline is.
KEITH: The second question is easy to answer: it belongs to the discipline of logic.
ALEXANDER: And how do you answer the first question?
KEITH: The objective is one of potentiality: making it
possible to infer possibility. Now since possibility
is sufficiency of resources for beginning or opening an
inquiry or a line of thought, the objective of the
premiss is potential overture of a line of thought.
ALEXANDER: Good. Let us suppose your premiss is correctly formed and turn to questions about its use. For
it is meant to be an instrument whose use is to conduct
affairs appropriate to logic. Our question is accordingly whether logic should keep the premiss in use; our
task is to conduct an inquiry sufficient to show whether logic should license its continued use. We consider
its use in two steps: application and following. To
take the two steps let us tell a story such as the following. The Chancellor asserts the certainty that the
name of that cat is George. Enough is thereby done to
make application of your premiss. Now how are we to
evaluate the following conversation? The Chancellor
says, "That cat is called George." I would like to
know how we are to think of the continuity of the conversation if you continue, "It may be called George."
Listen to yourself saying this: "It may indeed be
called George."
KEITH: I don't know what to say.
ALEXANDER: Does a good conversation have a beginning,
a middle and an end?
KEITH: Yes, I suppose so.
ALEXANDER: The Chancellor makes a beginning when he

says, "We call that cat George." Do you continue and
develop the conversation by saying, "Yes, and it may be
George"?
KEITH: It would be ridiculous to think there would be
continuousness.
ALEXANDER: You are quick to use the word "ridiculous".
Can we get our criticism precise?
KEITH: What do you mean?
ALEXANDER: If you do say, "...may be George," do you
stretch or shrink the conversation?
KEITH: I would set it back.
ALEXANDER: Then are we to criticize the use of your
premiss for defect or for excess?
KEITH: For defect. Having made a start it would put
us behind the starting line.
ALEXANDER: Then let us ban use of the second premiss.
KEITH: So my premiss has been convicted of some species of defect; we should accordingly free our new
academy of it. I think there are logicians who would
be moved to disquiet upon seeing it removed from their
games. I can hear Aristotle reply as follows. "If the
premiss is not true, it is false. If false, then, as
you yourselves say, a consequence of its use leads to
inconsistency. So much has not been shown. Even if
inconsistency were shown, we should seek resolution by
denying the given possibility. You would then have
abandoned a secure premiss for an impossible one, namely that what is certain is sometimes certainly not so."
Can't you hear some such reply arising from the pages
of Aristotle's On Interpretation?
RECORDER: I can.
KATHERINE: Of course you can, Julian. When any philosophical issue is raised, you hear a thousand voices
raised from a thousand texts. How are we to reply,
Professor Alexander?
ALEXANDER: The reply reasons from an excessive principle.
KATHERINE: You mean the law of the excluded middle.
ALEXANDER: Yes. For to say that any statement is true
or false is to say either that there are resources ade-
quate for a certain objective or that there are other
resources adequate for the objective. But it is excessive to assume as much.
KEITH: I am satisfied with your answer to the reply.
What about my first premiss, that what is possibly so
is possibly not so?
ALEXANDER: I think it can be convicted not of defect
but of excess.
KEITH: How?
ALEXANDER: I think it runs afoul of a general princi-

ple which I hope you can accept. Suppose we wish to
know whether to keep a certain premiss in use. Suppose
further that application is made without causing inconsistency. But by following the premiss inconsistency
does arise. The principle is that if we are not willing to make anything else superfluous, then we should
criticize use of the premiss for excess.
KEITH: I can accept the principle without hesitation.
It naturally hangs together with our discussion of indifference, consistency and inconsistency.
ALEXANDER: Suppose Katherine asks you, "What is the
name of that cat?" You reply, "I don't know. It may
be called George." The Chancellor, overhearing your
conversation, turns and says, "It is called George."
Shall we say that there is inconsistency between your
reply and his remark?
KEITH: According to our definition of inconsistency
there is none. I am not prepared to say that there is
consistency either.
ALEXANDER: It doesn't matter so long as you agree that
there is either indifference or consistency.
KEITH: I do.
ALEXANDER: Let us now make use of your first premiss.
We make application by allowing that it is possible
that that cat is George. The premiss is applied after
you give your answer, let us imagine, and before the
Chancellor makes his remark. It follows that the cat
may not be George. But the inference and the Chancellor's remark are inconsistent.
KEITH: We can resolve the inconsistency either by setting aside the Chancellor's remark or by banning the
use of my premiss. For what reason should we choose
one alternative over the other?
ALEXANDER: Use of your premiss makes it possible to
criticize the development of the conversation for excessive speed.
KEITH: What do you mean?
ALEXANDER: According to our use of your premiss we
should say the Chancellor went too far or jumped too
fast; for he carried the conversation into excess,
namely that of inconsistency.
KEITH: I see. But such criticism we should not try to
ground in advance of any particular conversation.
ALEXANDER: Are you satisfied with the analysis and the
resolution of your argument?
KEITH: Yes. It is extraordinary how many odd conclusions are generated by means of premisses which employ
words indicating power or possibility. Many arguments
are defective, I suppose, because of equivocation.
RECORDER: What are you thinking of?

KEITH: Just now I was thinking of an argument which I
have heard given for the principle of plenitude. The
principle is that any potentiality is realized in the
long run.
KATHERINE: Now there is an implausible principle.
KEITH: There is a derivative of the principle which
fits you, Katherine: it is called Murphy's Law. "Whatever can go wrong will go wrong."
RECORDER: I think we see the principle, not the law,
at work in Aquinas's third way of proving God's existence. Some of the things we come across can be but
need not be. For we find them springing up and dying
away. Now everything cannot be like this; for a thing
that need not be once was not, and if everything need
not be, once upon a time there was nothing. So much is
not true; so there must be something necessary.
KATHERINE: And guess who that is.
KEITH: So the principle of plenitude is used in this
way: anything corruptible will, during infinite time,
cease to be. It follows that there would be a time at
which all corruptible things would cease to be.
KATHERINE: I'm no great theologian, as you people
know. But even I can see what's wrong with that argument. Doesn't the principle require meeting two conditions in order to be applicable? I mean potentiality
and unrestricted duration?
RECORDER: Yes.
KATHERINE: Suppose, as I believe Aquinas held, that
the universe began and that God in fact caused it to
begin. Between then and now a certain duration has
elapsed. On the day of creation an angel says, "The
sun that Katherine Woods will one day see can burn out.
Therefore, by the principle of plenitude it one day
will burn out." Surely the principle is not meant to
predict the day of actuality as falling within a limited duration.
RECORDER: Indeed not.
KATHERINE: Then Aquinas is not right in arguing that
between then and now there would have been nothing if
everything had been contingent and corruptible.
RECORDER: I suppose not.
KEITH: It's not worth your time getting so fine a
point straight. The principle rests upon an argument
in which there is equivocation. As Aristotle delivers
the argument, it goes something like this: it is inconsistent both to say, "He might be at home" and to say,
"But he is not." Therefore, if the first is true, the
second is false. It accordingly follows that if there
is potentiality, there is sometimes actuality. You can
see that the argument begins with possibility and ends

with power and potentiality.

RECORDER: (During Keith's last remark the Porter entered and began to serve brandy and coffee. When he came to Katherine, he said:)

PORTER: And what have you been talking about the last hour?

KATHERINE: Skepticism. You remember, when you were here at five o'clock, I told you a story about a gardener who moves around our framework, cutting away stems of falsity.

PORTER: Yes.

KATHERINE: Well, we've found out he can't cut the whole tree down. He only cuts when he also preserves.

PORTER: So not everything can be false. Consoling thought, isn't it? When your gardener goes to work, he has triads of tools on his back, doesn't he?

KATHERINE: Yes.

PORTER: He looks for defect, sufficiency or excess.

KATHERINE: Right.

PORTER: Even if he can't cut the whole tree down, can't he deny that there is a single blossom on it?

KATHERINE: What do you mean?

PORTER: Isn't the objective even of the critical work of your gardener the achievement of knowledge?

KATHERINE: Yes, and if not that, then opening and continuing inquiry. I still don't follow your use of my analogy.

PORTER: To trim is to find false; but one can't trim one stem without conserving another. I very well see why such a trimmer would not make a great skeptic. But imagine a gardener who finds your tree weak, unhealthy and impotent.

KATHERINE: I see: it's growth is not adequate for knowledge. Not because stems are false; because they are exiguous. (turning to Alexander) Have we already considered such a possibility for skepticism?

ALEXANDER: I don't think so. Julian will know for sure.

RECORDER: I have nothing in my record.

ALEXANDER: I don't think we have time tonight. Perhaps we can take the new suggestion up another time.

KATHERINE: Yes, I think we should. (The Porter left.)

(9)

ALEXANDER: We have sufficiently considered skepticism in relation to our accounts of the stages of knowledge. Let us consider in a summary way philosophical positions which are open to us. We can then conclude our conversation by considering schools of philosophy which in one way or another are defective or excessive. We may succeed in protecting ourselves both against too much skepticism and also against too much dogmatism.

Our interests today have been predominantly meta-physical, logical and epistemological. With respect to metaphysics we consider particulars and universals and also mind and matter. Both considerations have been organized by means of certain metaphysical premises. The first concerns sameness and otherness, and the second, bridgework which carries the mind from the first minor family--that of sameness and otherness--to the second or the third.

On the epistemological side we ask ourselves what means are sufficient for reaching achievements of knowledge and disclosure. Rationalist philosophers answer, "By thought alone;" empiricist philosophers answer, "In part by perception." On the logical side, finally, we ask ourselves what truth is. Correspondence gives an answer in terms of sameness; coherence, in terms of consistency, and neo-pragmatism, in terms of sufficiency.

I touch upon questions and issues which we have discussed today in one way or another and in more or less detail. I would like to know whether you have any particular interest in any school which works out a position on the issues which concern us.

CHANCELLOR: We're willing to follow your lead. You must know what it is important for us to emphasize.

RECORDER: Perhaps I can help us to articulate our interests. You know I'm partial to graphs that can lay out all the possibilities.

KEITH: Do you think you'll ever go from keeping your records of conversations to writing a systematic treatise, Julian?

RECORDER: I don't know. To make clear what the possible schools of thought are let me consider mind and matter. For every great school of thought will have a central position regarding mind and matter. All schools fall into one of two possible classes: monistic and pluralistic. In the first class there are two possible schools: spiritual monism and materialistic monism. In the second class there are two sub-classes. The first holds that mind and matter are distinct and mutually dependent; the second sub-class holds that mind and matter are distinct and dependent but one alone on the other. In the first sub-class is the third possible school of thought; let us call it interactionism. In the second sub-class are the fourth and fifth possible schools of thought. The fourth is that mind depends upon matter but matter not upon mind. The fourth we can call epiphenomenalism. The fifth, finally, is that matter depends upon mind but mind not upon

204

matter.
KEITH: Whatever are you going to call the fifth?
KATHERINE: Natural theology.
RECORDER: I don't mind. Let us arrange them along a
line; at the ends of the line are two extreme positions: spiritual monism and materialistic monism. Put
spiritual monism at the far left. Next comes natural
theology; next to materialistic monism place epiphenomenalism. In the middle place interactionism.
KATHERINE: Which is suitable, since it happens to hit
the Mean and, even more accidentally, is your position.
Right?
ALEXANDER: The art of display does not teach us what
we ought to believe. Let us by all means cast an eye
along Julian's line and ask ourselves where the burden
of proof or of disproof lies.
RECORDER: It is surely helpful to locate and to refute, if possible, extreme positions.
(10)
ALEXANDER: You remarked this morning, Keith, that when
you went to college, you became an idealist. Were you
influenced by your reading of George Berkeley?
KEITH: I was overwhelmed.
ALEXANDER: I would like to have us consider idealism.
We have been considering excessive skepticism; it was
our intention to consider excessive dogmatism. I suppose you are by now immunized against severe idealism,
despite its newly found life. Are you willing to try
to regain a portion of your early enthusiasm and interest?
KEITH: Of course. It seemed to me that idealism rests
upon three pillars. The first is the premiss that to
perceive is to perceive sensible qualities; the second
is a definition of existence or reality: to be is to be
perceived. The third is a conceptual experiment to
reveal the neglected point of view. How do you wish to
have us order our discussion?
ALEXANDER: Let us begin with the definition; for its
use surely reveals the heart of idealism. Are you
quite sure you are willing to assume an old habit of
thought and do what you can do to state and defend it?
KEITH: Yes. I said I'm willing.
ALEXANDER: Taking account of our distinction between
perceptions and thought how would you state your definition of existence?
KEITH: To exist is either to think or to perceive or
to be thought or perceived. Whatever exists is a mind
or an object of a mind.
ALEXANDER: Suppose I assert, "This book exists." Its
existence is its being seen. So when I make the asser-

tion, I must mean, "I can see it."
KEITH: Yes. Berkeley himself writes as much. Explicating the term "exist" when applied to sensible things he writes, "The table I write on exists; that is, I see and feel it."
ALEXANDER: You know that we sometimes say something like the following: I could not see that book if it did not exist. Do we talk nonsense when we say such things?
KEITH: No.
ALEXANDER: If the one has the same meaning as the other, then one would be saying: I could not see that book if I did not see it. Do you think that I issue the same piece of reasoning twice?
KEITH: No.
ALEXANDER: Then can "exist" mean "see" or "be seen"?
KEITH: No.
ALEXANDER: Nor is it in your interest to answer in the affirmative. For you wish to say, "Whatever is apart from any mind does not exist" and not thereby mean, "Whatever is apart from any mind is not an object of a mind." Rather than repeat yourself you wish to make a metaphysical point.
KEITH: Of course. You're quite right.
ALEXANDER: Suppose Katherine returns home one day with something wrapped up. She undoes the wrapping and shows you what she has bought. You say, "What beautiful flowers!" She replies, "They are not real flowers." Do you act upon what she has in her hands differently before than after her reply?
KEITH: No. I look at and keep in sight what she shows me. Her denial of reality does not concern looking at, seeing or their object. I see whatever it is I see, whether or not she is right in holding that these are not real flowers. But although there is no difference with respect to perception, there is a difference with respect to thought. For I think different things. First I think, "What beautiful flowers;" I then think, "They are not real flowers." My second object of thought is not an object of perception.
ALEXANDER: Then to deny the reality of the flowers is not to deny that a certain thing is an object of perception.
KEITH: I meant to concede as much.
ALEXANDER: Then is to deny the reality of the flowers to deny that a certain thing is an object of thought?
KEITH: Sorry, I'm having a hard time following.
ALEXANDER: If to assert the reality of something is to assert that it is an object of perception or thought, then to deny the reality of something is to deny that

it is an object of either perception or thought.
KEITH: I see. The consequence surely does follow from
my definition.
ALEXANDER: Then when you think, "They are not real
flowers," you deny that the sentence "They are flowers"
reveals an object of thought. Have I given you a
plausible interpretation of what one means when one
says, "They are not real flowers" or "Unicorns are not
real"?
KEITH: No.
ALEXANDER: Then can use of your definition be sufficient for helping to account for what we mean when we
assert or deny existence and reality?
KEITH: No, it cannot be sufficient.
ALEXANDER: And for what have I criticized the definition: for defect or for excess?
KEITH: I have been taking it for granted that if use
of an instrument of reason leads to defect and if its
application is sufficient, then we should criticize the
instrument itself for defect. If, on the other hand,
use of an instrument leads to excess and if its application is sufficient, then we should criticize the instrument itself for excess.
ALEXANDER: Surely you do nothing more than adapt
statements of modus tollens in light of our earlier
discussions.
KEITH: Then I would say that consequences of the use
of the idealist definition of existence and reality
conflict with assumptions of good sense. The definition is therefore excessive. It should accordingly be
set aside in favor of another.
KATHERINE: I think it's fun refuting idealism--an old
enemy of mine anyway, you know. There is another ridiculous consequence. Suppose I deny reality when I
say, "Unicorns do not exist." Now, Keith, play the
role of a dummy in one of Plato's early dialogues.
Julian envies Plato his style of dialogue; he'll write
you above yourself.
KEITH: You all hate me. First Bill gets me to put on
old clothes--clothes I've not worn for five years.
Then, when I'm undressing, you mock me.
KATHERINE: Nonsense! Now listen. I say, "Unicorns do
not exist." When I say, "unicorns," do I say something
or nothing?
KEITH: Something.
KATHERINE: Something that is or something that isn't?
KEITH: Now you mock not only me but Plato too.
KATHERINE: Something that is or something that isn't?
KEITH: Something that is.
KATHERINE: And does it not follow in two ways that the

207

thing said is an object of mind?

KEITH: What do you mean, "in two ways"?

KATHERINE: If I succeed in saying something, then the thing said is an object of mind; second, since the thing said is, then by your definition of reality it is an object of mind.

KEITH: Yes, I see.

KATHERINE: I then go on to deny both that what is is and, second, that what is an object of mind is an object of mind. Now can it be my meaning, when I deny that unicorns exist, to contradict myself twice?

KEITH: No.

KATHERINE: So once again we see that your definition is excessive.

CHANCELLOR: The spirit of refutation is evidently contagious. Surely the definition does not deserve a third round of refutation. I would have students as much encouraged to build up as to tear down.

KEITH: Indeed. And I really would like to get out of these old clothes.

ALEXANDER: If you take them to a pawn shop, I assure you they'll be bought up. We are not done with idealism. The Chancellor will see it rise in his new academy.

KATHERINE: Even in Alberta?

RECORDER: That is the remark of an American.

KATHERINE: And that, of a Canadian.

KEITH: (turning to Alexander) Let us dampen the spirit of controversy. You do see how its bonds come undone. So I should ask you: What is it to assert or to deny the existence or the reality of something?

CHANCELLOR: Yes, do say. Delivery from error is only secured by positive, adequate theory.

(11)

ALEXANDER: Existence or reality is sufficiency of subject for objective. Subjects and objectives are both of potentiality and of actuality. Our first example was "This book exists." To assert existence is to assert sufficiency of the coordinated use of the word "book" for reaching a certain goal; so the subject is coordinated use of a certain expression and the objective is reaching a certain goal.

KEITH: Are you willing to have me try to examine your definition in a way parallel to that in which you examined mine?

ALEXANDER: Of course. The spirit of refutation must not be dampened in order to protect my definitions.

KEITH: From my definition it followed that whatever exists is a mind or an object of a mind. Something parallel surely follows from yours: whenever existence

is asserted, sufficiency is asserted of coordinated use of an expression for an objective. So when I assert, "This book exists," I must mean, "Use of the word 'book' is adequate for saying of this what it is."
ALEXANDER: Such a consequence is forthcoming.
KEITH: Now surely I actually put the word to a use I claim is adequate for reaching an end I actually reach. So I claim that that can be done that I actually do do. Would I not make a similar demonstration of adequacy by asserting, "This is a book"?
ALEXANDER: Yes.
KEITH: Then what is the difference between asserting, "This book exists" and asserting "This is a book"?
ALEXANDER: In the first instance you claim resources adequate for doing what you do do; in the second you do do what you do not claim resources adequate for doing.
KEITH: There must be a fine distinction between being and existence which I still fail to grasp.
ALEXANDER: When I assert that this is a book, I assert the adequacy of a subject, namely the use of "this", gesturing and the use of "a book" for an objective. When I assert that this book exists, I assert the adequacy of a subject, namely the use of "book", further coordinated, for an objective. The subject of being is completely specified; that of existence is not.
KEITH: I'm satisfied with your reply. Let me try something else. I would not be right in asserting of this that it is a book if it did not exist. Is my premiss a sufficiently good one?
ALEXANDER: I think so.
KEITH: According to your definition I would not be right in asserting of this that it is a book if use of the word "this" were not adequate for making clear what, for example, is before us.
ALEXANDER: Does thus making use of the definition lead to defect or excess?
KEITH: No.
ALEXANDER: Then have I given you a satisfying replacement for your old definition of existence and reality?
KEITH: Yes. But is there a great difference between your definition and that of idealism?
ALEXANDER: There is a difference. By my account it does not follow that anything which exists is an object of experience.
KEITH: But such a premiss we cannot unseat from our thought. Berkeley proved as much. You say nothing is easier than to imagine trees in a park and no one by to perceive them. Berkeley draws us close to our thought-experiment: we frame in our minds certain ideas we call trees and at the same time omit to frame the idea of

anyone who perceives them. But do not you yourself perceive or think of them all the while? This, therefore, is nothing to the purpose; you have not shown that you can conceive it possible that the objects of your thought exist without the mind; to do so you would have to conceive them existing unconceived or unthought of--which is a manifest repugnancy.

In light of Berkeley's argument I ask you how you mean to purge your account of the premiss that anything which exists is an object of experience.

ALEXANDER: By showing that its use leads to falsity. Suppose I assert that there exists a tree in that forest which has never been experienced by people nor animals nor yet thought of or about by anyone.

KEITH: By your definition it follows that use of the words "a tree", together with the use of certain other resources, is adequate for a certain end. What would be an example of reaching an appropriate end?

ALEXANDER: Suppose we walk through the forest tomorrow. You point to something and say, "There is a tree which has never been seen before nor yet thought about." Such a coordinated use of your words would be enough to demonstrate the adequacy which was promised but not realized by the consequence of my definition of existence and reality.

KEITH: But when you say, "There exists a tree in that forest," are you not thinking of the tree which we eventually find?

ALEXANDER: Are you serious?

KEITH: Yes.

ALEXANDER: I was supposing that we walk through the forest tomorrow. Would you be serious if you said, "I wonder whether this is the tree of which you were yesterday thinking when you said, 'There exists a tree in the forest which is unthought of'?"

KEITH: It would be absurd to say so.

ALEXANDER: Then when I say, "There exists a tree in that forest of which mankind has had no experience," I do not myself realize potential use of the words "a tree" in saying what it is to which I now refer, think of or speak about. I do assert that such a goal can be reached; I do not claim that I thereby reach it.

KATHERINE: You may know of a journal recently founded in Edmonton: The Compass. In the recent issue William Bowman Piper published a paper on Berkeley and the style of common sense. He argues that Berkeley manages a proof within polite conversation. It seems to me that Piper accedes to the experiment which you discuss. He concludes his paper by summarizing a discussion between the two characters of Berkeley's dialogue,

210

Philonous and Hylas. Piper remarks, as I remember,
that Hylas puzzles out the explanation of his original
error, that is, his neglect of his own conceptual in-
volvement in the case. Hylas thus helps to compose the
philosophy which he had set out to destroy. As he does
so, he accommodates to common sense the opinion he at
first pronounced to be the most extravagant that ever
entered the mind of man.
KEITH: Accommodates to common sense?
KATHERINE: His writing those words led me to say that
Piper accedes to the experiment.
KEITH: Can he really have been led by Berkeley's argument to disown the reaction of a man of good sense?
KATHERINE: What do you mean?
KEITH: Suppose you say to me, "Tomorrow, if I decide
to remain in Edmonton, I shall look for an apartment."
Suppose we meet tomorrow afternoon. Would I show good
sense if I said, "Did you find the apartment to which
you made reference when you said, 'I shall look for an
apartment'?"
KATHERINE: No, you would not.
KEITH: Everyone owes himself enough philosophy to master a distinction between the two following conceptual
experiments. First, suppose you have lost a pencil;
you look about and find it; you say, "I have found the
pencil which I was looking for." Second, suppose you
are looking for an apartment; you look about town; you
find--not "it" but--one; you say, "I have found one."
KATHERINE: Indeed. We owe ourselves--Piper owes him-
self--an understanding of saying, in the one case, "I
found it" and saying, in the other, "I found one."
ALEXANDER: I think we have finished with idealism.
When we opened our discussion, Keith said that idealism
rests upon three pillars. The first, that to perceive
is to perceive sensible qualities, we have torn down
long ago. The second is a definition which we have replaced, and the third, is a conceptual experiment which
we have diagnosed and set aside.
KATHERINE: Things feel slightly unreal to me at the
moment.
KEITH: (looking surprised) Why?
KATHERINE: You and Bill have settled the question what
existence is or what reality is, as if someone had
asked you what your name is. Philosophers have grap-
pled with the question what existence is. Can it be
answered so easily?
ALEXANDER: I hope you are not misplacing difficulty.
I have already had occasion today to remind you that to
define truth is not to say what in particular is true.
Similarly, to define existence is not to say what in

211

particular exists. You also know our method according
to which we make a transition from defining reality,
for example, to accounting for what it is to assert reality. Knowing the definition is one subject sufficient in its own way for knowing what it is to assert
reality.
RECORDER: It seems to be taking me a long time to get
an account of your method through my head. Plato too
undertook to define reality. Reality is a form distinct from sameness and otherness. Some of us thus understand his Sophist. So far there is agreement with
Plato. You part company, I take it, when he further
inquires about the relation between reality and other
things. For when you say that reality is sufficiency
of something for something, your method does not invite
the question, "What is the relation between sufficiency
and other things?"
ALEXANDER: Right. Arguments have been given today for
saying that such a question is defective. Plato's interest in the question is misplaced; it wants placing
at a later stage.
RECORDER: Plato would assert that sameness and otherness exist and underwrite the assertion by an account
of a relation between sameness or otherness and existence. The account is developed, I believe, by means
of a notion of combination and one of part and whole.
ALEXANDER: But we too mean to assert that sameness and
otherness exist. An examination of the assertion for
adequacy is posterior to an account of what it is to
make the assertion: namely to assert the adequacy of
cooperative use of the word "same" or the word "other"
for certain objectives. No question arises as to a relation between sufficiency and sameness.
RECORDER: So your method leads us along a metaphysical
inquiry to doors leading on to critical inquiries. The
chamber in which our metaphysics was done does not have
resources adequate for completing those critical inquiries. Have I correctly represented your view?
ALEXANDER: Yes.
KEITH: Then if we are agreed about how to define existence, I think we are done with idealism.
(12)
RECORDER: Keith is obviously anxious to shed the
clothes of idealism. I don't think you defend Berkeley
as well as one can. His was a mind of great bril-
liance. Making him appear in dull clothes is neither
good history nor good philosophy.
KEITH: You are an historian of philosophy. You raise
Berkeley from the dead. I've had enough.
KATHERINE: And I.

CHANCELLOR: Let us be more tolerant; I am to administer an academy, and Mr. Ingram, my department of philosophy. We must not slight the work of a philosopher of genius. So I think Ingram should play the part of Berkeley; I will have Professor Alexander examine his idealism.
ALEXANDER: Fine. Let us begin here: either your ideas are the same as or others in addition to ideas of God.
RECORDER: You state a premiss which is undeniable.
ALEXANDER: Do you not also hold a version of the principle of atomism: that whatever is distinct may be separate?
RECORDER: Yes. For if there is a distinction, then I can separately conceive two things; if I can separately conceive them, it is possible that they should exist so separated. But I deny that I can abstract one from another or conceive separately those things which it is impossible should exist so separated.
ALEXANDER: And what is distinct is other and what is other is distinct?
RECORDER: Yes.
ALEXANDER: Perhaps we can agree on something else in addition to a premiss and a principle. Our minds and God's mind are distinct. For it would be a heresy to say that your mind is a part of the divine Mind.
RECORDER: Indeed, it would be.
ALEXANDER: And since distinct, separate.
RECORDER: Yes.
ALEXANDER: So there is, if you'll permit me to say it, a metaphysical void between your mind and mine and between each of our minds and God's mind.
RECORDER: Yes.
ALEXANDER: Now let us suppose the first alternative of our premiss: your ideas are the same as some of God's ideas. How did you come to have one of them? How did God give you one of His ideas? Would it not have to pass through a metaphysical void?
RECORDER: Yes, it would have to, if our minds are distinct and separate.
ALEXANDER: And is an idea in a void anything at all?
RECORDER: No, nothing. For to be is either to perceive or to be perceived.
ALEXANDER: So you cannot have acquired any of your ideas from God.
RECORDER: No, none.
ALEXANDER: But our supposition is that all your ideas are the same as some of God's. Can you have acquired any of them?
RECORDER: Not according to our previous argument.
ALEXANDER: Then you are a bare monad, innocent of

213

ideas.

RECORDER: So it would seem. So the supposition must be wrong.

ALEXANDER: Then let us take the second alternative: your ideas are others in addition to ideas of God. You must yourself be the source of all of them.

RECORDER: No other source is possible.

ALEXANDER: Then you are really rather like a god yourself, a creator of a world.

RECORDER: So it would seem.

ALEXANDER: But an odd world.

RECORDER: Why do you say so?

ALEXANDER: Do you not say that an idea and its mind are distinct?

RECORDER: Yes. Spirits and ideas are things so wholly different that when we say, "They exist; they are known," these words must not be thought to signify anything common to both; there is nothing alike or common in them.

ALEXANDER: But if distinct, it is possible that they exist apart. It is therefore false that to be is to be perceived.

RECORDER: They cannot exist apart.

ALEXANDER: Then there are only spirits and nothing else. So once again you would be a bare monad, innocent of ideas.

RECORDER: So it would seem.

ALEXANDER: Then at least one of our instruments used in our metaphysical discussion is excessive. Before you tell me which you would name, I should ask you about a recent remark of yours. You said that when we say of spirits and ideas, "They exist," we must not think that anything in common is signified. Now since you claimed that there is a distinction, you must presuppose use of a common term. Or have you given up our account of sameness and otherness?

RECORDER: No, not at all.

ALEXANDER: Then in stating your distinction you presuppose first that minds are a kind of thing, and, second, that ideas are a kind of thing.

RECORDER: So much must be presupposed.

ALEXANDER: But do I use the words "a kind of thing" in the same sense twice?

RECORDER: No.

ALEXANDER: Then there is inadequate support for taking a path of otherness.

RECORDER: Indeed.

ALEXANDER: So your statement of a distinction is defective.

RECORDER: So it would seem.

ALEXANDER: And how are we to seek resolution?
RECORDER: I think that you have today shown us how to
proceed. We must give up the principle of atomism. It
has been amply shown that it is a principle of excess.
ALEXANDER: And what remains of Berkeley's work? I
don't mean to tamper with your record; nor would I dis-
courage you from hiring someone who can teach Berkeley.
I'm sure the Chancellor and you will help keep
Berkeley's work and thought alive. But I ask you: what
remains of his work which is sufficient and neither defective nor excessive?
RECORDER: Very little.
ALEXANDER: Have we any reason to think highly of his
spiritual monism?
RECORDER: No.
ALEXANDER: Then can we count ourselves free of such an
excess?
RECORDER: Yes, I would say so.
ALEXANDER: Then I think we should turn to the other
form of monism: materialism.
(13)
KATHERINE: (She touches Alexander on the arm) You
move too quickly. It's as if, in one single day, you
want to give Julian a record to publish. Does anyone
here fear for his advancement? (She turns to look at
Keith) I wish I had a camera. I would photograph you
and Julian. You show the pride of someone who had resolved at last to set aside a bad habit.
KEITH: And have we not? (sounding impatient)
KATHERINE: I think you have set aside spiritual monism, but I don't believe for a moment you've freed
yourself from what one might call linguistic idealism.
One of my teachers seemed to me to make Wittgenstein
read like a linguistic idealist. And I think I've
heard Julian come close to such a position when he asserts that to speak correctly is to reveal how the world
is.
KEITH: But today, Katherine, we have made a new resolve. Test us on today's commitments.
KATHERINE: I think you've today committed yourself to
a linguistic idealism which one might put something
like this: to create a language is to create a reality.
KEITH: Come now, Katherine. You're making fun of us.
KATHERINE: You surely hold the following premiss. If
anything is blue, then there is a word "blue" whose use
is adequate for saying of it what color it is.
KEITH: Yes, I do.
KATHERINE: Suppose Descartes's Demon carries us and
your metaphysical premiss into another world. Suppose,
in that world, that there exists no word "blue" use of
which is adequate for the stated objective. By the

215

premiss and modus tollens it follows that nothing in
that world would be blue. Indeed, we can very easily
imagine that no resources have been developed for realizing such an objective. To the extent to which we so
exercise our imagination we also suppose that there
would be nothing of the same color as the sky in our
world. But suppose we come upon a pool of water. I
assert, "Look, Keith! The water has the same color as
our sky does at high noon." It follows that the water
is blue. But according to the conclusion of the argument I just gave the consequence of the second argument
is false.

To relieve the tension created by the arguments
something must be given up. It would be absurd to give
up the assertion that our sky is blue. It would be
equally absurd to give up the claim that this water and
that sky have the same color. So you must either hold
that there have always and everywhere been resources
adequate for disclosing their color or hold that your
metaphysical premiss is false. The first is the exit
of someone mad or desperate. So the reasonable thing
to do would be to give up your metaphysical premiss.
Well, Keith, what do you say?
KEITH: One would think that you had been at the hair-
dresser's while we were discussing truth and falsity.
KATHERINE: (turning to Julian) He's either angry or
frightened. Can you tell which it is?
RECORDER: Leave me out of this.
KEITH: One of your early conclusions you put this way:
"Nothing in that world would be blue." You deny sufficiency in favor of what? In favor of criticizing for
defect or in favor of criticizing for excess?
KATHERINE: I took it that your premiss, a supposition
and modus tollens are capable of generating something
false. I meant to say: it follows that it is false
that in that world there would be something blue. It
further follows that this pool of water must be of some
other color than blue.
KEITH: But nothing guarantees that the premiss generates falsity rather than exiguousness. For in truth
what follows from the premiss is not that this pool has
a color other than blue but rather that use of the sentence "This is blue" is defective for saying of it what
color it is.
ALEXANDER: If we are done with one of two extreme positions, let us turn to the second one.
RECORDER: (As it turned nine o'clock, the Porter arrived and served us drinks.)
(14)
ALEXANDER: Let us turn to materialism.

CHANCELLOR: We spent a very long time on idealism. And I think I understand your pedagogy: examine and refute extreme positions. Seek the Mean. Right?

ALEXANDER: Right.

CHANCELLOR: A monistic position which denies the adequacy of a framework of otherness is extreme. It is becoming late and we have completed a discussion of only one of two monistic positions.

KATHERINE: All the odder in light of something obvious: a large number of people incline towards materialism. There is a kind of philosophical mind that inclines towards giving up dualism in favor of materialism.

KEITH: (turning to Alexander) Do you know that when I first met Katherine at college, she had recently become a materialist?

ALEXANDER: No.

RECORDER: Your friendship must have been raised upon an odd basis: one of you believing only in body and the other only in mind. Was there any union?

KEITH: You made me put on old clothes; I think Katherine should do the same.

KATHERINE: I returned mine to Winnipeg, where I bought them.

KEITH: I gather they're still in style there.

RECORDER: Or in Australia, and I think in any season.

ALEXANDER: Are you willing to present the case, Katherine?

KATHERINE: No. You wouldn't take me seriously anyway. In the course of today's conversations we have crossed many bridges each one inconsistent with an assumption of materialism or some version of materialism. It is implicit in this morning's discussion that there is a distinction between the mind and the brain. In particular there is a distinction between uses of parts of the brain and acts of thought and language. To mark such a distinction is to cross the first bridge. The second concerns the relationships between the two levels. First, there is dependency of mind upon the brain with respect to power: one would not be able to perform acts of thought without the use of mechanisms of the brain. Second, there is dependency of the brain upon mind with respect to intentionality: one would not in fact use certain mechanisms without the intention to perform certain acts of thought. And third, there is no relation of part to whole with respect to the brain and the mind.

ALEXANDER: There is inconsistency, as you say. But we cannot simply dismiss materialism as defective or excessive without argumentation. You would not yourself

217

have become a materialist out of whim.
KATHERINE: Not at all out of whim. I was moved by the
ambition of materialists to construct a unified physi-
calist science; I was moved by their desire for economy
and simplicity. I'm not sure any more of the order of
my development, but one theory I took up is that of
identity: mental phenomena are brain processes.
ALEXANDER: I wonder whether your premiss of identity
can cooperate with other instruments of reason.
KATHERINE: What do you mean?
ALEXANDER: You remember, when we discussed sameness
and otherness, that I laid out a law of sufficiency for
continuance (V.4). Meeting a condition of sameness and
meeting another condition are said to be sufficient for
a conclusion.
KATHERINE: I remember.
ALEXANDER: If you were faced either with defect or
with excess and could resolve your predicament only by
giving up your premiss of identity or by giving up the
law of continuance, how would you proceed?
KATHERINE: I would resolve the difficulty by declaring
my premiss an instrument of defect or excess.
ALEXANDER: I'm relieved to hear you say so. Let us
use your premiss in order to use the law. According to
your premiss to have a thought is for the brain to be
in a certain state. Have I correctly applied and followed your premiss?
KATHERINE: Yes.
ALEXANDER: Then I can also apply and follow the law:
if I know the thought, then I also know the state. Now
I do know the thought; it is that the law is valid. It
therefore follows that I know the state. But to know a
thought, namely that the law is valid, is not to know
a state. For the thought is a universal; many can have
the same thought. But the state is a particular event
of my brain, arising at a time and at a place. The
event is not also in your brain. There is therefore a
distinction between two achievements of knowledge:
knowing the thought and knowing the state. Since there
is a distinction, it is possible to reach the first
achievement without reaching the second.
      In point of fact I do reach the first achievement
without reaching the second. So the consequence of
using your premiss and my law is false. But it is true
that I do know the thought I had. It therefore follows
either that your premiss is excessive or that my law is
excessive. But you said you would not sacrifice the
law. It follows we should abandon your premiss on the
proved charge of excess.
KATHERINE: I stand by my agreement. The argument does

incline me to the giving up of my premiss of sameness.
Perhaps I am no longer a good person to make out the
case on behalf of materialism. I will be quite frank
with you. I have been deeply moved by your efforts to
clarify four families of notions. As distinctions became clear to me between the family of sameness and
otherness and that of combination and separation, I
wondered whether I had taken up materialism in college
simply confused about otherness and separation. I am
now inclined to agree with you in your theory of a modified pluralism: there is otherness with mutual dependency.

I now think it a frightful mistake to confuse otherness and separation. I can't imagine anyone willing-
ly and knowingly doing so. I also think it an equally
frightful mistake to confuse combination and dependence. I do suspect many people make that mistake,
thinking, for example, that since thought depends upon
behavior of the brain, thinking consists of brain behavior.
KEITH: Katherine is releasing herself from her agreement to make out a case for materialism and, in particular, the theory of identity.
KATHERINE: There is a paper which I found persuasive:
"Mental Events" by Donald Davidson. He argues the
identity of a mental with a physical event on behalf of
resolving apparent inconsistency among three principles. The first principle is that some mental events
interact causally with physical events. The second
principle is that whenever there is causality, there
must be a law. The third is that there are no strict
deterministic laws on the basis of which mental events
can be predicted and explained. So by the second two
principles and modus tollens there is no causality between mental and physical events. But the conclusion
conflicts with the first principle.
KEITH: How does Davidson mean to effect a reconciliation?
KATHERINE: Suppose m, a mental event, caused p, a
physical event. By the second principle and under some
description m and p instantiate a strict law. But this
law can only be physical. Since m falls under a physical law, it has a physical description; which is to
say it is a physical event. So every mental event that
is causally related to a physical event is a physical
event.

Davidson sketches a position of anomalous monism
for reconciling the three principles. Causality and
identity are relations between individual events no
matter how described. But laws are linguistic; so

events can instantiate laws, and hence be explained or predicted in light of laws only as those events are described in one or another way. The principle of causal interaction deals with events in extension and is therefore blind to the mental-physical dichotomy. The principle of the anomalism of the mental concerns events described as mental; for events are mental only as described. The principle of the nomological character of causality must be read carefully: it says that when events are related as cause and effect, they have descriptions that instantiate a law. It does not say that every true singular statement of causality instantiates a law.

KEITH: Perhaps you can clarify Davidson's use of the word "instantiate": first you quote him as saying that events instantiate a law and then as saying that descriptions of events instantiate a law.

KATHERINE: I'm not sure whether it matters which one means. What does matter is Davidson's premiss that if one event causes another, there is a strict law which those events instantiate when properly described.

KEITH: I think it matters. We have passed the day trying to become clear how to think about the use of instruments of reason. A law is evidently an instrument of reason. According to our account one applies and follows it. If Davidson's use of "instantiation" implies an alternative account, then he should mean that descriptions instantiate a law. I don't very well see how events could do so.

KATHERINE: Fine. Have it your way: descriptions instantiate laws.

KEITH: Can you tell me again how the second principle goes?

KATHERINE: Where there is causality, there must be a law: events related as cause and effect fall under strict deterministic laws.

KEITH: In light of our agreement you actually mean that when there is causality, there are descriptions of given events which descriptions instantiate a strict deterministic law. Now the principle can hardly be adequate as it stands. For an allowance of causality is sometimes made in the absence of appropriate deterministic laws.

KATHERINE: Someone in our mythical community could have observed that turning up the heat caused the water to boil without there being an appropriate law. But if one allows causality, it is not inconsistent to allow that there is a law whose use would have explained and predicted something about the given effect.

ALEXANDER: Before you continue your discussion, I

think it would be useful to define causation. You will
then perhaps be in a better position to examine
Davidson's third principle. (turning to Keith) What
then is a cause?
(15)
KEITH: A cause is a range of subjects each necessary
for and jointly sufficient for an effect. By "necessary for" I mean that the effect depends upon each subject.
ALEXANDER: You evidently do not mean to say that a
cause is a kind of sufficiency.
KEITH: Right. I presume that a cause is a particular
or a universal: a range of one or more subjects upon
which an effect depends.
ALEXANDER: So at a certain level one lays out a path
of sufficiency; at a lower level one lays out a path of
dependence. Is it your view that the word "cause" indicates both sufficiency and dependence?
KEITH: Yes.
ALEXANDER: So if one claims causation and if in fact
there is independence, the claim is defective?
KEITH: Yes.
ALEXANDER: Suppose someone claims that smoking is the
cause of lung-cancer. If in fact there is independence
between smoking and developing lung-cancer, the claim
is defective.
KEITH: Yes.
ALEXANDER: Suppose the development of lung-cancer depends upon smoking. In order to claim causality the
supposition must be subordinated to another: that smoking is sufficient for the development of lung-cancer.
KEITH: Yes.
ALEXANDER: Suppose someone asks why this table-top
maintains its position.
KEITH: The question presupposes that it depends upon
the position and the strength of its legs. One would
then claim that their position and strength are together adequate for the top to maintain its position.
ALEXANDER: Would you accordingly want to say that the
position and the strength of the four legs are the
cause of the top maintaining its position?
KEITH: Yes, I think so.
ALEXANDER: Having defined causality let us return to
our examination.
(15.1)
KEITH: (looking at Alexander, silent and then speaking
up) I hope I don't annoy you. One issue leads to another. We are friends and still have leisure.
KATHERINE: What is it now, Keith? I was afraid, when
we started discussing causation, that we would never

finish.

KEITH: We distinguish between a cause and a law. Now with respect to causes of such events as we commonly observe I suppose we would say that a cause is a complex range of subjects each adequate in its own way and which range is sufficient by itself for a certain event. A young science, wishing to explain the cause of a certain event, might offer the world certain laws. It is likely such a law, meaning to explain an effect, would mention only some but not all the subjects which jointly make up the cause. Is my surmise outrageous?

ALEXANDER: By no means.

KEITH: Let me give an example which is friendly to our own inquiries both this afternoon and this morning. I issue the following premiss to Katherine who is looking for something: "If you look carefully enough, you will see it." It turns out that she does not see it. By modus tollens it follows either that she was not looking carefully enough or that use of my premiss is not adequate for one of its tasks: namely explaining why she didn't see it. For the sake of a good story we can surely allow that she was looking carefully enough to see it, even though she did not in fact see it. Can we make the allowance?

ALEXANDER: Of course.

KEITH: Then it follows that use of the premiss is not adequate. Are we to charge defect or excess?

ALEXANDER: Defect. For according to your story we can say that its use is inadequate for the objective of providing a complete explanation. The task of doing so must fall upon the shoulders of another premiss, principle or law which mentions other subjects of the causal range; for we must evidently look elsewhere to find a subject defective or excessive for Katherine's having seen what she was looking for.

KEITH: I think I follow you. So suppose that the cause of an event E is a range of at least two subjects; suppose we have a law which mentions one subject and the event: "If S, then E." But we observe that the event does not arise. By modus tollens we are entitled to an inference of two alternatives: if the law is itself adequate, then either the subject S is not adequate in its own way or, if it is, use of the law on this occasion is not adequate for giving a complete explanation of why the event did not arise. If the first alternative is taken, we have no further guidance as to whether to look for defect or excess; if the second, we charge defect.

Am I still following you, or have I run away with your answer to my question?

ALEXANDER: You've nicely built upon it.
KEITH: I still have a further worry. Consider a formula such as "If this coffee is hot enough, I can solve
a certain problem of logic." Meeting the condition is
sufficient for using the formula. But since solving
the problem does not depend upon this coffee having a
certain temperature, its having a certain temperature
is no part of the cause of my solving the problem.
ALEXANDER: Indeed. For although a certain subject may
be adequate in its own way for a certain objective, it
does not follow that the objective depends upon the
subject.
KEITH: I've been wondering whether in such cases too
we have two alternatives: if the formula is sound, then
either this coffee is not hot enough or use of the formula is defective for giving an appropriate or complete
explanation.
KATHERINE: However is one to come clear about so sub-
tle a matter with so silly an example? Of course the
coffee is hot enough for you to solve the problem; any
temperature would be great enough. It would be ridiculous to think that you didn't solve the problem because
the coffee was too hot or too cold. Defect lies in the
use of such a ridiculous formula: it's of no use at all
for explaining why you didn't solve the problem.
KEITH: Then are you prepared to leap to a universal
conclusion?
KATHERINE: Yes, of course. What is it?
KEITH: Let us write the formula "If A, then B." Suppose the state or event indicated by "B" does not depend upon that indicated by "A". Our conclusion would
be that if the formula is sound and if it is not true
that B, then either it is not true that A or use of the
formula is defective for explanatory purposes. But
suppose the formula is sound and that it is not true
that B. But since the state or event indicated by "B"
is independent of that indicated by "A", the subject
revealed by "A" is adequate for the state or event revealed by "B". It further follows from our conclusion
that use of the formula is defective for explanatory
purposes.
RECORDER: (looking at Katherine) Are you full of admiration for your friend?
KATHERINE: Why should I be?
RECORDER: When we charge use of an instrument with defect, we look for supplementation; when we charge excess, elimination. Suppose a scientific kit has only
one law in it. What Keith has helped us to see is a
difference of some interest: whether we enlarge the kit
or change the one tool in it for another. Do you see?

KATHERINE: (smiling at Keith) My admiration grows.
(turning to Julian) I like the image, Julian. It
helps one see the predicament a scientist or a philosopher may be in: whether to enlarge his repertory or to
cast aside what he has as false. One may not know
whether modus tollens should lead to replacement or
amplification.
(16)
KEITH: When we digressed, we were discussing
Davidson's second principle that when there is causality, there must be a law. In light of our discussion of
causality it seems doubtful that the principle is worthy of assent. We would then resolve Davidson's puzzle
not by trying to reconcile the three principles but by
dismissing the second one. And surely we are justified
in doing so. We allow that every event has a cause.
But for every event we do not have an explanation.
Further, two classes of explanations are given: the
first without and the second with the help of strict
laws. The first kind is retrospective and particular;
the second, prospective and general.
    Suppose I now make a decision as to whether to re-
main in Edmonton tomorrow. Since the decision is a
mental event, it has a cause; its cause is a range of
subjects. Let us distinguish its subjects according to
our picture of a hierarchy of levels. It will do to
consider only two levels: what we call a level of mind
and a supporting natural level at which brain mechanisms are employed. Let us say accordingly that some
subjects of the range are on a horizontal plane with
the mental event; others are on a vertical plane. In
an even more abbreviated way we can say that some subjects are horizontal and others are vertical. You
would expect me to explain why I made my decision not
by citing the full range of subjects (anyway I don't
know it) but by selectively citing horizontal subjects
of the range. I do in fact give you my reason when I
say that I wish to visit another day with Julian.
KATHERINE: Then your reason for deciding to stay is
not the cause of your decision.
KEITH: It is not the cause.
KATHERINE: (turning to Alexander) I'm satisfied with
Keith's resolution of Davidson's puzzle. I do think it
right to resolve the puzzle not by trying to reconcile
the three principles but by dismissing the second one.
I accept a distinction between allowing universal causality and allowing that there is a law use of which is
sufficient for predicting and explaining something
about a particular cause or effect. But I think we now
face an even greater perplexity: namely how there can

224

be freedom. How are we to reconcile freedom and causal determinism? Surely, as Davidson writes at the beginning of his paper, freedom requires escape from the nomological net. Davidson does not effect a reconciliation; for by confusing the language of mental events with mental events his nomological net captures mental events and re-describes them; that friendly creature he calls anomalous monism captures the language of mental events and doesn't know what to do with it.

ALEXANDER: (turning to Katherine) I think your question introduces an inquiry fit for another day. May I take it that we are done with a discussion of monism in the form of materialism?

KATHERINE: Yes. And spiritualism as well.

(17)

ALEXANDER: So, as we move back from the two extreme positions, we consider three pluralist positions.

KATHERINE: With handkerchiefs in our hands, Keith, we wave goodbye to the extremism of our late youth. You know, when we first met, we were not as extreme as we forced one another to become. A wonderful thing, isn't it? Prolonged argumentation drives the arguers into opposing species of excess.

RECORDER: One sees an example of what you mean in the argument between Augustine and Pelagius. Augustine moves to a position of extreme dependence of man upon God, and Pelagius, to one of extreme independence of man from God. The first too little and the second too much affirms free will.

KATHERINE: (turning to Alexander) I guess we've decided that monism rests in part upon corrupt metaphysical thinking. Is a principal instrument of that thought either the principle of atomism or the modified principle of atomism?

ALEXANDER: For a real answer to the question we should depend upon Julian; an answer deserves a serious study. I hope someone will do it.

We have set aside two extreme positions; I suppose it is clear to you that in setting them aside I fix myself firmly in the middle, arguing, I suppose, for interactionism and reciprocal causality. Perhaps we should still look a little from side to side. I'm certainly willing to ask you what you think of theism, on the one side and, on the other, naturalism.

RECORDER: For the sake of completeness we ought to consider four pluralist positions. It would feel natural to me to follow the procedure you have already laid down. First consider theism, a position close to spiritual monism; consider, second, naturalism, a position close to materialism; third, interactionism, and fourth

225

parallelism.
KATHERINE: Please, Julian. It's 11:00, and I'm becom-
ing tired. Has anyone here ever been inclined to par-
allelism?
KEITH: Not I.
CHANCELLOR: Nor I.
KATHERINE: (turning again to Julian) You see: no one
since Leibniz has held that mind and matter are dis-
tinct and independent one of the other. Leibniz must
have thought he was even more clever than he was. Lord
knows he was clever enough.
KEITH: Enough for what?
KATHERINE: For silencing you. Let's not discuss par-
allelism.
RECORDER: I can follow your suggestion.
KATHERINE: And do we really need to discuss theism?
Is such a discussion necessary or wanted in our day?
I'll wager you that no one here believes with any seri-
ousness at all that every part of the physical universe
depends at all times upon spirit and mind.
KEITH: As a boy I thought so.
KATHERINE: As a boy! Now you are a man, aren't you?
Do you think so now?
KEITH: No. Upon abandoning idealism I have also given
up theism. But perhaps Julian has taken up what I have
given up.
RECORDER: Whether I hold a relevant position or not,
is not entirely to the point. I think all students at
our new academy should think the position through, as
we all think they should think the two extreme monistic
positions through.
KATHERINE: I think it is too much in one day to try to
do justice to the pluralist positions.
CHANCELLOR: Perhaps you would be willing to meet later. I would prefer not to rush through positions
which I have taken seriously. Further, you might expect me to try to defend my own. So I think it would
be sensible to postpone a discussion of the pluralist
positions.
ALEXANDER: I'm prepared to do as you say. We can decide tomorrow when we should again meet.
KATHERINE: Before we stop for the day, there is one
last thing.
ALEXANDER: What is it?
(18)
KATHERINE: This morning (III.9) Julian gave some arguments according to which either there is no knowledge
or your account of means for reaching knowledge is irrelevant.
ALEXANDER: I remember. I agreed to reply after we

discussed idealism and materialism.
KATHERINE: Julian opened your discussion by putting a
question which of course I've forgotten. What was the
question, Julian?
RECORDER: Is the thing which one knows, knowing a
length, the same thing which the table has? Bill replied, "When I know the length of the table, I know
that length which the table actually has." He then de-
clined to say what "has" means.
KATHERINE: But an account of its meaning and use
emerged in our discussion of the correspondence theory
of truth (VII.5). When one says that this table has a
length, the word "has" indicates sufficiency. Its objective is of potentiality: initiating an inquiry whose
end is the management of the achievement of knowing or
disclosing a length. Its subject is potential use of
resources.
ALEXANDER: (turning to Julian) In light of
Katherine's summary you perhaps understand why my answer to your question does not raise more metaphysical
dust than it lowers. The word "has", employed in saying, "...which the table actually has," does not indicate a relation of combination. My answer does not
prepare ground for use of the premiss "What is other is
combined or separate." The rest of your argument turns
upon use of that premiss--a premiss which we have abandoned.
KATHERINE: Setting Julian's arguments aside is like
sweeping down cobwebs from an attic little used. Cobwebs spun from the premiss that what is distinct is
combined or separate. The attic, free of cobwebs and
junk, with its windows cleaned and polished, looks
bare. What is left hardly furnishes the place. Universals exist and are distinct both from substances and
from minds. That's not much to sit on--or to sit in
with a feeling of luxuriance.
KEITH: But we should learn how much to expect from
philosophy and thereby expect neither too little nor
too much. We know what truth is. To know the definition is not to know what in particular is true; to know
the definition is to know enough to structure and to
initiate particular inquiries; to complete them special
and appropriate disciplines are necessary. When we
acknowledge that there is a transition from metaphysics
to a particular discipline, we acknowledge both its
help and its limitations. Your attic may look bare;
but metaphysics tries to hold on to too much ground
when it invites us to consider relations between
substances and universals and between minds and universals. It is enough if metaphysics can carry us from

itself to a court where inquiry can be structured and
initiated and sent on its way.
CHANCELLOR: Some time ago we were invited to a consideration of certain schools of philosophy in order, once
again, to find a mean between defect and excess. It
has become late. I appreciate that philosophical discussion resists closure. There is always more to be
said, but more tonight is too much more. The Premier's
friend expects us in a few minutes; let us not disappoint him. I hope we have something of a philosophical
nature to tell him.
KATHERINE: Tell him that modes of criticism come in
triads. Tell him the highest virtue of his province is
sufficiency and not otherness: in particular, enough
wealth for a certain kind of life and not more and more
and more. I think there are many things to say.

analogy, 192f
appearance, 111
Aquinas, on truth, 152f
Armstrong, D.M., on realism, 168f
Augustine, on time, 49ff
being, 61ff
Berkeley, a discussion between Hylas and Philonous,
    37ff; idealism, 327ff; setting words aside, 52ff
Confucius, the Doctrine of the Mean, 90
consistency, 144ff
causality, definition, 26, 221
Davidson, D., on materialism, 219ff
Descartes, role of dreams, 20f; modified principle of
    atomism, 125f
Dummett, M., on the equivalence thesis, 153f
existence, definition of, 92f, 208f
expressions, kinds of, 30ff; "this", 31f; T-expres-
    sions, 32ff; O-expressions, 33ff; U- and A-expres-
    sions, 42f
having, meaning of "have", 156f
Hume, reasoning, 180; skeptical argumentation, 197f
identity, as a relation, 95ff
induction, 188ff
laws, the first triadic law, 82f, 83f; the law of non-
    contradiction, 83f; a law of sufficiency, 102f;
    second law of sufficiency (Leibniz's Law), 104ff
Leibniz, universal harmony, 84f
Liar's Paradox, 172f
method, of inquiry, 6f
modus ponens, 68ff
paradoxes, 172ff; Russell's paradox, 174f
Peirce, as pragmatist, 161
perception, as an hypothesis, 107ff; whether universals
    are perceptible, 133ff
philosophy, a definition of, 2; two ways of, 32f
Plato, an argument from the Phaedo, 17ff; getting along
    without words, 52ff; skepticism, 85ff
plenitude, principle of, 202
possibility, 194ff; definitions of possibility, proba-
    bility and certainty, 194f
positions, six positions regarding particulars and uni-
    versals (cf. II.5, II.7, VI.4, VI.5, VII.7) 45f;
    six corresponding epistemological positions (cf.
    VII.6.1) regarding time, 50ff
principles, the principle of atomism, 24ff; 124ff; in
    Ockham, 125; in Hume, 125f; 141; the principle of
    distinguishable resources, 28ff
sameness and otherness, distinctions between acts and